Patterns of Conflict

American University Studies

Series II
Romance Languages and Literature

Vol. 105

PETER LANG
New York • Bern • Frankfurt am Main • Paris

Sheila R. Ackerlind

Patterns of Conflict

The Individual and Society in Spanish Literature to 1700

PETER LANG

New York • Bern • Frankfurt am Main • Paris

Library of Congress Cataloging-in-Publication Data

Ackerlind, Sheila R.
    Patterns of conflict : the individual and society in
Spanish literature to 1700 / Sheila R. Ackerlind.
    p. cm. – (American university studies.   Series II,
Romance languages and literature ; v. 105)
    Bibliography: p.
    Includes index.
    1. Spanish literature – To 1500 – History and criticism.
2. Spanish literature – Classical period, 1500-1700 –
History and criticism.   3. Individuality in literature.
4. Conflict (Psychology) in literature.   5. Social conflict
in literature.   6. Social structure – Spain – History.
I. Title.   II. Series.
PQ6060.A25   1989   860'.9'355 – dc19   88-23423
ISBN 0-8204-0879-4   CIP
ISSN 0740-9257

CIP-Titelaufnahme der Deutschen Bibliothek

Ackerlind, Sheila R.:
Patterns of conflict : the individual and society
in Spanish literature to 1700 / Sheila R. Acker-
lind. – New York; Bern; Frankfurt am Main;
Paris: Lang, 1989.
  (American University Studies: Ser. 2,
  Romance Languages and Literature; Vol. 105)
  ISBN 0-8204-0879-4

NE: American University Studies / 02

© Peter Lang Publishing, Inc., New York 1989

Printed by Weihert-Druck GmbH, Darmstadt, West Germany

For Frank

Acknowledgments

The individual in conflict with society is a theme that first sparked my interest during my senior year at Georgetown University, when Professor Yolanda R. Solé suggested that I incorporate it in my bachelor's degree thesis. I followed her suggestion and have been intrigued by the theme ever since.

I am deeply indebted to my husband, Frank Lobosco, for his unflagging patience and good humor, as well as for his astute editorial comments; to my father, Professor Francis M. Rogers (who introduced me to Spain and to her literature), for his invaluable encouragement and advice; and to Professors John E. Keller, Samuel G. Saldívar, Sara DeGregorio, and the late Stephen Gilman, all of whom painstakingly read the manuscript and offered helpful recommendations. I am also grateful to Anita A. Wayne, Susan P. Waide, Sylvia Adams, and Brigitte McDonald (my editor at Peter Lang Publishing) for their editorial assistance.

S. R. A.

Bayside, New York
17 August 1988

Table of Contents

Preface

This book examines the patterns of conflict between the individual and society as depicted in Peninsular literature written in Castilian during Spain's Middle (c. 1140–1492) and Golden (c. 1492–1700) Ages. The theme of the individual in conflict with society is a most significant one since it reflects the human condition and consequently serves as the foundation for numerous plays, novels, short stories, poems, and treatises written during those six centuries.

This thematic overview of early Spanish literature would be especially useful to nonspecialists as well as to undergraduate and graduate students of Spanish literature, comparative literature, and Hispanic culture. Besides providing an introduction to the societal ideals and values underlying medieval and Golden Age writings (ideals and values that have survived well into the twentieth century as powerful constraints on the individual), this book schematizes the basic types of conflict revealed in literary works and attempts to clarify why authors selected particular solutions to the kinds of conflict they chose to treat.

As a professor of Spanish literature, I have learned that a person unfamiliar with the complexities of the theme of conflict fails to grasp the true meaning of the works in which it appears. The purpose of this book, therefore, is to assist the reader in understanding and appreciating early Spanish literary masterpieces and to acquaint him or her with lesser known works that involve this theme.

Because the scope of this book is indeed broad, I have purposely not analyzed those subplots and topics that do not bear directly on the theme of conflict. With few exceptions, I have also avoided discussing modern literary theories and criticisms; however, if the reader cares to learn more about a certain author, work, or genre, I urge him to consult the Selected Reading List, which I have arranged chapter by chapter and which contains complete bibliographical information about secondary sources mentioned in the chapter endnotes.

The Index lists all authors and literary works discussed in the text and endnotes, and it includes the authors' dates of birth and death, as well as the dates of the first appearance in manuscript or print of all anonymous works.

Bearing in mind that readers of this book may have a limited knowledge of Spanish, I have modernized the punctuation and orthography of certain quotations *except* in those cases where modernization would seriously affect rhyme or meter, and I have paraphrased in English all quoted material.

Abbreviations

Arbor	*Arbor: Ciencia, Pensamiento y Cultura*
ArH	*Archivo Hispalense: Revista Histórica, Literaria y Artística*
BAE	Biblioteca de Autores Españoles
BBMP	*Boletín de la Biblioteca de Menéndez Pelayo*
BCom	*Bulletin of the Comediantes*
BH	*Bulletin Hispanique*
BHS	*Bulletin of Hispanic Studies*
BSCE	Biblioteca Selecta de Clásicos Españoles
CC	Clásicos Castellanos
C.H.	Cultura Hispánica
CHA	*Cuadernos Hispanoamericanos: Revista Mensual de Cultura Hispánica*
C.S.I.C.	Consejo Superior de Investigaciones Científicas
EFil	*Estudios Filológicos*
F.C.E.	Fondo de Cultura Económica
F.U.E.	Fundación Universitaria Española
Hispano	*Hispanófila* (Chapel Hill, NC)
HR	*Hispanic Review*
I&L	*Ideologies and Literature: A Journal of Hispanic and Luso-Brazilian Studies*
JHP	*Journal of Hispanic Philology* (Tallahassee, FL)
KRQ	*Kentucky Romance Quarterly*
LdD	*Letras de Deusto*
MLN	*Modern Language Notes*
MLR	*Modern Language Review*

MP	*Modern Philology: A Journal Devoted to Research in Medieval and Modern Literature*
NBAE	Nueva Biblioteca de Autores Españoles
NRFH	*Nueva Revista de Filología Hispánica* (Mexico City)
PMLA	*Publications of the Modern Language Association of America*
R.A.E.	Real Academia Española
RCEH	*Revista Canadiense de Estudios Hispánicos*
REH	*Revista de Estudios Hispánicos* (Univ. of Alabama)
RF	*Romanische Forschungen*
RFE	*Revista de Filología Española*
RO	*Revista de Occidente*
RPh	*Romance Philology*
RR	*Romanic Review*
TDR	*Tulane Drama Review*
U.P.	University Press
ZRP	*Zeitschrift für Romanische Philologie*

Introduction

The individual is a member of society from the moment of his or her birth. Despite the measures that society takes to shape and regulate the individual in accordance with its dictates, the individual, nevertheless, feels the need to exert his individuality: he may protest the written and unwritten laws that restrict him; he may strive to influence society in a positive way; his actions may even have a negative effect on society.

The conflict between the individual and society forms an integral part of the human condition. It is not surprising, therefore, that it has traditionally appeared under diverse guises as an essential theme in European literature and, specifically, in Spanish literature written during the Middle and Golden Ages.

This book explores the ways in which Spanish literary works of those periods reflect the age-old and universal theme of conflict. I have sought to examine how characters respond to the ideals and values of their world and how their world, in turn, responds to their individuality.

Although this book refers to the social structures, institutions, and organizations of the twelfth through the seventeenth centuries, it is not a sociological study of Spain but a study of her literature. With few exceptions, my primary sources are literary works, not historical documents or official records. However, the reader who is interested in learning about the realities of Spanish society—in particular, its standards and attitudes, as well as the modes of behavior it expected of the individual—will discover that these works offer a wealth of information; indeed, they complement documents and records in contributing to the body of knowledge concerning Spain's past.

While it is reasonable to conclude that the ideals and values revealed in Spanish medieval and Golden Age literature echo the societal beliefs of those times, the reader should be cautioned not to interpret a single work, the literary production of a single author, or even a single genre as a mirror image of social life. Verisimilitude, or the appearance of truth, was meant to originate in what what was probable rather than in what was necessarily real in an objective sense. Consequently, literary works represent the subjectivity and the creativity of writers who perceived their world from perspectives as varied as their own circumstances, experiences, and aspirations. As a result, a character's journey through a particular phase of life may well reflect a distillation of the author's life as it was or as it might have been. Writers, for instance, who were members in good standing of mainstream society were inclined to accept without serious question the social structure and tenets of their times, an ideology they shared with their literary patrons and with many of their readers. These authors tended to criticize only the hollow and superficial nature of certain values, like the excessive importance their contemporaries attached to wealth and appearances. On the other hand, writers whose personal beliefs and goals were at odds with those of established society often created characters who reenact metaphorically the drama of their creators as individuals alienated by the hostility of the world around them.

The established society that literature depicts was hierarchical in structure and Roman Catholic in official religious belief. It comprised different groups, each one based on such ancestral factors or common interests as the family (whose members were usually linked by territorial proximity), membership in any one of the three estates (clergy, nobility, and commonfolk), and Old Christian origin (of "pure" Christian stock, not "tainted" by Jewish or Moslem blood).

Established society was inherently exclusive. It attempted to bar from participating in its mainstream certain groups of people whose ethnic and/or religious ancestry, as well as their life-styles, it considered unacceptable. Among these marginal groups figured slaves, gypsies, witches, *pícaros*, Jews, *Conversos* (New Christians of Jewish origin), Moslems, and *Moriscos* (New Christians of Moslem origin). Literature bears ample witness indeed to the alienation that characterized their lives.

Through their membership from birth in group life, literary characters, like real-life men and women, become socialized: society teaches them the principles and values that influence them to conform to the patterns of conduct befitting the groups to which they belong. For example, characters learn the significance of reputation, which serves to constrain them from acting in a manner deemed improper by their families, peers, and social superiors.

Spanish literature also reveals how particular social institutions and groups seek to mold the individual into an image of their own ideals and attitudes. The Church imparts the religious doctrines that she established to provide the groundwork for spiritual life and the salvation of mankind. The State promulgates laws to ensure social order and justice. In its role as microcosm of society, the family not only furnishes its young with models of interpersonal relationships, which teach them how to behave in society, but also instructs them in the norms and modes of conduct that they must follow in order to secure individual and social well-being.

Church, State, and family frequently work together in an effort to socialize their members. The family strives to rear its young in keeping with the mandates of Church and State; these institutions generally endorse the teachings of the family. Chastity in a female character, for instance, is one of several ideals to which Church, State, and family lend their fervent support.

Occasionally, however, religion and secular society instill in their members conflicting beliefs. During the sixteenth and seventeenth centuries, discrimination on the part of Old Christians against New Christians was widespread, and yet it exemplifies a perversion of a fundamental Church doctrine. Nonetheless, the State and even some religious orders forbade converts and their descendants from joining their ranks, a point to which numerous Golden Age literary works attest. Like this obsession with an individual's "purity" of blood, vengeance in the case of a wife's alleged infidelity also runs counter to Christ's laws and even to the formal secular laws in effect during medieval and Golden Age Spain; nevertheless, monarchs in nonreligious works sanction wife murder and, in doing so, place the societal code of honor above the Christian code of forgiveness and the legal code they ought to uphold.

Literary characters share with real-life individuals the need to acquire the teachings of their world in order to master the social roles they are to play.

A female character's role usually pertains to her marital status: she is defined as single or married. If single, she must safeguard her virginity. If married, she must remain faithful to her husband. (A married woman seldom appears in her role as mother, since motherhood has less dramatic potential than does her fidelity, which is often at stake.)

A male character's roles are determined by the groups to which he belongs. He may be father and king, or wronged husband and loyal subject of a lustful prince. Of special significance in literature is the inner conflict that ensues when his two roles clash. Will the king enforce the law and punish his wayward son? Will the husband permit the prince to seduce his wife? The way in which an author resolves his protagonist's dilemma can be helpful to us in ascertaining the social roles and, by implication, the principles and values that the writer and/or his public considered of greater importance.

One reason why Spaniards have shown a continued interest in their medieval and Golden Age literature is that they are familiar with the characters' roles and with the societal ideals and attitudes embodied in them. Many of these standards and values have proved highly resistant to change. The honor code, for instance, not only provides the thematic framework for a multitude of Golden Age plays but has survived well into the twentieth century as a powerful restraint on illicit sexual activity. Bravery and loyalty appear as essential ingredients of manliness in medieval literature, and their worthiness has never been seriously challenged. And even anti-Semitism, which manifests itself in Golden Age works, has not entirely disappeared from Spain; in fact, it is not unusual to hear modern-day Spaniards vociferously deny Jewish ancestry, and many a Spaniard is still keenly aware of which surnames denote Jewish origin and which place-names signify a formerly Jewish populace.

In addition to its norms of conduct and its attitudes, society instructs the individual in its traditional customs and usages, which are more subject to change and less crucial to the welfare of the individual and society than are its mores.

One custom that often emerges in Golden Age comedies of intrigue (also known as "cloak-and-dagger" comedies) concerns parental coercion in the case of a marriageable daughter's choice of a husband. The daughter, however, rebels against wedding the wealthy suitor whom her materialistic father has forced on her, and she plots to wed her truelove. Although she has momentarily provoked papa's consternation, if not his wrath, all ends happily for the lovers. The young man may be lucky enough to inherit his uncle's fortune, and his newly acquired wealth now makes him a desirable match in the eyes of the young lady's father, who is only too happy to see in their marriage his own honor enhanced.

The usages that society teaches involve the rules of etiquette and decorum appropriate to each social group. One usage that appears in Spanish literature dictates that a nobleman refrain from violence and extramarital sex while in the royal presence or palace. Should he challenge a rival to a duel or seduce a woman, the king might imprison or banish him, but at least he generally manages to survive with his life intact.

Society's responsibilities toward its members, however, extend far beyond merely socializing them and providing them with role models. Besides these important tasks, society must also restrain those individuals who threaten its well-being. Consequently, it empowers the Church, the State, and the family to control their members and to punish any individuals who deviate from their norms.

The monarch, the mayor, and the bailiff commonly represent the State in Spanish literature and bring to justice negative individuals who disobey society's formal and even informal rules. The Spanish Inquisition, which was established to oversee the orthodoxy of Church-members' religious beliefs, also makes its presence felt in literary works, especially in Golden Age novels.

The Spanish Church and State not only endorsed the teachings of the family but tended to strengthen the authority of one another. The social order was regarded as a reflection, albeit imperfect, of the divine; therefore, a crime against society was deemed a sin against God, a precept that Church and State long used to their mutual advantage. Religious beliefs have traditionally fostered an individual's willingness to respect secular authority; the State, in return, rewarded the Church for her support not only by contributing to her wealth and conferring tax-exempt status on her but by protecting her from the potentially corroding influence of other religious persuasions. Literature attests to this alliance of religious and secular authority. In several Golden Age dramas, for example, God allies Himself with society in punishing the wicked, nonrepentant disrupter of the divine and social orders.

Spanish literature, however, reveals that the individual's family and network of friends and acquaintances are even more instrumental than Church and State in controlling him or her. For instance, it is common in the comedies of intrigue for a father to keep his flirtatious daughter under lock and key; he judges flirting unseemly since it may ruin her chances of snaring an eligible bachelor. Other girls risk death at the hands of their irate fathers, who believe rightly or wrongly that their daughters have brought them shame. A young lady's neighbors also keep her under close surveillance and publicize anything she may do or say that they construe to be improper. (Fortunately for her, neighbors are not always able to read her mind!) Responding to gossip, the family hastens to restrain the young woman member whose behavior it feels may sully its reputation.

Like religious doctrines, the societal tenets reflected in literature wield great power over the individual. Infractions of the concrete modes of conduct associated with society's norms—especially with those regulating extramarital sexual relations—are punishable, even by death. Characters know a priori that sexual misconduct violates the honor code, which prescribes harsh measures for the offenders: the convent for an unmarried girl whose seducer refuses to marry her, and death for her erstwhile lover as well as for an adulteress and her paramour.

Lest it be thought that death is the severest form of punishment to appear in literature, however, society avails itself of yet another form, one that the individual considers a fate worse than death: it bars guilty and even suspect members from its ranks. Exclusion from social life spells doom for literary characters because it is tantamount to temporal nonlife, to death on earth.

Fear of ostracism, which serves as a powerful constraint on the individual, is the key to understanding the significance of shame and reputation, values whose strength may puzzle the young, modern-day reader. Clearly, formal laws are and must be powerful deterrents to antisocial behavior, but how can the idle gossip of one's neighbor (the *¿qué dirán?* 'what will people say?'), which is often indicative of society's unwritten laws, be allowed to exert the same degree of power, if not more? The answer lies, once again, in the essence of the individual's relationship to his world. A social being, he depends on the favorable opinion his neighbors hold of him. Society instructs him to avert scandal in order not to exist as a social outcast in a state of nonlife. This fear of rejection compels numerous characters to conform to society's dictates, for they know that conformity guarantees them the essence of temporal life—a sense of belonging.

Spanish medieval and Golden Age literature has been criticized for having produced an abundance of types who personify societal ideals and values, and a scarcity of benevolent individuals whose decisions are determined not by their preordained social roles but by goals that are theirs alone. In view of the importance attached to conformity, nevertheless, it is understandable why few characters are capable of sustaining their unique individuality without relenting to society or bringing on themselves punishment of one form or another. Individuality is, at best, difficult to nurture in a world where the mandates of society take precedence over the aspirations of the individual and where the rigid social structure curtails the freedom to live as one would wish.

As a medieval or Golden Age writer mapped out his character's journey through a particular phase of life, he was guided by the principle of verisimilitude. His portrayal of the individual, society, and the relationships between the two must be probable. Hence, the author must endow his character with a semblance of free will; at the same time, he must also take into account the limitations that real-life society would have placed on the individual.

A fictional character, like his nonfictional counterpart, is constantly confronted with decisions. His world has taught him to elect what it deems acceptable and has warned him of the consequences of any unacceptable decision he might make. As a result, he is left with few true choices. If he did not feel the need to conform to the rules governing his social roles, he would have a greater opportunity to exercise his free will so that he could strive to become what he might want to be.

This will to break free of restricting social roles is an important theme in Spanish medieval and Golden Age literature and is related to the universal conflict between the individual, who endeavors to live as he wants, and society, which expects him to live as it wants. Despite the measures that society takes to thwart them, however, it is not at all unusual for characters to exert their individuality. Indeed, their defiance of society provides a justification for the very existence of most plays, novels, and short stories.

Medieval and Golden Age literature recreates many kinds and degrees of conflict that ensues when individuals challenge the attitudes, norms, and customs of established society.

One type of conflict results when a commoner and a noble fall in love and wish to wed one another. But the mainstream society to which they belong frowns on socially mixed marriages. How the lovers triumph, while respecting social convention at the same time, is the subject matter discussed in Pt. I of this book.

Pt. II concerns New Christians, prisoners, and *pícaros*, all of whom live outside or on the fringes of established society. The plight of these marginal individuals confirms the inflexibility of mainstream society, which frustrates their efforts to gain a foothold in the world of their aspirations. Treated with intolerance and injustice by an unyielding world, and impotent in the face of circumstances beyond their control, these alienated and outcast individuals are inclined to fall prey to feelings of negative solitude. Many of these men and women are excluded from established society because they lack the religious and social credentials necessary for admittance. If these hapless individuals lack money as well, they can never buy the fraudulent documents and the other trappings of respectability that will enable them to pass themselves off as full-fledged members of the world they hope to join.

For an individual born into mainstream society, as we shall see in Pt. III, money also makes the difference between society's acceptance or its rejection of him, between his being treated with dignity or with abuse. Poverty estranges a nobleman from the world of his birth. Derided and ridiculed, many an impoverished but titled protagonist realizes that his future security depends on winning his affluent ladylove's hand in marriage. He may have to feign the appearance of wealth to court her, and she may have to lie to her father to avoid wedding a suitor whom she loathes. But society tolerates these relatively minor deceptions since the lovers have not clashed with its fundamental laws. The poor nobleman eventually marries his rich noblewoman and lives opulently ever after; what is more, his new-found riches allow him to enjoy a harmonious relationship with his world.

The nobleman's good fortune, however, contrasts radically with the fate of the destitute commoners portrayed in Spanish literature. Their existence is fraught with helplessness. Poverty subjects these lowly individuals to the oppression of the mighty, and they have little to alleviate their suffering. Despairing of justice in this life, they can only pray that God will treat them with justice in the next.

Marginal and impoverished victims of negative solitude dream of finding security, prosperity, and justice within mainstream society. Other men and women depicted in Spanish literature, to the contrary, yearn to disassociate themselves from established society, especially from the corruption of courtly and urban circles. These individuals seek an idealized, rustic life-style in which they can be true to themselves instead of being slaves to greed, deception, and artifice. Only in the country will they encounter positive solitude, the solitude they themselves willingly choose in order to live free of the societal values they so abhor. Society, as we shall see in Pt. IV, permits these individuals to pursue their goals because they have not disobeyed its mores.

Many of Miguel de Cervantes' characters also defy the customs of their worlds so that they can live in accordance with their consciences. They flee the societal restraints their preordained roles have imposed on them. In the end, however, only such *thoroughly* undeceived individuals as the dying Don Quijote realize that the quest for individuality and freedom is ultimately meaningless unless it is firmly rooted in the pursuit of eternal life.

While the completely undeceived individuals who appear in Spanish literature shun those aspects of society that might jeopardize the salvation of their souls, numerous other characters remain oblivious to spiritual matters; their sole concern is to live in harmony with society, and they choose not to question whether the dictates they must follow in order to ensure their continued membership in society pose a danger to their souls.

Of the various modes of conduct prescribed in medieval and Golden Age literature, the societal code of honor is the one that most governs the individual's membership in his world. The honor code, which is treated in Pt. V, determines how characters should lead their lives if they wish to avert social ostracism or death.

Sometimes honor clashes with love, and the characters involved in this conflict must choose between the course of action that they, as individuals, would like to take and the one that society expects them to take. Spanish literary works also present the collision between honor and inordinate sexual passion. The catalyst of this conflict is an antagonist who selfishly pursues a single or a married woman without regard for her reputation. In profaning the sanctity of chastity, friendship, marriage, and family, he violates the religious and societal precepts on which they are based. Examples of this negatively individualistic type permeate Spanish literature, especially the theater, and he often appears as a monarch, a donjuanesque nobleman, or a *bandolero* 'outlaw'. His antisocial behavior threatens his female victim's life as well as his own. Having rebelled against society, he must pay the price that his crime warrants—either marriage to the young lady or death.

In the following chapters, we will examine how individuals in medieval and Golden Age Spanish literature play the roles that direct their relationships with society, and we will see why the destinies of these characters usually depend on which of the societal ideals, values, and norms of conduct they have respected and which ones they have challenged.

I

The Theory of
Estate Society and
the Problem of
Social Ascent

1

Estate Society

The thirteenth-century King Alfonso X "the Learned" and his nephew Prince Juan Manuel were the foremost Castilian theorists of the hierarchical society in which they lived. Alfonso, who directed the compilation of the legal encyclopedia *Las siete partidas*, and Juan Manuel, the author of the *Libro de los estados*, realized that each person needed to know how his social system functioned if he was to have a clear understanding of his role within it. Accordingly, Alfonso and Juan Manuel enumerated in their treatises the subgroups of each estate, or broad social group, and the duties incumbent on them and their members. By providing us with a detailed view of society as it was meant to be, these works assist us in appreciating the relationships between medieval and Golden Age literary characters and their world.

The society that Alfonso and Juan Manuel summarized was vertical in structure. It stratified its members in three estates, each of which had a specific function to perform. The first estate comprised the clergy (*oradores*); the second, the nobility (*defensores*); the third, the common people (*labradores*). Depending on his lineage, over which he obviously exercised no control, a person was born into the second or third estate. He could, however, elect to become a member of the clergy regardless of his ancestry, provided that he met the requisite qualifications.

Membership in an estate bestowed on an individual legal and social classification. It also assigned him certain duties, which he was expected to carry out for two purposes: the salvation of his soul and the common good. Considered a social being, he functioned not as an individual but as a part of and in relation to society.

Although members of different estates did not share social equality, they were linked together in a network of rights and obligations, which were intended to protect the integrity of society as a whole and to insure justice for all.

Estate society was monarchical in governance. Just as God reigns supreme over the divine order, so did the king reign over the social order. Since the social order originated in the divine, and since the authority of the king emanated from divine law, the king therefore ruled in God's name as His temporal regent; in the words of Alfonso X, "debe el Pueblo conocer al Rey primeramente en el mismo, como es temporalmente Señor; y otrosí, como es escogido de Dios, y que en su nombre tiene lugar en tierra."[1]

Alfonso expresses great concern in the *Partidas* about the specific ways in which subjects should respect their monarch: in word and deed. Any disrespect shown him, ranging from lack of decorum to treason, should be appropriately punished. (Ironically, the reality of Alfonso's reign bore little resemblance to the legal ideal he reiterates in the *Partidas*, for several of his brothers and sons did him the great dishonor of rebelling against him.)

Of the three estates, the clergy was the one deemed most worthy of respect, for its duties in society pertain to man's ultimate destiny, the salvation of his soul. Notwithstanding its lofty mission, the clergy traditionally was associated with great wealth because, like the nobility, it was exempt from paying taxes. The clergy is the estate least represented in literature. Exemplary priests or nuns, like mothers, do not normally afford much dramatic potential since they should be immune from concerns about love, worldly honor, and power. When clergymen do appear, however, they are often portrayed as greedy abusers of the common people, for which they are the objects of biting satire.

The clergy and the nobility, or second estate, joined forces during the Crusades and the Reconquest (the crusade begun in 711 and concluded in 1492 to liberate the Iberian Peninsula from the Moslems) to form the religious-military orders. They were, nevertheless, wont to disdain one another's way of life. Literature makes use of the pen-versus-sword motif to illustrate the rivalry between the educated cleric or clerk (two words derived from the Latin *"clericus"*) and the illiterate knight-soldier. In the satirical, thirteenth-century *Disputa de Elena y María*, for example, the priest's girl friend extols the material comforts of her lover's existence, in marked contrast to the hazardous realities of life that the soldier must confront. Needless to say, the soldier appears to be the more self-sacrificing and deserving of eternal reward. Several centuries later, Don Quijote discourses with more impartiality on the relative merits of letters and arms. Both, he concludes, are as mutually dependent as the notions of theory and practice that they exemplify.[2]

Like the clergy, the nobility was organized hierarchically, a reflection of estate society and the divine order on which it in turn was patterned. It comprised three subgroups, or strata:

1. *Títulos* (such noblemen as marquesses who inherited their titles) and *grandes* 'grandees'; known in the Middle Ages as *ricos hombres* 'men of means', grandees were allowed the privilege of keeping on their hats while in the king's presence.

2. *Caballeros* (cavaliers); the Golden Age descendants of these medieval knights were entitled to a coat of arms as outward proof of their nobility.

3. *Hidalgos* (squires); known during medieval times as *hijos dalgo* 'sons of the worthy', they constituted the lowest stratum of the aristocracy. They generally resided in the countryside, where they were landowners. Literature stereotypes them as poor, vain, and ridiculous. They try to obscure their poverty with the outward appearance of extreme gentility, and they act with excessive punctiliousness in matters regarding their honor. Medieval *hidalgos* had been prohibited from earning money. As their sixteenth- and seventeenth-century descendants were accustomed to a life of leisure, they considered most demeaning indeed the possibility of working for a living, an attitude that Golden Age authors ascribed not only to pride but to laziness.

Medieval noblemen were required to defend the faith and the realm at the king's bidding and to protect the defenseless. Notwithstanding Don Quijote's efforts to the contrary, however, medieval chivalry by the late sixteenth century was but a memory of the past. A new breed of aristocrat had begun to emerge from the three traditional ranks of the nobility, the *cortesano* 'courtier' (whom Baldassare Castiglione describes in his treatise *Il Cortegiano*). Extensively depicted in literature, he represents the decadence of chivalry, which had been the guiding principle of knighthood. With the advent of the courtier, the battlefield has given way to the palace. Like the medieval knight, the courtier hopes to win the favor of the king. To that end, unlike the knight, he must now resort to intrigue as he can find few battles in which to display his prowess.

The third estate comprised the common people, who then, as now, were the laborers and taxpayers of society. During the Middle Ages, manual laborers were closely identified with agriculture and included farmers and those merchants who traded in agricultural goods. This estate gradually broadened to encompass the bourgeoisie, or incipient middle class, which had become more numerous with the increase of commerce and with the subsequent growth of cities. Literature introduces us to the gamut of commoners: landowning and tenant farmers, journeymen, merchants, craftsmen, doctors, lawyers, notaries, innkeepers, soldiers, and servants.

ENDNOTES

[1] King Alfonso X, *Las siete partidas*, Partida II, Title XIII, Law xiii, in *Los códigos españoles concordados y anotados* (Madrid: n.p., 1848), II, 395.

[2] Miguel de Cervantes, *El ingenioso hidalgo don Quijote de la Mancha*, Pt. I, Ch. xxxviii, in *Obras completas*, ed. A. Valbuena Prat, 12th ed. (Madrid: Aguilar, 1962), pp. 1205–1207.

2

Literary Treatments of Social Ascent

In theory, the medieval social structure restricted the individual to his own estate, which fixed his place in society. In practice, however, social ascent was not uncommon. During the first five centuries of the Reconquest, numerous commoners who had acquired land formerly owned by Moslems were able to attain *hidalgo* status. From the fourteenth century on, the gap between social theory and practice widened even more. Many wealthy commoners fraudulently obtained *ejecutorias* 'letters patent of nobility' so that they could become *hidalgos* and thus reap the benefits of tax-exemption. Numerous affluent bourgeois, Jews, and *Conversos* married urban nobles and also ascended the social ladder. After all, what could be more mutually advantageous than the merger of a fortune-hunting aristocrat and a wealthy social climber?

Despite such "contamination" within its ranks, the nobility professed to scorn the wealth of the bourgeoisie, whose desire to amass money was considered sinful. More pertinent, however, to the reality of the times than this quasi-religious pretext is the fact that noblemen sought to protect their privileges in the face of a more fluid economy and the resultant increase in the number of affluent nonnobles. Exemplified by Prince Juan Manuel in his defense of the estate system, they feared the upheaval that would ensue from a disturbance of the "natural order of things", that is, of the established social order, which the ideals of lineage and inherited—not earned—wealth helped to preserve.

The desire to ascend socially is a recurrent literary motif of the Golden Age. It reflects the very human desire to better one's condition and to gain the respect of one's peers and superiors.

Commoner and noble characters who strive to climb within their own estates often meet with success. Owning land enables a peasant to acquire wealth and the favorable opinion of his peers. Through good fortune, a poor cavalier may win the heart and hand of a duchess. Reflecting the tenets of the sixteenth and seventeenth centuries, literature condones these instances of upward mobility because they do not promote social unrest.

What literature infrequently tolerates is the marginal individual—the *pícaro* or the *Converso*, for example—who determines to break into established society from without. We shall see in Pt. II that novelists depict the world this individual hopes to enter as one that thwarts him at every step.

With the exception of the occasional slave, Golden Age theater rarely presents us with characters born outside or on the fringes of established society. The lives of *pícaros* and *Conversos* are the subject of novels, not of plays. As a result, dramatists spared themselves the dilemma of handling such controversial topics as the ambitious marginal man or woman, or a *Converso*'s love affair with an old Christian.

The *gracioso* (the stock, comic servant character of Golden Age theater) shares some of the attributes of the *pícaro*. He is concerned with day-to-day survival and yearns to improve his financial state. He is a realist, and his mundane values are diametrically opposed to the lofty ideals of honor that the principal male character upholds. Several important differences, nonetheless, distinguish the *gracioso* from the *pícaro*. The *gracioso* is a member of the third estate, and his blood is "pure". Birth has endowed him with what the *pícaro* covets, a place in established society. The *pícaro* marries for convenience or simple passion; the *gracioso*, for love (albeit crudely expressed!). He weds another servant; never does he marry above him. Nor does he attempt to climb the social ladder in any other way, unlike the *pícaro*.[1]

Respectful of the inherent inequality between members of the second and third estates, playwrights treat relatively few

20

cases of commoners who succeed in attaining noble status. One commoner type who tries to succeed and who often fails is the wealthy, middle-aged or elderly merchant. A stock character in the comedies of intrigue, he conspires with an aristocrat to marry the latter's daughter. The heroine happily outwits her materialistic father and her lecherous suitor. Asserting her will, she marries her truelove, a fellow noble of sometimes reduced means.[2]

Peasant protagonists, on the other hand, seldom harbor a desire to leave their estate. The older and wealthier ones are especially content to cleave to their ancestral niches, from which they derive great satisfaction. They are proud of their "purity of blood", a heritage that imbues them with a kind of honor and that distinguishes them from merchants and urban aristocrats, whose blood they suspect is "tainted". They know their place in society and cherish their peaceful existence, which in their opinion emanates from an unperturbed social order.

Lope de Vega, the father of the *Comedia nueva* (the corpus of Spanish plays written during the late sixteenth and the seventeenth centuries), penned several plays concerning the *villano* 'villein' who dreams of nothing more than to live in the tranquility of his beloved countryside, far removed from the intrigue and falsity of the court. In one such play, *El cuerdo en su casa*, Lope contrasts the prudent (*cuerdo*) shepherd Mendo with his friend, the *hidalgo* Don Leonardo, who tells Mendo to acquire some of the trappings of the aristocracy. External display is important to Leonardo because it creates the aura of privilege and prestige. Mendo replies that he was born a peasant and will die a peasant and that Leonardo is foolish to think that what befits his role—damask in his home (*casa*)—would also befit Mendo's. True to himself and his peasant stock, Mendo refuses to don the proverbial kid gloves.

Although dramatists tend to portray peasants as content with their station in life, they do permit a token number to climb a rung or two to the lower strata of the nobility. Even more extraordinary are the truly exceptional cases of commoners who manage to scale the social ladder.

One way for a commoner to rise is to display qualities traditionally associated with the aristocracy: the respect of one's peers, loyalty above and beyond the requisite paying of taxes, honor, and courage. If these attributes catch the king's attention, he may reward the commoner by bestowing on him honors that he would normally accord only a noble.

One example of an ennobled peasant is Peribáñez, the hero of the play that Lope de Vega named after him. Peribáñez is happily married to Casilda, with whom the Knight Commander falls passionately in love. Realizing that he cannot seduce her under the watchful eyes of her husband, he hatches a plot, which ultimately leads to his own ruination: he names Peribáñez captain of a band of soldiers and assigns him to lead an expedition that will force him to be absent from his home. Peribáñez discovers the ruse and kills the Commander. The King not only sanctions Peribáñez' deed but honors him by confirming his captaincy.

Another example is Pedro Crespo, the heroic mayor of Pedro Calderón de la Barca's drama *El alcalde de Zalamea*. The wicked Captain has carried off Crespo's daughter against her will. In his capacity as mayor, Crespo orders him executed. The King condones Crespo's act and names him mayor for life.

Peribáñez and Crespo do not rebel against the nobility in general or against the estate system. They merely oppose those noblemen who fail to recognize that peasants are just as entitled as they to defend their honor and to be treated with justice. The monarchs of these plays uphold the peasants' dignity and ratify the righteous punishment the two lowly members of society have meted out to their social superiors.

Although the older peasants are proud to be simple, plain folk, their offspring are often not. Pedro Crespo's son Juan, for example, tries to persuade Crespo to purchase letters of nobility, to which Crespo replies that honor born of genuine nobility, by its very nature, cannot be bought: "Que honra no la compra nadie."[3] He knows what he is and what he is not, and a false title would not fool anyone.

Tempted by the lure of adventure and of courtly life, the

young are eager to savor more of the world than their rustic villages. The generation gap widens when a youthful peasant and an aristocrat fall in love. Matrimony would allow the commoner access to the world of the nobility, but such marriages are infrequent in Golden Age drama. The lovers must first override the objections of their fathers, who think it unnatural for love and marriage to cross social barriers. Then the king normally must give his assent. As his duty is to preserve what he believes to be a divinely inspired system, he ennobles the commoner in order to give their marriage a semblance of social equality. Love indeed triumphs over obstacles that society has imposed, but at the same time it has not seriously disrupted the status quo.[4]

Several of Lope de Vega's plays deal with a peasant and a noble whose love bridges the gulf between the two worlds they represent: the country and the court. One such play is *El villano en su rincón*. Juan Labrador, the protagonist, extols the virtues of rural life and cannot understand why his children would forsake the serenity of the country for the excitement of the court. Meanwhile, the King has heard favorable reports about Juan and invites him to visit him in his palace. Juan refuses to leave his home. Intrigued that a humble villein embodies such haughtiness, the King pays *him* a visit and asks him to send his children to the court. The King has swallowed his pride in seeking out Juan, and now Juan must reciprocate. He reluctantly accedes to the King's request, but his life will never be the same. Once at court, his daughter and the noble Otón fall in love. The King supplies her with a dowry so that she may marry Otón in style, and he raises Juan's son to the rank of cavalier; what is more, he names Juan his majordomo. We sympathize with poor Juan. His children's dreams have come true, but he must sacrifice what he holds most dear, his own little corner (*rincón*) of the world, for an honor he never sought.[5]

El villano en su rincón inspired Francisco de Rojas Zorrilla to write his famous drama *Del rey abajo, ninguno*. García, the protagonist, shares Juan Labrador's dislike of courtly life, but for different reasons. Unlike Juan, García and his wife Blanca are both noble-born. Their fathers had incurred the King's wrath and had found refuge in the country, where they and their children have lived as peasants. Curious to know why García has avoided meeting him, the King determines to visit him incognito. After a tense episode in which García mistakenly thinks that the King plans to seduce Blanca, all ends well. The King learns the couple's true identity and magnanimously restores them to his favor and to the position their forefathers had once enjoyed.

Tirso de Molina gives a new twist to the story of the peasant and the aristocrat in his *Mari-Hernández la gallega*. Mari is a conniving peasant girl who schemes to marry Don Álvaro. In love with Marchioness Beatriz, Álvaro is a most reluctant bridegroom. Only through deception and the intervention of the King, who also loves Beatriz and hopes to rid himself of a rival, will Mari be able to entrap him. Lying to the King, she tells him that Álvaro seduced her with the promise of making her his wife. Deceit and two love triangles combine to produce happiness for Mari and misery for her two victims. The King raises Mari to the nobility and forces Álvaro to wed her. He then gives the crestfallen Beatriz in marriage to another noble. Mari scores a victory of sorts, but one that condemns Álvaro and Beatriz to live apart, each in a state of blissless matrimony.

Miguel de Cervantes also penned a story about an astute, ambitious peasant girl, Dorotea, and her plot to snare the nobleman whom she loves; Cervantes incorporated this tale in his masterpiece *El ingenioso hidalgo don Quijote de la Mancha*.

Contemplating what she hopes is her forthcoming wedding, Dorotea recognizes that she is not the first to use marriage as a vehicle of social ascent: "No seré yo la primera que por vía de matrimonio haya subido de humilde a grande estado."[6] In order to ensure that her dreams come true, Dorotea hides witnesses in her bedroom and then invites Don Fernando to a rendezvous. The witnesses overhear Fernando promise to marry her just before she lets him make love to her. Unfortunately, however, he reneges on his promise and abandons her. Dishonored but still determined to win Fernando and the social status he represents, Dorotea sets out to pursue him. After many adventures (during which time she meets Don Quijote), she finally tracks him down. Her perseverance fills him with admiration and respect, and his conscience tells him what the witnesses would have confirmed—that she is his wife. Accordingly, he vows to cherish her for the rest of his life, and the two return home together.

With the exception of a comparatively small number of works, Golden Age literature reflects the widespread disapproval of socially mixed marriages. Yet writers were well aware of the dramatic potential to be found in the conflict between love and societal customs. In presenting the romance of two *apparently* unequal lovers and the discovery in the denouement that the commoner is *really* a noble, authors made use of an ingenious solution that would respect society, on the one hand, and allow love to triumph, on the other.

Cervantes employs this device in two of his short "exemplary" novels (*Novelas ejemplares*). "La gitanilla" is a story about the noble Don Juan, who is enamored of the "gypsy" girl (*gitanilla*) Preciosa. He leaves home and willingly assumes a new identity as the gypsy Andrés so that he may prove himself worthy of her love. As it turns out, the gypsies had abducted the noble-born Preciosa as an infant and have raised her as their own. Daughter and parents are reunited, and she marries Juan/Andrés with the approval of her family and his. The plot of "La ilustre fregona" is essentially the same: Constanza, a washerwoman (*fregona*), is revealed to be of illustrious lineage and marries Avendaño, who is not a *pícaro* at all but as noble as she.

The lovers of both stories have assumed temporary identities, which do not correspond to their true social status. Although these roles are but a brief interlude in their lives, they are crucial as a means of testing the strength of their love, a love that would have prevailed despite their seeming differences. Cervantes, however, respects convention and does not permit the lovers to wed until they have resumed the roles befitting their heritage.[7]

Bartolomé de Torres Naharro, a precursor of the *Comedia nueva*, wrote two plays, *Comedia calamita* and *Comedia aquilana*, that make use of this technique. To heighten the dramatic appeal of these dramas, he emphasizes the dishonor that would befall the noble's and the King's families, respectively, if the "ill-matched" lovers were to marry. Calamita, the heroine of the play bearing her name, is ostensibly a peasant girl. The noble-born Floribundo has fallen in love with her and wishes to marry her, much to the consternation of his father, who would rather him dead than wed beneath him:

> Pues vengo determinado
> De matarle [a Floribundo] si no muero;
> Que al mal hijo más lo quiero
> So tierra que mal casado.[8]

The King of *Comedia aquilana* discovers that his squire Aquilano has won his daughter's heart. Their relationship, he fears, might cause the esteem in which he is held to plummet: "¿Qué dirán? / ¿Qué estima de mí harán?"[9] Parental anger turns to joy in the two plays when it is discovered that Calamita is noble-born and that Aquilano is a Hungarian prince in disguise. Only with the removal of social barriers can love find fulfillment in marriage.

Lope de Vega also enables his characters to wed in a way that satisfies the demands of their world. His *La moza del cántaro* is particularly interesting in that the heroine, Doña María, is one of the few avenging women to appear in Golden Age theater. Fearing capture after she kills the man who has dishonored her father, she disguises herself as a washerwoman; her trademark is the bucket (*cántaro*) she carries to fetch water. Although Don Juan courts her with great persistence, she feels compelled to refuse his love because she cannot make known her real name; nor does she deem it proper for him to marry a "servant" (*moza*). But the story has a happy ending. Pardoned for the murder that her outraged honor forced her to commit, she reveals her true identity (which Juan claims to have suspected all along) and finally marries her beloved.

In two of Lope's plays, *El perro del hortelano* and *La vengadora de las mujeres*, women of high rank fall in love with their secretaries. They vacillate between the extremes of social convention, which dictates that they reject their admirers, and love. Although they profess to disdain their suitors, they cannot bring themselves to relinquish them altogether.

Lope stresses the ambivalent behavior of this kind of woman in the title he gave to the first of these plays. *"El perro del hortelano"* derives from a refrain about a mean-tempered gardener's dog that neither eats nor permits any other creature to eat. Lope likens the central character, Countess Diana, to the cur in that she removes herself from the object of her desire but selfishly refuses to relinquish him to another lady. Gradually, nastiness and pride give way to love, and she resolves to wed him. She knows that her beloved is not of her social stature, even though Count Ludovico has mistakenly proclaimed him his long-lost son. Her truelove's origins, however, matter less to her than the fact that the world believes him to be her equal. She is not about to repudiate Ludovico's claim, since the truth would jeopardize her reputation. Only the lovers know the full significance of their impending marriage—that it will effectively transform a sham count into a real one.

Princess Diana, the avenger (*vengadora*) of women (*mujeres*), hates all men at the outset of the play, and she resolves to write of men's defects in order to punish them for the wrongs they have inflicted on women. Lope, of course, must then avenge men by humiliating her: he makes her fall in love despite her liberated attitude, a dilemma compounded by her lover's ostensible social inferiority. Knowing that she cannot live without him, she has no choice but to wed him. That he is really the Prince of Transylvania in disguise does, nevertheless, assuage the punishing blow to her pride.

To this device of truth revealed, Tirso de Molina introduces a new and personal note, the vindication of the disinherited, bastard child of political exiles. Tirso, perhaps himself the illegitimate son of the Duke of Osuna, created individuals who intuitively sense that they are to the palace born. As peasants, they fall in love with highborn young men and women. Once they discover their ancestry, they cast off their false, peasant roles, which society and circumstances had forced on them, and they claim what is theirs by birth.

Tirso's *El vergonzoso en palacio* concerns the ambitious Portuguese "shepherd" Mireno. Eager to taste courtly life, he leaves the countryside and changes his name to the regal "Dionís". His fortune begins to improve when Duchess Magdalena makes him her secretary, but his arrogant nature turns bashful (*vergonzoso*) when she aggressively pursues him. For them to marry, he first must overcome his timidness. Then they both must defy convention. Only after they wed do they find out that Mireno/Dionís is in fact Prince Dionís, whose father had been wrongly accused of murder and had fled the court to lead the life of a humble shepherd. Dionís' royal blood, never fully suppressed, emerges victorious.

Rogerio, the lead character of Tirso's *El melancólico*, also abandons the countryside, and eventually he discovers that he is the illegitimate son of the Duke of Britanny. Courtly life, however, fills him with melancholy. He yearns to succeed on his own merits, but his friends at the court respect him for his inheritance, not for his ingenuity, which he fears his newly discovered title will obscure:

> Yo con la industria mía,
> Lo que no a la fortuna, le debía
> A la naturaleza,
> Ambicioso de fama y de grandeza
> No heredada, adquirida
> Con noble ingenio y estudiosa vida,
> Que ilustra más la personal nobleza.[10]

What is more, Rogerio longs for the peasant girl Leonisa, and he decides to forsake convention in order to wed her. Leonisa has also long harbored a secret uncertainty about her origins.

The fortuitous discovery that she is Rogerio's cousin confirms her suspicion and facilitates their marriage.[11]

Such revelations concerning the true provenance of ostensible commoners liberate them from a way of life that the wrongdoings of others have imposed on them. Once vindicated, these innocent victims may lay claim to a world their birthright has preordained for them, and they may enjoy the freedom to wed whom they so desire. Truth also serves to placate society, which otherwise would have placed obstacles in their paths.

ENDNOTES

[1] See J.A. Maravall, "Relaciones de dependencia e integración social: Criados, graciosos y pícaros."

[2] Another commoner whose efforts to ascend the social ladder are thwarted is the arrogant protagonist of Lope de Vega's *El caballero del milagro.*

[3] Pedro Calderón de la Barca, *El alcalde de Zalamea*, Act I, in *Obras completas*, ed. A. Valbuena Briones, 5th ed. (Madrid: Aguilar, 1969), I, 545.

[4] For more information on the drama as a vehicle to propagandize the social status quo, see J.A. Maravall, *Teatro y literatura en la sociedad barroca*, espec. pp. 57–77, 85–86; J.M. Díez Borque, *Sociología de la comedia española del siglo XVII*, espec. pp. 70–71, 346–351; and G.H. Szanto, *Theater and Propaganda*, espec. pp. 23–24, 75.

[5] Another play about a content, conservative peasant is Lope's *Los Tellos de Meneses*, Pt. I.

[6] Miguel de Cervantes, *El ingenioso hidalgo don Quijote de la Mancha*, Pt. I, Ch. xxviii, in *Obras completas*, ed. A. Valbuena Prat, 12th ed. (Madrid: Aguilar, 1962), p. 1151.

[7] See A.E. Wiltrout, "Role Playing and Rites of Passage: *La ilustre fregona* and *La gitanilla.*"

[8] Bartolomé de Torres Naharro, *Comedia calamita*, Act V, in *Teatro selecto*, ed. H. López Morales (Madrid: Las Américas, 1970), p. 316.

[9] Ibid., *Comedia aquilana*, Act IV, p. 409.

[10] Tirso de Molina, *El melancólico*, Act II, in *Obras dramáticas completas*, ed. B. de los Ríos, 3rd ed. (Madrid: Aguilar, 1969), I, 234.

[11] Another play about the noble origins of a "peasant" is Tirso's *Averígüelo Vargas.*

II

The Plight of the Alienated and the Outcast

3

Negative Solitude and the
Marginal Individual

Historians have traditionally depicted the vertical structure
of society in the form of a triangle: the king represented the
apex; the nobility, the stratum immediately beneath him; and
the commoners, the base. Américo Castro, one of the foremost
twentieth-century historians of Spain, viewed Spanish history
from a different perspective. For him, medieval society was
structured horizontally into three *castas*, or groups determined
by racial-religious criteria.[1] During the Middle Ages, each of
these three *castas*—Christians, Moslems, and Jews—performed
functions essential to the well-being of society. In very broad
terms, Christians were knights, soldiers, and farmers; Moslems
were farmers and artisans; and Jews were doctors, intellectuals,
merchants, and financiers.

Castro did not intend to disprove the existence of the hierarchical estate system but to show that an analysis of medieval
Spain *solely* in terms of estates fails to take into account the fact
that Moslems and Jews also played a vital role in weaving the
fabric of Spanish society, a role historians prior to Castro tended
to disregard. Although established society treated Moslems and
Jews as marginal, these groups did form an integral part of
Spanish society as a whole. Indeed, affirmed Castro, a knowledge of the interplay among the three medieval *castas* is crucial
to an understanding of the Golden Age, since the presence of
non-Catholics profoundly affected the psyche of sixteenth- and
seventeenth-century Spain.[2]

As a consequence of the Reconquest, the expulsion of the
Moslem population and of many Jews, and the forced conver-

sion of those Jews who chose to remain in Spain, Catholicism would emerge as the official religion of all Spaniards. Thus, the delicate balance among the *castas*, one that mutual dependency had fostered, would give way to the supremacy of the Christian *casta*. It took the Christians some nine hundred years, however, to achieve total dominance of Spain.

MORISCOS

The Moors had begun their invasion of the Iberian Peninsula in 711 and in the course of only a few years had conquered most of what is present-day Spain and Portugal, save for a small area in the North. Immediately following the invasion, the Christians initiated their Reconquest. Granted Crusade status by the Church, the Reconquest lasted for nearly eight hundred years. During that time, in a sporadic succession of battles, the Christians moved slowly southward reconquering Moorish lands in their paths. January 2, 1492, signaled the end of the Reconquest, for on that day Granada, the last Moorish stronghold of the Peninsula, fell to the Christians.

Not all Moors acquiesced to Christian domination. The *Mudéjares* (Moslems who lived in reconquered lands) of Granada revolted in 1499–1500. As a result, Queen Isabel (Isabella) I of Castile ordered them to convert or to face expulsion. As many *Mudéjares* were unable or understandably reluctant to leave their ancestral homes, they accepted baptism. In 1568–1570, however, the *Moriscos* (the name given these converted *Mudéjares* and their descendants) staged a second uprising in Granada to protest decrees prohibiting them from speaking Arabic and wearing Moorish dress. That they resisted full assimilation to Catholic traditions led the Old Christian populace to doubt the sincerity of their newly acquired religious beliefs. Old Christians assumed that the *Moriscos*, notwithstanding their "conversion", might look to the Turks as liberators and that they would act as a fifth column in lending their support to a Turkish invasion. Fearing such a possibility, King Felipe (Philip) III made the momentous decision in 1609 to expel the *Moriscos*. During the course of the next five years, some 275,000–300,000 *Moriscos*, of a total population of 7,500,000–10,000,000 Spaniards, were escorted to the port cities and frontiers of Spain. The majority of them settled in North Africa, the land of their forefathers. After 1614, only some 10,000 stragglers remained, pocketed chiefly in Castile.

Spain had achieved her goal—political and religious unity—by effectively ridding herself of the descendants of Islam, and this final epilogue to the Reconquest drew to a close. From an economic point of view, nevertheless, the expulsion of the *Moriscos* spelled disaster, especially for Valencia where agriculture suffered an irreparable decline.

Moors appear in medieval Spanish epic poetry, though rarely as heroic protagonists; after all, they were the sworn enemy of Christendom. In the years following the Christian victory at Granada, however, the Reconquest became but a memory of the past. It was then that the spirit of magnanimity combined with the nostalgia of an idealized, chivalrous past to produce the so-called "Moorish" ballads (*romances*) and novels, which flourished during the last two decades of the sixteenth century. The Christian novelists who wrote these tales chose Granada as their setting, and they portray the Moor as a heroic knight and a courtly lover whom war compels to take leave of his beloved. His gallantry and faithfulness are rewarded when more fortunate circumstances at long last permit the lovers to reunite.[3]

Moriscos, unlike Moors, do not figure prominently as literary characters. Despite the havoc that forced conversion and later expulsion wrought in their lives, established society continued to view them with distrust.

The *Morisco* with whom readers of Spanish literature are probably most familiar is Ricote, who makes a brief appearance in Pt. II of *Don Quijote de la Mancha*. Sancho Panza, Don Quijote's loyal squire, has been Ricote's friend and neighbor. Ricote tells Sancho of the *Moriscos'* plight in general and of his own sadness as he prepares to bid farewell to his country. We sense Cervantes' mixed reaction to the expulsion, ordered only six years before he published this final part of the novel. On the one hand, Ricote seems to voice the sentiments of Catholic Spain. He agrees with the decree of 1609 since, by his own admission, most *Moriscos* were false converts and posed a potential threat to the unity of Spain. On the other hand, and on a personal level, Sancho sympathizes with his friend.[4]

Ricote's story is the lament of a group of people so marginal that not even formal conversion was sufficient to warrant their fitting into the mosaic of Spanish society. The Jews, as we shall see, could at least choose whether to go into exile or not, but the *Moriscos*, despite their overt Catholicism, were left with no alternative but to endure the hardships of banishment. Wherever they are, *Moriscos* cry for Spain, Ricote tells Sancho, for Spain is their homeland, their birthplace. And what is equally tragic is that they never find elsewhere the welcome they so desire: "Doquiera que estamos lloramos por España; que, en fin, nacimos en ella y es nuestra patria natural; en ninguna parte hallamos el acogimiento que nuestra desventura desea."[5]

Ricote has decided to settle with his family in Germany, where he hopes to live in a peaceful environment of religious tolerance. He has secretly returned to his former home to unearth the treasure he had hidden, and he asks Sancho's help. Sancho refuses on the grounds that to aid an enemy of the State is treason. Nonetheless, he will not betray Ricote, and the two men remain friends as they take their leave of one another.

Sancho's feelings toward Ricote may be ambivalent, but most Old Christian characters regard *Moriscos* with utter contempt, as we read in a passage from Lope de Vega's *El duque de Viseo*. When a young noblewoman learns, to her dismay, that her fiancé is half Moorish, she resolves to end their engagement at once, for she will not deign to enter such a lowly marriage. What is more, she even begins to wonder whether she ever loved him at all. What, she asks herself, could have attracted her to such an infamous man in the first place?:

¡Casada! No lo permita
El cielo, ni que yo venga
A casarme con quien tenga
Tal nota de infamia escrita.
¡Afuera, vil pensamiento!
Amor, si hubo amor alguno,
No me seas importuno
Con tan bajo casamiento.[6]

The young lady talks herself out of love because she owes it to herself, her family, and her *casta* not to besmirch her good reputation. She brushes aside her feelings, which matter little in the face of weightier social considerations.

CONVERSOS

The history of the Spanish Jews is as turbulent as that of the Moslems. Although Jews seemed to coexist peacefully with Christians during the Middle Ages, the Christian nobility and peasantry envied their positions of wealth and power, and they derided them as avaricious usurers. The mendicant religious, preaching that Jews were *matacristos* 'killers of Christ', encouraged the hostility of Christians, whose hatred toward Jews grew to such a crescendo that they accused Jewish doctors of poisoning their Christian patients. They even found in the Jews a scapegoat for the plagues of the fourteenth century, and they charged them with tainting their wells. This anti-Semitism culminated in the violent pogroms of 1391. Fearful of further reprisals against them, thousands of Jews immediately converted to Christianity.

Except for their newly adopted religion (as a result of which many *Conversos* rose to positions of distinction in the Church), their life-styles remained virtually unchanged. They continued to engage in the same professions as their Jewish brethren. Their intellectual acumen, like that of their forefathers, enabled them to exercise their influence in matters of State, and their wealth still made it possible for them to marry Old Christian merchants and nobles.

The numerous conversions of fifteenth-century Jews, however, failed to extinguish the smoldering fires of anti-Semitism. To the contrary, hatred toward the Jews reached its tragic peak on March 30 of that historic year 1492 when King Fernando (Ferdinand) II of Aragon and his wife Queen Isabel declared that they would no longer tolerate the presence of Judaism within their realms. In decrees similar to those they issued their Moslem subjects, they banished all Jews who chose not to renounce their ancestral faith.

With the expulsion of some 150,000 Jews, Catholic Spaniards scored what they thought was a significant victory: the clergy rejoiced to see its dream of religious unity fulfilled, at least officially; the nobility rid itself of a threat to its predominance; and the commoners (in particular, those of Castile) bid good riddance to a sector of society that they were inclined to blame for their own misfortunes. The price, however, that Catholic Spain paid for her triumph was steep—the weakening of her economy, which would never fully recover.

The religious sincerity of the *Conversos* was a matter that troubled both Church and State during the fifteenth, sixteenth, and seventeenth centuries. Many *Conversos* did wholeheartedly embrace Catholicism, and several went on to become Inquisitors (Tomás de Torquemada), bishops (the Hieronymite Hernando de Talavera, who was also Queen Isabel's confessor), and saints (Teresa de Ávila). But Old Christians and zealous New Christians, recognizing that coercion provided a poor basis for religious sincerity, took for granted (as they had in the case of the *Moriscos*) that large numbers of *Conversos*, especially the less educated, were in reality *Marranos* (crypto-Jews). That *Marranos* secretly clung to Jewish dietary laws and observed the Sabbath hurt the credibility of authentic *Conversos*, a point that the aforementioned Hernando de Talavera makes in his religious treatise *Católica impugnación*. Talavera defends *all* sincere Catholics and vehemently denounces Old Christians who insultingly refer to faithful *Conversos* as *Marranos* (literally "swine") and heretics:

"Que yerra gravemente el que denuesta a los cristianos nue-
vamente convertidos, llamándoles marranos y marrandíes y
mucho más llamándoles herejes."[7]

Talavera was not alone in advocating the cause of the faithful
Converso. The sixteenth-century Augustinian *Converso*, humanist, poet, and theologian Fray Luis de León affirms in his *De
los nombres de Cristo* that all Christians, irrespective of their birth,
belong to the kingdom of God, Who considers no one's lineage
vile:

> El mando de Cristo universalmente comprende a todos los hombres y
> a todas las criaturas, así las buenas como las malas, sin que ninguna
> de ellas pueda eximirse de su sujeción, o se contente de ello o le pese;
> . . . ningún vasallo es ni vil en linaje ni afrentado por condición, ni
> menos bien nacido el uno que el otro.[8]

Santa Teresa also reiterates the same point in a chapter of a
book she wrote for her Carmelite novices, *Camino de perfección;*
the chapter heading reads: "En que trata lo mucho que importa
no hacer ningún caso del linaje las que de veras quieren ser
hijas de Dios" ("Which treats how important it is for women
who truly desire to be God's daughters not to pay attention to
lineage").[9]

Despite such affirmations of the spiritual equality of all true
Christians, the fact remained that many *Marranos*, who were
Christians in name only, never did reject in their hearts the
Jewish faith. Indeed, the presence of crypto-Judaism contrib-
uted to the establishment in 1483 of the Spanish Inquisition.[10]

Spanish monarchs exercised direct control over the Inquisition by appointing Inquisitors-General, whose duty it was to
protect Catholicism from witches, heretics, and false converts.[11]
Because *Conversos* in the sixteenth century numbered some
350,000, or roughly three to five percent of the Spanish population, the Inquisition kept itself well occupied as it watched
over their religious life and punished those who, in its judgment, were *Marranos*.

Following the expulsion decree of 1492, many Jews fled to
Portugal in the hope of finding there what the fictional Ricote

would seek in Germany. But their dreams were short-lived, for in 1497 the Portuguese King Manoel I forced all Jews, Portuguese and Spaniards alike, to convert. Notwithstanding his edict, crypto-Judaism thrived, since Portugal did not establish her own Inquisition until 1536. When Spain annexed Portugal forty-four years later, there ensued a veritable surge of *autos-da-fé* (public Inquisitorial trials and executions). Numerous *Marranos* fled Portugal. Although it seems ironic that many of them sought refuge in Spain, they knew that they could live there free from fear of the Portuguese Inquisition, which had no jurisdiction outside Portugal.[12] These *Marranos* encouraged Castilian *Conversos* to practice the Jewish faith in secret. Try as it did, the Spanish Inquisition was not able to effectively suppress crypto-Judaism until the second half of the seventeenth century.

Old Christian peasants felt secure in the knowledge that very little Jewish blood had "contaminated" their ranks, but townsfolk and nobles knew differently. Because marriage of the largely urban *caballeros* to Jews and *Conversos* was commonplace during the late Middle Ages, Golden Age cavaliers often aspired to membership in the prestigious religious orders so that they could prove to the world their requisite "purity of blood". This cult of "purity" became formalized in a series of statutes issued during the sixteenth and seventeenth centuries, which barred New Christians from holding positions of State and from entering certain religious orders (though not all: several *Conversos* rose to power in the Dominican Order, which supplied the Inquisition with its Inquisitors-General). These statutes, which would remain in effect until the nineteenth century, required that a candidate prove matri- and patrilineal "purity". If the testimony of witnesses and the investigation of parish records substantiated the candidate's claim, he was awarded the coveted certificate of "purity". If, to the contrary, documentary investigation unearthed damaging evidence, or if a vindictive witness gave false testimony, the hapless individual would have to bear for life the stigma attached to his *Converso* status.

The divisive cult of "purity" widened the rift between Old and New Christians. The *Converso*'s existence was, at best, uneasy, for he lived in fear of betraying his heritage. Fear fostered in him the need to appear as Catholic as Old Christians, regardless of the sincerity of his convictions. To this end, he made a point of attending Mass regularly, eating pork publicly, and disregarding the Sabbath altogether.

The cult also forced many *Conversos* to practice another form of deception: in order to attain the desired certificate, they frequently falsified their ancestry by changing their surnames and places of birth and residence and by bribing witnesses. From the second half of the sixteenth century on, wealthy *Conversos* found it increasingly more difficult to marry into noble families; consequently, they tried to buy letters of nobility since noble status, albeit fraudulent, helped to provide the means of achieving a modicum of security in a threatening world.

The estrangement from society that the *Converso* was wont to experience profoundly affected his psyche. The conflict between outward patterns of behavior, on the one hand, and inward sentiments, on the other, resulted in a feeling of alienation from self. Neither belonging fully to established society nor able to disassociate himself from his past, the *Converso* was apt to live in a spiritual, cultural limbo. His was a state of negative solitude, not the solitude of his choosing but one that circumstances and society imposed on him.

The writings of certain New Christians bear witness to the *Converso*'s alienation from self and from his Old Christian neighbors.

The fifteenth-century poet and recent convert Antón de Montoro dons the mask of sardonic humor to hide his suffering. In one poem, he declares that he has dutifully recited the Apostles' Creed, attended Mass, made the sign of the Cross, prayed on his knees, recited the rosary, and eaten pork. Notwithstanding his impressive efforts to appear as Catholic as Old Christians, he has yet to lose the epithet "Jew bastard":

Hice el Credo y adorar,
Ollas de tocino grueso,
Torreznos a medio asar,
Oír misas y rezar,
Santiguar y persignar,
Y nunca pude matar
Este rastro de confeso.
Los hinojos encorvados
Y con muy gran devoción,
En los días señalados,
Con gran devoción contados
Y rezados
Los nudos de la Pasión.

. . .

No pude perder el nombre
De viejo puto y judío.[13]

Montoro directed another poem against the more assimilated New Christian poet Rodrigo de Cota in reply to sarcastic verses the latter had penned about *Marranos* who adhered to Jewish dietary practices. Montoro confesses that he too spoke out against *Marranos*, but only because he was a prisoner of insecurity, fear, and necessity. Cota, to the contrary, has blended in with established society and has subsequently lived free of such duress. Even so, Montoro feels that Cota should be more understanding of the extent to which societal pressures can force a man to denounce his own people:

Retraté contra los míos
De miedo o necesidad;
Más huyendo que alcanzando
Con poca seguridad,
Mi perdición recelando,
Mas no como vos estando
En la vuestra libertad.

. . .

Digo, que con gran misterio
Diréis mal de cuanto hice,
Mas, según cuenta Valerio,
Quien otorga en cautiverio
Es ninguno lo que dice.[14]

Those Jews who submitted to the pressures Montoro describes and who converted outwardly are truly sad creatures, for they neither preserved their old law nor accepted the new one: "Que estos tristes . . . ni conservaron su ley, / Ni tomaron de la nueva."[15]

Montoro derives great pleasure from noting that he and the dapper Cota (whom he facetiously addresses as "muy lindo galán" and "varón de muy linda vista") both descend from the Jewish Medinas and the Benatavés, not from the Old Christian Guzmanes and the Velascos. Cota may pretend to be what he is not, but he cannot fool Montoro. The habit does not make the monk, Montoro pointedly reminds him: "El hábito no hace fraile."[16] And in a final blow to Cota's façade, Montoro suggests that Cota would be better suited to chronicle Moses' deeds than to serve as the Sicilian King's chronicler (a position he apparently held):

> Dicen que sois coronista
> Del Señor Rey de Sicilia;
> Mas no vos pese, señor,
> Porque este golpe vos den;
> Sé que fuérades [fuerais] mejor
> Para ser memorador
> De los hechos de Moisén.[17]

Antonio Enríquez Gómez was a well-known seventeenth-century poet, playwright, and novelist whose *Converso* heritage contributed to his reknown and lent a touching, personal quality to a number of his works. His paternal grandfather, a crypto-Jew, had been arrested by the Inquisition and had died in prison. His father, also a condemned *Marrano*, managed to flee to France, where Enríquez Gómez himself would later spend thirteen years in self-imposed exile.[18]

While in France, Enríquez Gómez composed several poems evocative of the pain that exile and negative solitude have brought him. Through no fault of his own, rivals have persecuted him and have caused him to fall from glory, he writes plaintively in one poem. Estranged from his fatherland, disconsolate, he attributes his plight to the unfortunate circumstances of his birth:[19]

> Despeñado caí de un alto cerro,
> Pero puedo decir seguramente
> Que no nació de mí tan grande yerro.
> Lloro mi patria, y de ella estoy ausente,
> Desgracia del nacer lo había causado,
> Pensión original del que no siente.[20]

He tells us that he has lost the most precious things a man can possess: his home, his good name, and his freedom:

> Perdí mi libertad, perdí mi nido,
> Perdió mi alma el centro más dichoso.
> Y a mí mismo también, pues me ha perdido
> . . .
> Perdí mi estimación, parte primera,
> Del cortesano estilo noble llave,
> . . .
> Perdí lo más precioso de mi estado,
> Perdí mi libertad; con esto digo
> Cuanto puede decir un desdichado.[21]

When he contemplates what he was and the depths to which he has fallen, his agony increases doublefold:

> Cuando me paro a contemplar de asiento
> Lo que al presente soy y lo que he sido,
> El ansia se me dobla y el tormento.
> Cuando me veo solo y perseguido,
> Reparo si yo soy el que merezco
> La imagen de mi ser en tanto olvido.[22]

Enríquez Gómez observes the resemblance between his plight and the Biblical Job's. Like Job, he will place his trust only in the Lord, Who will reward him justly for the tribulations he has patiently endured.[23]

It is difficult to understand why Enríquez Gómez dared to

return to Spain in 1649. He knew firsthand how perilous the religious and political climate of Spain could prove for the grandson and son of crypto-Jews. Did he think that time would erase his past and that he could begin life anew? (He did, upon his return, take the precaution of writing plays under a pseudonym.) Did he hope that Spain would respect him for the honors that France, according to his own testimony, had accorded him? Or did nostalgia for Spain so overpower his fears that he decided to risk the dangers that might lie ahead? Whatever his motivations, he went back to Spain, only to meet the same fate that had befallen his grandfather. Burned in effigy in a Sevillian *auto-da-fé* of 1660, he was arrested one year later as a Judaizer. The Inquisition condemned him in 1663, and within a few days he died in prison while awaiting sentence. He was posthumously reconciled to the Church, however, in 1665.

A play attributed to Enríquez Gómez, *Fernán Méndez Pinto*, is particularly interesting from the standpoint of the individual in a hostile world. It concerns the travels of a sixteenth-century Portuguese, Fernão Mendes Pinto, who left Portugal for mysterious reasons in 1537 (one year after the establishment of the Inquisition in that country) and embarked on a journey to India and the Far East. After he returned to Portugal some thirty years later (just before the Inquisition was established in Portuguese India), Mendes Pinto wrote the story of his adventures, the *Peregrinaçam*, which would provide Enríquez Gómez with the source material for his play. The playwright limits the scope of Mendes Pinto's travels to China, where he has been shipwrecked. But the wheel of Fortune spins again, and he quickly rises to become the Chinese King's captain of the guard.

Enríquez Gómez discovered in Mendes Pinto (who might himself have been a *Converso*) a kindred soul. Both men shared a desire to obscure their genealogies. The hero of the play, reflecting Enríquez Gómez' tragic family history, remarks that to speak of one's grandparents is to tempt fate all the more:

> Que al que ha sido desgraciado
> Blasonar de sus abuelos

> Es incitar la fortuna
> A mayores desaciertos.[24]

Fortune compelled both Mendes Pinto and Enríquez Gómez to a life of travel and travail and beset them with great woes. Through their own merits, however, the two overcame adversity to achieve recognition and respect in exile. It is when they went home that their paths parted ways: Mendes Pinto received widespread acclaim, whereas Enríquez Gómez faced imprisonment.[25]

Misfortune and negative solitude are themes that also set the framework for the so-called "Byzantine" novels. These tales, which enjoyed immense popularity during the Golden Age, relate the afflictions of heroes and heroines whom Fortune and society have condemned to a life of wandering.

One of these novels is Alonso Núñez de Reinoso's *La historia de los amores de Clareo y Florisea y de los trabajos de la sin ventura Isea.* Just as Enríquez Gómez identified with Job and with Mendes Pinto, so too did Núñez, a *Converso* exiled in Italy, identify with Isea, the heroine of his book.

Shipwrecked, buffeted, and rejected, Isea wanders from country to country until she eventually seeks refuge in Spain. She dreams of ending her years of conflict and turmoil in the tranquility of a convent, but the Abbess, echoing the prejudices of established society, soon dashes her hopes. She refuses Isea a permanent haven, for she deems this poor woman of dubious background to be unworthy of associating with the wealthy, pedigreed nuns.[26]

 One of the most popular Spanish dramas ever written is the *Tragicomedia de Calisto y Melibea,* which appeared in print in 1499 and is commonly called *La Celestina* after the fascinating bawd character it portrays. The author of *La Celestina* is the *Converso* Fernando de Rojas, whose father and father-in-law, like Enríquez Gómez and his forefathers, were condemned by the Inquisition for alleged crypto-Judaism.

The principal plot of *La Celestina* concerns the illicit, ill-fated love affair between Calisto and Melibea, which we shall examine in depth in Ch. 12. For now, however, suffice it to say that the lovers perish—Calisto falls off a ladder, whereupon Melibea takes her own life.

Upon witnessing Melibea's suicide, her father Pleberio sadly reflects on the circumstances that have led to her death. Too late does he realize that life is not orderly and rational. In reality, he concludes, it is ruled by unbridled passion, strife, and the vicissitudes of Fortune. His own life has fallen to pieces, and his dreams have turned into nightmares. He amassed great wealth in order to bequeath it to Melibea; now that she is dead, he questions the purpose of his life. As materialistic as his values may seem, he is still a broken, pitiful man whose outlook on life, once optimistic, is now steeped in pessimism. Prior to Melibea's demise, he thought that he had life firmly in control; now, he sees that life has deceived him. Tragically undeceived, he now believes that the nature of the human condition destines men and women to live alienated from one another and from their worlds.

Literary critics have traced the source of Pleberio's pessimistic views to Petrarch's *De remediis utriusque fortunae*. Nonetheless, many scholars are convinced that *La Celestina* is more than a simple reworking of an older text (or texts). Some critics feel that the pessimism of *La Celestina*, especially Pleberio's lament, reflects the *Converso* state of mind: an attitude of insecurity, inner resentment toward a hostile society that exacerbates the travails of human existence, and outward resignation in the face of an ever-changing Fortune.[27]

Another character of *La Celestina* who voices distrust of and disillusionment with the world is the independent-minded prostitute Areusa. Unlike Pleberio, however, her pessimism has arisen early in life. As a result, she has been able to shield herself from much of the suffering that afflicts her friends and acquaintances.

Although nowhere is it stated that Areusa is a New Christian, her profession has relegated her to marginal status, which her outlook on established society reflects. She refutes, for example, the notion that honor is synonymous with lineage. Like Fray Luis de León and Santa Teresa, she asserts that all persons are children of Adam and Eve and that deeds, not ancestry, ought to determine honor. Consequently, she says, each person should endeavor to be good and should not extol his noble forefathers' virtue as proof of his own: "Las obras hacen linaje, que al fin todos somos hijos de Adán y Eva. Procure de ser cada uno bueno por sí y no vaya a buscar en la nobleza de sus pasados la virtud."[28]

What has stirred Areusa to comment on lineage is a discussion of Melibea's physical attributes. According to Areusa, Melibea is not nearly as beautiful as people think. Since Melibea is wealthy, however, people overlook her defects. Areusa's opinions undoubtedly betray a certain degree of jealousy, but they also contain a kernel of truth, a truth that marginal members of society are apt to sense more acutely than members of established society: a person's wealth or pedigree, she implies, distorts the true facts about him or, in this case, her.

Was Miguel de Cervantes, like Fernando de Rojas, also a New Christian? While there is no conclusive evidence to substantiate his claim, Américo Castro concluded that he was. Castro based his opinion on certain details of Cervantes' biography (the fact that his father was a doctor, for example) and on internal, textual evidence. Indeed, many of the themes and motifs that permeate Cervantes' stories (solitude, the conflict of the individual in a hostile world, the individual's need to be recognized for his achievements regardless of his lineage, his disdain of genealogy, and his desire for freedom and justice) are typical of the *Converso* outlook on life.[29]

What offered Castro proof beyond doubt of Cervantes' Jewish origin was a short, farcical play he wrote entitled *El retablo de las maravillas*. This *entremés* 'dramatic interlude' is a hilarious parody of Old Christians and their zealous concern for "purity of blood", on which were based their good reputation and their sense of identity.

Cervantes sets the scene of his *entremés* at a puppet show. In this variation on the same medieval motif that Hans Christian Andersen incorporated in "The Emperor's New Clothes", the Director informs the audience that only legitimately born Old Christians will be able to see the marvellous wonders (*maravillas*) of the show (*retablo*). The curtain rises, the spectators see nothing, and each one, to his horror, believes that he is really an illegitimate *Converso*! Yet all must pretend to see, for their honor is at stake, as the Governor reminds himself: "Basta; que todos ven lo que yo no veo; pero al fin habré de decir que lo veo, por la negra honrilla. . . . ¿Mas si viniera yo a ser bastardo entre tantos legítimos?"[30] No one wants to be excluded from his world, even if inclusion means blinding himself to reality. And when one spectator finally does muster the courage to tell the truth, the others say of him, *"ex illis"*—one of *those*!

Whether or not Cervantes descended from Jews, he was, nevertheless, a partial outsider vis à vis mainstream Spanish society. A soldier, he had fought bravely for Spain and in 1571 had lost the use of his left hand at the Battle of Lepanto. On his way home four years later, Turkish corsairs seized him and carried him off to Algiers. During the five years Cervantes spent in captivity, he gallantly helped other prisoners to escape, although his efforts on his own behalf failed. Ransomed at long last, he returned to Spain. He expected his country to reward him for the services he had rendered her, but official recognition never came his way, and life did not progress for him as he had hoped. His physical handicap precluded a military career, and he could not support himself and his family on the meager earnings from his writings.

He did manage to land a position as commissary of military provisions, only to be charged with misappropriating government funds. Released on bail, he appealed his sentence. He then settled on a career as tax collector and was *again* arrested and released on bail. (Biographers of Cervantes agree that he was most probably innocent of both charges; it was his bookkeeping that was faulty, not his scruples.) And to add insult to injury, the government denied him his petition for a position in the Indies, despite his exemplary military record.

The world treated Cervantes unjustly and forced him to swallow many a bitter pill of disappointment. Fortunately for posterity, however, Cervantes transformed the glories and disillusionments of his life into literary masterworks, as we shall see throughout this book and particularly in Ch. 8.

PRISONERS

Justice seems to have miscarried as far as Cervantes was concerned, and his case was by no means unique. When we consider that the Spanish sixteenth and seventeenth centuries were an age of war, undisputed obedience to authority, struggle for religious orthodoxy, and political and professional intrigue, it comes as no surprise that such other Spanish writers as Enríquez Gómez also found themselves behind bars. A variety of factors led them to imprisonment. In their writings, some lash out in anger at those who have victimized, betrayed, and oppressed them. But what all these authors share in common— and with their *Morisco* and *Converso* brethren—is a radical form of negative solitude and a sense of impotence in the face of circumstances beyond their control.

Let us return to Cervantes, who spent five years in an Algerian bagnio. After two years had elapsed, he wrote his friend Mateo Vázquez a poetic epistle ("Epístola a Mateo Vázquez") in which he describes his plight. He knows firsthand what hardship is, for he has traveled along the worst of roads in the darkest and coldest of nights. Nevertheless, he sees no way out of the blind alley of his present state, no way out of the bitterly unbearable Turkish dungeon. He is losing his youth, he laments, and is dying in a land of barbarian unbelievers:

> Yo, que el camino más bajo y grosero
> He caminado en fría noche oscura,
> He dado en manos del atolladero;

Y en la esquiva prisión, amarga y dura,
Adonde ahora quedo, estoy llorando
Mi corta infelicísima ventura,

. . .

Vida es ésta, señor, do [donde] estoy muriendo,
Entre bárbara gente descreída,
La malograda juventud perdiendo.[31]

Cervantes implores Vázquez to intercede with King Felipe (Philip) II on behalf of himself and of the other twenty thousand Christian prisoners who await ransom or rescue. Cervantes would eventually be ransomed, but in the interim he would have to endure three more years of the tribulations he so movingly depicts.

This period of captivity makes it appearance under the guise of fiction in several of Cervantes' works. One well-known reference to the Turkish dungeons is the "Captive's Tale", contained in *Don Quijote.* Safely back in Spain, the ex-Captive relates the feeling of solitude that engulfed him when pirates seized him. Suddenly he found himself alone in the midst of his enemies, the only unhappy man among so many happy ones, the only captive among so many free men: "Me hallé solo entre mis enemigos a quienes no pude resistir, por ser tantos; . . . y sólo fui el triste entre tantos alegres, y el cautivo entre tantos libres."[32] The "Captive's Tale" is similar in plot to two of Cervantes' dramas about Spaniards imprisoned in Algerian bagnios, *Los baños de Argel* and *Los tratos de Argel.* The same motif recurs in yet another work, his short "exemplary" novel "El amante liberal". In this story, however, Cervantes shifts the scene of action to Turkey and changes the characters' nationality to Sicilian.

The fact that Cervantes fictionalized his episode of captivity on four occasions is significant, for it reveals how traumatic an experience his prolonged incarceration must have been.

An earlier example of the prisoner's solitude is found in a famous anonymous Spanish ballad, the "Romance del prisionero". We do not know why the prisoner is confined, nor does it matter. The ballad takes place in the month of May, when love blossoms and life is born anew. But the prisoner cannot partake of the hope that spring offers. His only consolation is a little bird, which sings to him at dawn. One day, a thoughtless archer kills the bird. Deprived of his only companion, the prisoner in his despair prays for justice—that God punish the archer. With these words the ballad abruptly ends, and we are left with a most poignant reminder of the prisoner's desolation:

> Que por mayo era por mayo,
> Cuando hace la calor,
> Cuando los trigos encañan
> Y están los campos en flor,
> Cuando canta la calandria
> Y responde el ruiseñor,
> Cuando los enamorados
> Van a servir al amor;
> Sino yo, triste, cuitado,
> Que vivo en esta prisión;
> Que ni sé cuándo es de día
> Ni cuándo las noches son,
> Sino por una avecilla
> Que me cantaba al albor.
> Matómela un ballestero;
> Déle Dios mal galardón.[33]

The famed sixteenth-century soldier and poet Garcilaso de la Vega was also imprisoned. His "crime" was that he had witnessed his nephew's betrothal ceremony; as a result, he incurred the wrath of King Carlos I (Emperor Charles V), who was displeased at the match. King Carlos banished Garcilaso to a dungeon on the Danube River. Forced against his will to languish in a distant land, and distraught that the jailer can do with him as he pleases, Garcilaso writes of his loneliness and his helplessness:

> Aquí estuve yo puesto,
> O por mejor decirlo,
> Preso y forzado y solo en tierra ajena;
> . . .
> El cuerpo está en poder
> Y en manos de quien puede
> Hacer a su placer lo que quisiere;[34]

Another prisoner, the aforementioned Augustinian monk Fray Luis de León, was brought to trial by the Inquisition in 1572. What were the charges against this illustrious poet and scholar? For one thing, he had made a private rendering into Spanish of the Old Testament Song of Songs, despite the prohibitions of the Council of Trent against unauthorized translations. For another, he had shown disrespect to the Vulgate of Saint Jerome. A Hebraist, Fray Luis had compared the Vulgate to Hebrew texts of the Bible and had pointed out certain errors in Saint Jerome's translation. Fray Luis had exercised intellectual freedom in a milieu that frowned on such activities, especially if they smacked of heresy or challenged a Church Father's authority. The fact that the Inquisition had denounced his great-grandmother as a crypto-Jewess might not have helped his cause, nor did the jealousy of his Dominican colleagues, who were instrumental in denouncing him.[35]

Fray Luis refers on several occasions to the five years he spent incarcerated. In one poem, he portrays himself as an innocent victim on whom malice has imposed the bleakness of enforced solitude. In words reminscent of the "Romance del prisionero", he writes that the dark prison cell bars him from enjoying the brightness of a new day, the springtime, and the nightingale's song:

> No pinta el prado aquí la primavera,
> Ni nuevo sol jamás las nubes dora,
> Ni canta el ruiseñor lo que antes era.
> La noche aquí se vela, aquí se llora

El día miserable sin consuelo,
. . .
En mí la culpa ajena se castiga,
Y soy del malhechor ¡ah! prisionero,
Y quieren que de mí la fama diga.[36]

The years of imprisonment, however, enabled Fray Luis to work on a project that would occupy him until his death in 1591: a translation and textual commentary of the Book of Job (*Exposición del Libro de Job*). What we know of Fray Luis's struggle to persevere in the midst of conflict and affliction makes it understandable why he, like Enríquez Gómez, identified so deeply with Job.

ENDNOTES

[1] "Caste" is not a good translation of *"casta"* since it connotes a vertical rather than a horizontal social structure.

[2] See A. Castro, *La realidad histórica de España* and *Sobre el nombre y el quién de los españoles.*

[3] Three famous sixteenth-century "Moorish" novels are the anonymous *Historia del Abencerraje y la hermosa Jarifa*, which appeared in Jorge de Montemayor's *Los siete libros de la Diana* and in other works; Ginés Pérez de Hita's *Guerras civiles de Granada;* and Mateo Alemán's "Historia de Ozmín y Daraja", which he included in his *Guzmán de Alfarache*. Both the *Historia del Abencerraje* and *Guerras civiles* served as sources for Washington Irving's *Tales of the Alhambra.*

[4] See F. Márquez Villanueva, "El morisco Ricote o la hispana razón de estado."

[5] Miguel de Cervantes, *El ingenioso hidalgo don Quijote de la Mancha*, Pt. II, Ch. liv, in *Obras completas*, ed. A. Valbuena Prat, 12th ed. (Madrid: Aguilar, 1962), p. 1459.

[6] Lope de Vega, *El duque de Viseo*, Act I, in *Obras escogidas*, ed. F.C. Sainz de Robles, 3rd ed. (Madrid: Aguilar, 1974), III, 1078.

[7] Hernando de Talavera, *Católica impugnación*, Ch. viii, ed. F. Martín Hernández (Barcelona: Juan Flors, 1961), pp. 82–83.

[8] Fray Luis de León, *De los nombres de Cristo*, "Rey de Dios," 4th ed. (Madrid: Espasa-Calpe; Austral, 1968), pp. 166–167.

[9] Santa Teresa de Ávila, *Camino de perfección*, Ch. xlv, in *Obras completas*, ed. E. de la Madre de Dios, O.C.D., and O. Steggink, O. Carm., 2nd ed. (Madrid: Editorial Católica; Biblioteca de Autores Cristianos, 1967), p. 278.

[10] The Spanish Inquisition, also known as the Supreme and General Inquisition, should not be confused with the Papal Inquisition, founded in 1233 to root out heresy.

[11] For a recent and very informative, readable history of the Spanish Inquisition, see H. Kamen's *The Spanish Inquisition*.

[12] See J.H. Yerushalmi, *From Spanish Court to Italian Ghetto*, espec. Ch. 1: "Marranos in the Seventeenth Century."

[13] Antón de Montoro, "A la reina doña Isabel" (a.k.a. "Oh Ropero amargo"), in *Cancionero de Antón de Montoro (el Ropero de Córdoba)*, ed. E. Cotarelo y Mori (Madrid: n.p., 1900), p. 99.

[14] Ibid., "Del mismo a unas que hizo Rodrigo Cota de Maguaque," p. 284.

[15] Ibid., p. 287.

[16] Ibid.

[17] Ibid., p. 292.

[18] Why Enríquez Gómez went to France in 1635 or 1636 is not clear; his departure was probably hastened by his *Converso* status, the courtly intrigue in which he was involved, and/or the debts he owed. Nor is it known whether or not he was a crypto-Jew; T. Oelman, in his "The Religious Views of Antonio Enríquez Gómez: Profile of a Marrano," concludes that he was, and he bases his conclusion on Inquisitiorial documents, the fact that members of his family were *Marranos*, and the absence of Christological and New Testament references in his works.

[19] Enríquez Gómez' pessimism is reminiscent of Segismundo's in Calderón de la Barca's *La vida es sueño*.

[20] Antonio Enríquez Gómez, first "Elegía," in BAE, XLII, 366.

[21] Ibid., p. 367.

[22] Ibid.

[23] See Enríquez Gómez' third "Epístola de Job," in BAE, XLII, 388.

[24] Ibid., *Fernán Méndez Pinto*, Act I, ed. L.G. Cohen, F.M. Rogers, and C.H. Rose (Cambridge, MA: Harvard Univ.; Dept. of Romance Languages & Literatures, 1974), p. 83.

[25] For more information on the relationship between Enríquez Gómez' play and Mendes Pinto's *Peregrinaçam*, see F.M. Rogers, "Fernão Mendes Pinto, His *Peregrinaçam*, and the Spanish Play," and C.H. Rose, "Enríquez Gómez and the Literature of Exile."

[26] See C.H. Rose, *Alonso Núñez de Reinoso: The Lament of a Sixteenth-Century Exile*.

[27] For more on the *Converso* background of Fernando de Rojas and its influence on *La Celestina*, see S. Gilman, *The Spain of Fernando de Rojas: The Intellectual and Social Landscape of La Celestina*.

[28] Fernando de Rojas, *La Celestina*, Act IX, ed. J. Cejador y Frauca, 9th ed. (Madrid: Espasa-Calpe; CC, 1968), II, 34–35.

[29] See A. Castro, "Cervantes y el 'Quijote' a nueva luz."

[30] Cervantes, *El retablo de las maravillas*, in *Obras completas*, p. 583.

[31] Ibid., "Epístola a Mateo Vázquez, mi señor," p. 58.

[32] Ibid., *Don Quijote*, Pt. I, Ch. xxxix, p. 1209.

[33] "Romance del prisionero," in *Flor nueva de romances viejos*, ed. R. Menéndez Pidal, 15th ed. (Buenos Aires: Espasa-Calpe; Austral, 1965), p. 194.

[34] Garcilaso de la Vega, third "Canción," in *Obras*, ed. T. Navarro Tomás (Madrid: Espasa-Calpe; CC, 1963), pp. 181–182.

[35] See M. Durán, *Luis de León*, espec. Ch. 2: "Luis de León, the Man and the Humanist."

[36] Luis de León, "En una esperanza que salió vana," in *Poesía*, ed. J. M. Alda Tesán, 8th ed. (Zaragoza: Ebro, 1967), pp. 66–68.

4

Pícaros and *Pícaras*

The *Moriscos, Conversos*, and prisoners about whom we have read shared the common plight of negative solitude. Yet the dilemma of these estranged and sometimes outcast individuals appears only sporadically in Golden Age literature. If we are to catch more than merely a glimpse of the alienated, we should examine the picaresque novels, which sprang up in Spain in the sixteenth century and continued to flourish well into the seventeenth. This subgenre explores in greater depth than any other the lives of marginal men and women who could find in established society no permanent place for themselves.

The authentic *pícaro*[1] does not and cannot belong to mainstream society, for he was born either on its fringes or outside it altogether. His ancestry is usually tainted morally and/or religiously: his mother may have been a prostitute; his father, a drunkard, gambler, pimp, or thief; and one or both parents, *Conversos*. The child of infamy, the *pícaro* represents the antithesis of the values that established society espouses; he is, therefore, excluded a priori from its ranks.

The weight of his inherited dishonor makes a profound impression on the young *pícaro* and scars him for life. It has brought him shame, which the ridicule of others exacerbates. Try as he will, he can never fully put his past behind him. Moreover, he inexorably becomes what he has futilely attempted to escape. His story bears witness to the atavistic forces that condemn him from the moment he is born.

Other burdens contribute to mold his character. As a youth, he is poor and hungry, circumstances that may already have swayed his mother and father toward a life of moral irregularity. Society, however, does not judge his parents with compassion; when the law does apprehend them, it metes out severe punishments.

Even as a young boy, the *pícaro* is conscious of the poverty and injustice that shape his world. He knows that life offers him three alternatives: he can remain at home, where there is no breaking away from the chains of despair that bind him; he can cast his lot with members of the *hampa* (the infraworld of *pícaros*, beggars, and thieves);[2] or he can try to free himself of his heritage in order to get ahead in life, to *medrar*. Needless to say, the *pícaro* opts for the latter choice because it offers him the possibility of breaking into established society and, thereby, of rising socially and financially.

The *pícaro* bids farewell to his family and heads for the larger towns and cities, where it is easier for him to hide his past than in the countryside and villages. He soon happens upon a stranger in need of a servant. The innocent *pícaro* readily agrees to serve him since he sees in his new role an end to hunger and the beginning of a new and better future. To his immense disappointment, however, his master often proves greedy and cruel, and the *pícaro* leaves him to serve another, the second in what will be a series of masters.

Despite the setbacks and perils that his existence entails, the *pícaro* persists in his resolve to cut himself off completely from his parents' milieu. He determines to become a new person, to forge for himself an entirely new identity. Through his adventures as a servant, he studies the ways of his betters: their values, tastes, and mannerisms. His observations confirm to him what he has long held to be true—that the key to respectability lies not in virtuous behavior but in wealth and in social status. The occasionally good and altruistic deeds he has performed in his early years have, if anything, deterred him from his goals. In order to pass for a person whom established society would welcome as one of its own, he concludes, he must resort to fraud, theft, and other illicit means. He must appear to others to be what he is not, even if it means sacrificing his integrity.

His ambition to enter the mainstream of society distinguishes him from the comic *gracioso* of Golden Age theater, with whom he is often compared. Although the *gracioso* and the *pícaro* both desire wealth, the typical *gracioso* is born a commoner and has therefore no inherent marginal status to obscure. He may wish to have been born a nobleman like his master, but he belongs, nonetheless, to established society. The shame-ridden *pícaro*, on the other hand, yearns for the social acceptance that the *gracioso* has always possessed, and he will go to extraordinary lengths to achieve it.[3]

The world around him has taught the *pícaro* to practice deception. In addition, his masters have furnished him with examples of "success", and he envies them. Hardly paragons of virtue, they have distorted and perverted the ideals of charity, honor, justice, truth, and loyalty, which they outwardly profess. In emulating them, the *pícaro* becomes as hardened and corrupt as they.

The *pícaro*'s façade of deception, however, wears thin, and society generally exposes him as an impudent upstart. A rich *Converso* could use his wealth to buy his way into the Old Christian world, but the poor *pícaro* has no means with which to obtain social status other than to rely on his growing adeptness at delinquency and criminality. Society, however, condones his measures far less than a rich man's fraudulent schemes.

The *pícaro*'s heritage of moral baseness is another factor that distinguishes him from the *Converso*, and it also explains why society continually thwarts him.

Modern readers may take a more tolerant view of the *pícaro*'s immorality and unlawfulness, given the dire conditions of his poverty-stricken existence; they may also consider his antisocial behavior the end product of societal injustice. But Golden Age readers, especially if they belonged to established society, would have interpreted the *pícaro*'s acts in a different light: as the consequence of atavism rather than of social evils. The *pícaro*'s eventual loss of innocence would have struck them as inevitable, because his origins precluded any other possibility. Observant and honest readers of the sixteenth and seventeenth centuries might have conceded that certain members of mainstream society influenced the *pícaro* for the worse. In their judgment, however, he carried within him the seed of ignominy, which was bound to flower regardless of the path he followed.

The *pícaro* manages to climb a rung or two, and sooner or later mainstream society topples him off its ladder. He nurses his wounds and struggles to climb once again, only to find himself back where he started. Each rejection reinforces the limbo-like nature of his existence. Having tasted, if only for a moment, the fruits of the good life, he will not return to his childhood environment. Society, on the other hand, frustrates his efforts to find lasting material well-being, social status, and peace of mind. He is a "half outsider"[4] since he lives on the fringes of a world he hopes to call his own. He has tried to disassociate himself from his past, but he cannot fully realize his goal of a successful future. And even if he were able to carve a more permanent niche for himself, he would fear discovery. He knows that his position with regard to established society will always be tenuous.

The insecurity of his marginal condition fills him with loneliness. Women do play a part in his life, but they do not ease his solitude for long. Depicted as lustful, promiscuous, and avaricious, these women are looking to exploit the *pícaro* just as he has learned to exploit them. Rarely does he experience genuine love, for he has known few models of sincere, selfless affection. He understandably becomes disillusioned with women, to whom he is apt to refer in highly cynical terms. Trusting a woman and surrendering himself to her, body and soul, is the cause of man's downfall, one *pícaro* laments: "El fiarse el hombre y rendirse al amor de la mujer es causa de todo."[5] And this *pícaro*'s misogynism is by no means unique.

As he unfolds to us the story of his life, the *pícaro* voices his resentment of the world that has heaped on him humiliation, disappointment, and loneliness. He vents his anger at the closed society that foils him, and he resolves to keep storming its doors until he passes through them for good.

60

He takes particular delight in criticizing the hypocrisy of those who shun him. They are shams, he declares, no better and no worse than he. They have corrupted the ideal of true honor, which should be based on virtuous conduct and moral worth. They have scorned him for his lowly origins, and he reacts by proclaiming, like *Conversos*, that lineage alone does not constitute the groundwork of honor. The pedigree of those who abuse him may be illustrious, but as men they are no more honorable than he.

He ridicules their obsession with reputation, and he notes that they are not as free as they think they are, for they are slaves to *¿qué dirán?*, to what people will say about them. The *pícaro* craves freedom and does not want anything to shackle him. Experience has taught him that an enviable reputation is not worth the effort required to maintain it, and he determines to live unencumbered by those restricting preoccupations.

The *pícaro* needs to feel superior to the people who have taunted him. He stresses the freedom of movement and the carefree life he sometimes enjoys. In fact, however, he deceives himself. It is true that he has no honor to safeguard. But a man on the run with a past to hide only deludes himself if he believes that he is really free; when he least expects it, his past turns up to haunt him. He would like to think that he is his own person, but he is not. He has adopted the values of established society and has assumed a variety of roles and masks in order to blend in with the very people whom he criticizes. His function within mainstream society is to wait on his betters, and what could be more antithetical to freedom than dependence and subservience?

The grievances the *pícaro* airs throughout his story are the consequence of the alienation he feels: alienation from a milieu that continually frustrates him, and alienation from self. He has chosen to give in to society on its terms and to emulate those persons who, if they were to find him out, would remind him of his shame. He switches façades in accordance with his masters' expectations of him. He deceives his acquaintances and ends up deceiving himself, for he has lost sight of his conscience. He has readily agreed to conform to society, even if conformity means that society will dehumanize him. He gladly renounces part of his identity, the part associated with his humble and tainted ancestry, but he must also renounce his integrity. After each momentary achievement, he believes that he has triumphed, but in reality he has bartered his conscience for something of fleeting worth. Success quickly turns to failure, and in the end he has accomplished nothing. Permanent freedom, acceptance, and prosperity all elude him. He will always have his origins to confront, and he will find it difficult to retrieve the most precious attribute he once possessed—his integrity.

Most picaresque novels are pseudoautobiographical; that is, the *pícaros* who relate their lives are not the authors but rather fictional entities whom the authors have created.[6] Interesting to ponder and difficult to ascertain is the relationship between novelist and *pícaro*. How does the creator regard his character's purpose in life (to better himself socially and economically), the means by which he tries to reach his goal, and the society that almost invariably rejects him? To answer these questions, we should explore the following not unrelated factors:

1. *The readership to whom the author aimed his book*
Who read the book? Members of the upper crust, who would be loath to tolerate the underhanded schemes of an upstart rogue and who would smirk at his failures? Without doubt, and also bourgeois and New Christians, who might be slightly more tolerant of the *pícaro*'s aspirations.

2. *The author's motivations*
Why did he write his book? Simply to entertain? Possibly, and on occasion to open his readers' eyes to the world around them and to impart a lesson. But what lesson, if any, should his readership derive? The prologue of a picaresque novel often provides a clue to the author's intentions. We should not, however, take at face value everything he wrote. His was a difficult course to tread. He had to exercise discretion via à vis his official censors, and he would not have wished to alienate his readers

by stating explicitly what he could say in veiled terms or what he might better leave unsaid. It is up to us to read between his lines; yet, if we peruse the extensive collection of literary criticism concerning each major picaresque novel, we encounter varied and even contradictory interpretations. It seems that few critics form the same opinion of the author's motivations.

3. *The author's social and economic background*

Literary critics have fortunately unearthed a great deal of information about many of the novelists, and their discoveries do help us to draw limited conclusions regarding an author's outlook on his *pícaro*.

If we know, for example, that an author was a *Converso*, it would be reasonable to conclude that he might present serious issues in his book, issues that he would want the reader to consider. An author living on the outskirts of established society might ask his readership to address such questions as: whether an outsider has the right to dent the framework of established society; what reprisals, if any, society should take against this defiant individual; how society should resolve the conflicts his actions have produced; and the extent to which heredity and environment shape him (undoubtedly a very familiar subject of debate to the twentieth-century reader). A *Converso* author living in Spain could not, of course, have proffered any solution that would refute the theory of estate society. That writers raised these issues at all, however, indicates an increasing discomfort with the status quo that mainstream Spain was fighting to uphold and a recognition of the fact that times were beginning to change.

It is also reasonable to suppose that an author whose background and/or religious beliefs were not acceptable to established society might have felt a sense of solidarity with the *pícaro*. He and his character alike lived on the fringes of a world that would not accept them as they were and for what they were. Heredity relegated them to marginal status. They could not and would not go back to the world of their forefathers. Marriage or fraud might cover up their past and allow them access to the Old Christian world, but they would forfeit a part of their true identity in return for a false one. Both were alienated from themselves since they would have to pay lip service to the very values (concern for lineage and obsession with reputation, for example) that society had used against them, values they justifiably deplored. Moreover, the *Converso* could sympathize with the *pícaro*'s fear of discovery and subsequent rejection and with the loneliness that comes from a lifetime of hiding behind a mask.

Writers who were born into established society tend to advocate an adherence to the societal status quo. In their books, they punish their audacious *pícaros* for posing a threat to social stability. To allow a *pícaro* entry into a world that was not his through birth would mean violating the tenets of the estate system, the bedrock of order. To permit him to succeed in his attempts would signify condoning his antisocial measures. The *pícaro*, in this conservative way of thinking, should know his place and should accept his lot in life. He should recognize that his marginality has foreordained him to live on the outskirts of mainstream society. Thus, these authors push their *pícaros* off the road to success, a fitting end, in their estimation, to a short-lived career of defiance. These writers were not necessarily blind to the miserable conditions in which the *pícaro* grew up. But they could offer no solution to his dilemma other than that he accept his fate and make the best of it with whatever lawful means were at his disposal.

Regardless of their places in society, authors of true picaresque novels were cognizant of the rampant corruption around them. They realized that depravity breeds depravity and that all men, irrespective of their stations in life, are vulnerable to evil. They were also aware of the reality of society (a reality we will examine in greater depth in Pt.III)—that wealth and appearances took precedence over virtue and truth. Marginal individuals were no more or no less immune from ambition and presumption than nobles, commoners, and—yes—even clergymen. These writers criticize the duplicity and materialism that challenge Christianity as the guiding stars of social life. If society is base, it is because its members have corrupted it with their baseness. They in turn corrupt others, like the *pícaro*, who strive to imitate them.

Authors of many pseudopicaresque novels, on the other hand, tended to ignore the issue of the *pícaro*'s environment. They wrote for a monied readership, which was more interested in entertainment than in serious reflection, and they were not about to rock the boat of popularity. In their books, we see none of the character development that distinguishes these works from the picaresque masterpieces. The *pícaro* and the *pícara* (his female counterpart) do not *become* corrupt; rather, these writers depict them as corrupt from birth, and no benign influence on earth would have the power to deter them from their predetermined courses of infamy. That society might be responsible in some way for molding their values is a matter these writers simply ignore. The only determining influence on the *pícaro*'s life that they deem worthy of stressing is his heritage of immorality.

The picaresque offers us a panorama of sixteenth- and seventeenth-century society at large. We see parade before our eyes a variety of types and individuals. Some, like the cavaliers, squires, doctors, lawyers, and merchants, represent established society. Others—prostitutes, thieves, pimps, and swindlers—live in the infraworld of squalor and sordidness. They prey on the more fortunate in order to survive.

People are on the move. We sense that the world is in a state of flux, notwithstanding the efforts of conservative forces proclaiming the immutability of society. The degree to which the picaresque reflects the political crises and the economic decline of Golden Age Spain is a matter of considerable discussion, but the fact remains that upheaval and decay did contribute to the geographic mobility we witness in these novels. Soldiers are traveling to and from battles or are in wait of a battle to fight. Poor farmers, having sold their meager possessions to pay the tax collector, have left their lands in search of urban work. If they fail to find a job, they soon join with beggars, vagabonds, students, and other unemployed people who roam the highways and byways in search of a handout, a meal, or just a crumb or two.

For all the glimpses of sixteenth- and seventeenth-century life that it affords, however, a picaresque novel is not a mirror image of society. We must bear in mind that we are viewing the world through the biased eyes of the *pícaro*, who narrates his adventures from the vantage point of adulthood and experience. The prejudice and rejection he has endured may distort his perception of people, their roles, and their values. He will cast a critical eye on men and women who have shunned him, and he may blind himself to the deficiencies of those few who have treated him well. To complicate the matter further, we must contend with the presence of the author, whose position with regard to mainstream society may color his attitudes.

Although picaresque novels portray Spanish society subjectively, the masterpieces, at least, tend to recreate probable behavioral patterns of frustrated individuals who interact with an unyielding world. They realistically evoke the alienation that accompanies *pícaros* struggling through life in constant confrontation with hostile and debased men and women.

While *pícaros* may be guilty of exaggerating or generalizing, they do call attention to the real contradictions of Golden Age society, contradictions that were responsible for the *pícaros'* estrangement from the hypocritical world around them and, ultimately, from themselves. Their plight exemplifies the gulf that separated the theory from the reality of society. *Pícaros* learn that society closes its doors only to those who cannot pay the price of admission. They also realize that members of established society are all too often not what they claim to be. The clergyman whom a *pícaro* serves, for instance, hardly personifies charity, and the nobleman whom he encounters attends Mass daily at ten in the morning and spends the rest of the day neglecting his other duties.

Picaresque novels have retained their popularity through the years and have inspired modern writers to create their own antiestablishmentarian rogues. It is not difficult to understand why these tales have generated such sustained interest. Despite the fact that the socioeconomic conditions of Spain have undergone great change since the advent of the picaresque, the individual's frustrating struggle for dignity and well-being in a world that thwarts and corrupts him is an essential theme of the modern novel and one with which twentieth-century readers, especially those familiar with the plight of the urban underprivileged, can identify.

LAZARILLO DE TORMES

The first of the picaresque masterpieces is the anonymous, pseudoautobiographical *Lazarillo de Tormes*. From the moment of its appearance in 1554 to the present day, *Lazarillo* has enjoyed immense popularity and has been imitated and widely translated.[7]

Each of the seven chapters of the book represents a significant episode in Lazarillo's life, one that will indelibly mark his future.

In the first chapter, Lazarillo introduces us to his impoverished family. His father, a miller, was charged with stealing and later died in a military campaign. His widowed mother took as her lover a kindly black Moor, who also stole in order to feed his hungry family and was harshly punished for his "crime".

While still a young boy, Lazarillo meets a blind beggar in need of a guide, and the two set out together. The Blind Man teaches Lazarillo lessons that will stick with him for the rest of his life: how to live by his wits and how to deceive. Blindness has forced the beggar to fend for himself. He has suffered ridicule and abuse and has been the victim of many a malicious prank. He naturally distrusts mankind, even his guide boy Lazarillo, whom he mistreats on several occasions. Lazarillo resolves to look for an easier and more profitable life. Abandoning the Blind Man, he unwittingly jumps from the frying pan into the fire, for his second master is a priest whose miserliness and cruelty far surpass those of his first master.

Disillusioned, his hopes for a bright future dimmed, Lazarillo moves on to Toledo, where he meets up with his third master, the Squire. Striking in this third chapter are the parallels between Lazarillo's existence and the Squire's. Both are alone in the world and destitute. Only in serving prosperous gentlemen will they be able to find the security they so desire. Lazarillo, however, soon realizes that the Squire is not the epitome of prosperity he has pretended to be. Since the noble lineage he flaunts precludes manual labor of any sort, the Squire cannot support himself—much less Lazarillo—in the manner befitting his rank. He intends, therefore, to find a *caballero* to serve, although he considers repugnant the very thought of waiting on another man. So far, unfortunately, no cavalier has materialized, and both master and servant have no choice but to survive by their wits. They are parasites. Lazarillo lives off society as a beggar in order to feed himself and the Squire, and the Squire lives off Lazarillo's meager contributions. Thus, the roles of master and servant are reversed: instead of sustaining Lazarillo, the Squire depends on him for sustenance.

This chapter affords the author, speaking through Lazarillo, the opportunity to comment on the shallowness of worldly honor. In reality, the honor that the Squire represents has little to do with virtuous conduct and much to do with a person's pedigree and reputation. The Squire embodies the superficiality of worldly honor. He tacitly agrees to let Lazarillo beg on the condition that Lazarillo not reveal that he lives with the Squire: "Y solamente te encomiendo no sepan que vives conmigo, por lo que toca a mi honra."[8]

Although the Squire feigns the appearance of honor, he is thoroughly dishonorable. He lies to Lazarillo and others about his financial state and would readily lie to any cavalier whom he would have the good fortune to snare. He does nothing except maintain the semblance of a gentleman, while Lazarillo works day and night to provide for him. And, most ignobly, he abandons Lazarillo and disappears, thereby avoiding the rent collector (a pattern he has repeated on more than one occasion).

In spite of the Squire's despicable nature, Lazarillo understands him, cares for him, and reacts stoically to his ingratitude. The only complaint Lazarillo utters about him concerns his conceited airs. But he has come to recognize that pomposity is one of the rules of the honor game and that the Squire and others of his ilk will continue to live and die playing that game:

> Sólo tenía de él un poco de descontento. Que quisiera yo que no tuviera tanta presunción; mas que abajara un poco su fantasía con lo mucho que subía su necesidad. Mas, según me parece, es regla ya entre ellos usada y guardada. . . . El Señor lo remedie, que ya con este mal han de morir.[9]

Even though Lazarillo bears the Squire no ill will, he does react strongly to false honor in general. Whenever he sees a man like his master, Lazarillo tells us, he feels only pity for him, and he laments that honor has come to be an idol for which people endure more pain than they would for God himself: "¡Oh Señor, y cuántos de aquestos debéis tener Vos por el mundo derramados, que padecen por la negra que llaman honra lo que por Vos no sufrirían!"[10]

Poor Lazarillo! How unjustly the world has treated him! The authorities punished his father and stepfather for stealing, notwithstanding their desperate plight; yet the Priest and the Squire, truly loathsome human beings, managed to escape the long arms of the law.

Hunger, deprivation, and injustice impelled Lazarillo to a life of wandering. He has had to live by his wits and at the mercy of cruel, selfish masters. What has he gained? Nothing he had hoped for—neither security nor prosperity. He has, however, discovered for himself the validity of the Blind Man's lesson. He now knows that he cannot count on any other person or on society and that he must fend for himself: "Dije entre mí: 'Verdad dice éste [el ciego], que me cumple avivar el ojo y avisar, pues solo soy, y pensar cómo me sepa valer.'"[11]

Although circumstances have driven Lazarillo to a state of aloneness, he still relishes his moments of independence, which he wants to ensure by achieving lasting financial well-being.

Up to and including Ch. iii, Lazarillo has been the victim of adverse social conditions and of malice. From Ch. iv on, his fortune begins to improve. He briefly serves a nonexemplary friar who gallivants from place to place. But the Friar treats him better than the Priest did, and he generously gives Lázaro a pair of shoes. Then Lázaro meets an indulgence seller and accompanies him from town to town. No longer does Lázaro suffer from hunger. He eats at the expense of gullible people whom he and the Indulgence Seller have duped. He shows no remorse at stooping to immorality; in fact, he gloatingly remarks that he now *enjoys* tricking his victims and conning them out of their money.

In the sixth chapter, Lázaro becomes a chaplain's assistant and begins to thrive. Imitating the Squire, whose airs he once disparaged, Lázaro no longer cares to engage in manual work. He also dresses in the genteel manner that suits his new station in life.

The book culminates in Lázaro's social and economic ascent and in his moral descent. He is appointed town crier and supplements his income in the two lucrative ways the Blind Man had prophesied: he auctions wine, and he marries the lover of the Archpriest, his patron. The novel ends with Lázaro, wife-lover, and Archpriest settling down to a comfortable ménage à trois.

Lázaro believes that, like his namesake, he has arisen. From his one-dimensional viewpoint, he is correct. He has entered the mainstream of society on his own and has triumphed in a world that normally shuns a man of his background.

Lázaro is full of praise for himself and for other men who live by their wits. He has written the story of his life, he explains in the Prologue, to prove to the titled noblemen whom Fortune favored from birth that a lowly rogue can get ahead despite the misfortunes and conflicts that have plagued him:

> Y también porque consideren los que heredaron nobles estados cuán poco se les debe, pues Fortuna fue para ellos parcial, y cuánto más hicieron los que, siéndoles contraria, con fuerza y maña remando salieron a buen puerto.[12]

Lázaro points out that it is a virtue to know how to rise in the world; what he implies is that one should learn how to avail himself of any means, commendable or not, at his disposal. His story proves that he has practiced what he preaches, for he has delighted in defrauding the innocent and has willingly become a cuckold.

We may ask ourselves what caused the compassionate, generous Lazarillo of the first three chapters to mature into the corrupt Lázaro of the last four. The blame for his change rests in great part with the Squire, the Indulgence Seller, and the clergymen whom Lázaro has served. All members of established society, they have taught him to live not in accordance with the ideals that should govern society but rather with the social realities to which their own lives attest. These masters have perverted their roles in life. Pretending to abide by the spiritual principles of Christianity, they really embrace godless values. The social and moral obligations incumbent on noblemen and clergymen seem to have disappeared, in the view of the anonymous author, and a title is merely a façade that masks superficiality and baseness. As for the poor and the outcast, justice is little more than a synonym for victimization and abuse, and charity has risen to Heaven without leaving behind even a trace.

Lázaro's masters have taught him to assume the roles they expect of him. He knows that the fulfillment of his goals depends on his moral pliability. As his tale draws to a close, he reveals that he has learned society's lessons so well that he has become a living lie. In the last chapter, the townsfolk are gossiping about his wife. Lázaro questions the Archpriest, who confirms that the wife does indeed spend time at his home but that she does not jeopardize her honor or Lázaro's. Having assured Lázaro that he has nothing to worry about, the Archpriest then cautions him not to pay attention to what people say; rather, Lázaro should concern himself only with his own well-being:

> 'Lázaro de Tormes: quien ha de mirar a dichos de malas lenguas nunca medrará. Digo esto, porque no me maravillaría alguno, viendo entrar en mi casa a tu mujer y salir de ella. . . . Ella entra muy a tu honra y suya. Y esto te lo prometo. Por tanto, no mires a lo que pueden decir, sino a lo que te toca, digo, a tu provecho.'[13]

The Archpriest's advice is intentionally ironic and exemplifies the twisted code of ethics for which he and Lázaro stand. The wife's adultery brings Lázaro honor, he implies, since it nets him a tidy profit. The Archpriest has stripped honor of the integrity it is supposed to denote and has reduced it to the level of mere financial gain.

Given the evolution of his character, it is not surprising that Lázaro sees the wisdom of the Archpriest's words. He readily closes his eyes to what he would have found reprehensible as Lazarillo. His first master had used physical blindness as a tool for survival. Lázaro, to the contrary, has passed beyond the stage of mere survival. He no longer must use his wits to stave off hunger. Now he seeks prosperity, which moral blindness will guarantee. Deceived by his masters, he deceives others—and himself (a recurrent theme in the picaresque). He has mastered the art of hypocrisy so well that he blinds himself to his moral decline and to the baseness of the very kind of people whom he once criticized. Lazarillo, who distinguished right from wrong, has given way to Lázaro, who chooses not to see evil.

Lázaro is at peace with himself at the end of his story. Any conflict between integrity and corruption that might have arisen in Lazarillo has no chance of arising in Lázaro, since he will not allow his conscience to trouble him. The Archpriest has made him an offer of material success, and Lázaro will not refuse it. Lázaro is no hero, nor does he care to be one. Heroism has no place in his world, which will continue to bestow its favors on him as long as he keeps his part of the bargain. Lázaro thinks that he is finally his own master. He has freed himself of the shackles of hunger and poverty and has achieved acceptance and security. Yet he ignores the fact that he has bound himself with the more enduring chains of immorality.

Lázaro has let himself be corrupted by taking the path of least resistance. But to what extent can we blame him for what he has become? His masters were vile hypocrites, and he has never experienced the rewards of integrity. Mainstream society has never shown him how to succeed without forsaking his conscience. If we are to condemn him, the author suggests, we should also condemn his masters and, by extension, society. Saints and heroes follow exclusively the dictates of their consciences. Most mortals, however, who have known only degradation and injustice will understandably acquire the very values that society has used against them. They do not seek saintliness or heroism; rather, their goals are freedom and the material comforts that their oppressors possess. The author does not necessarily ask us to admire Lázaro but to reserve our judgment of him until we consider fully how and why he emerged from Lazarillo.

Lazarillo de Tormes is unique among the picaresque masterpieces in that Lázaro is the only *pícaro* whose creator permits him to accomplish on a permanent basis what he set out to do. This point, in addition to the extreme hypocrisy of the characters, has led several literary critics to conclude that the anonymous author was a *Converso* who saw in Lazarillo a kindred soul. Sympathetic to the quagmire of Lazarillo's existence, the author might have vicariously realized his own dream of belonging to established society. His New Christian status would also have led him to underscore the falsity of Lazarillo's masters in order to remind Old Christians that they were not of higher moral caliber than the New Christians and the destitute whom they shunned. If Old Christians had exemplified the justice and compassion that should have ruled their lives, many *Conversos* and *pícaros*, like Lazarillo, would not have felt the need to renounce their integrity in the hope of gaining entrance to a world that otherwise would have lain beyond their reach.

Other critics, however, stress the anticlerical nature of the book and affirm that the author was a Protestant or a disciple of Erasmus (the Dutch reformer of the Catholic Church, whose writings fell from official favor in Spain during the second half of the sixteenth century).

Whether or not he was a *Converso*, a Protestant, or an Erasmist, a man born on the outskirts of the mainstream or a disillusioned member of established society, the author has written a harsh indictment of godless men whose example of apparent success encourages others to follow in their base footsteps.

GUZMÁN DE ALFARACHE

Mateo Alemán is the author of the second great picaresque novel, *Guzmán de Alfarache*, the first part of which was published in 1599. The wide acclaim that the book received inspired an obscure writer named Juan Martí to pen a second part under the pseudonym "Mateo Luján de Sayavedra". Published in 1602, this apocryphal continuation so incensed Alemán that he wrote his own second part, which appeared in 1604.

Alemán's novel is much longer than *Lazarillo de Tormes*. It contains several intercalated short stories and numerous episodes of the *pícaro*'s life, in marked contrast to the scant seven episodes that the anonymous author related about Lazarillo.

The modern-day reader may find *Guzmán de Alfarache* less appealing than *Lazarillo* because of the many moral, religious, and philosophical digressions interspersed throughout the book. Unlike Lázaro, Guzmán claims to repent at the end of Alemán's second part, and these digressions represent the viewpoint of the newly reformed Guzmán; they also ensured that the Index would not proscribe the novel, as it had done in the case of *Lazarillo de Tormes*.

When we read *Guzmán de Alfarache*, we should bear in mind that three voices are speaking to us: the *pícaro* Guzmanillo, the reformed Guzmán, and Alemán, whose official beliefs correspond to Guzmán's but whose *Converso* status lends another perspective to the book.

To summarize as briefly as possible the plot of the book, Guzmanillo was born in Seville, a thriving metropolis noted for its infraworld of thieves, beggars, and prostitutes. His travels take him to Italy, where he serves a number of masters and immerses himself in gambling and criminality. He prospers, returns to Spain as a merchant, and marries for convenience. His wife soon dies, and Guzmanillo, having lost his fortune, decides to study for the priesthood in the hope of living the good life to which he has grown accustomed. He abandons his plan, however, when he falls in love and marries for a second time. This wife is a prostitute who supports herself and him on her earnings and who later leaves him. Reduced to destitution again, he resumes his low life. Ironically, the authorities apprehend him for a crime he did not commit. Sentenced to the galleys, he heeds God's voice and vows to emend his sinful ways. He promises to write a third installment of his "autobiography", which has never appeared.

Guzmanillo's ancestry is far more infamous than Lazarillo's. His mother, a *Conversa*, was a prostitute (as her mother had been and as Guzmanillo's second wife would be). His father, also a *Converso*, was a notorious swindler, opportunist, and thief (and Guzmanillo would follow suit).

From the theological viewpoint that Alemán (alias Guzmán) emphasizes, the dishonor into which Guzmanillo was born symbolizes the dishonor of mankind fallen from grace as a result of original sin. Mankind, which Guzmanillo represents, is destined to transgress but can be redeemed through free will fortified with grace. Guzmán's repentance bears witness to the redemption God promises to those who will to abide by his commandments.

From a personal point of view, Guzmanillo believes that he has inherited his family's inclination toward vice. He accepts the atavism inherent in society's attitudes concerning virtuous and wicked conduct. Defeated from the beginning, he feels that his ignominious heritage will make it impossible for him to achieve goodness; nor will any good come his way, he is convinced: "Se me puso en la cabeza que tan malos principios era imposible tener buenos fines ni podía ya sucederme cosa buena ni hacérseme bien."[14] His heritage will continue to doom him until he accepts the gift of hope that God has been offering him all the while.

Ashamed of his family, Guzmanillo leaves home in search of freedom from his past and from the malicious tongues that torment him. His wanderings through Spain and Italy convince him that he has found *gloriosa libertad*, the freedom to come and go as he pleases, to do what he wants when he wants to do it. But once he settles down, as he must if he is to get ahead, he forfeits his freedom, for he must respond to the biddings of others, not only to his own instincts.

He does, however, possess another form of freedom, the freedom to disregard social conventions and usages. Unhampered by the values restricting the men and women whom he serves, Guzmanillo is proud not to be a slave to worldly honor. As he was born without honor, he has none to lose; he needs not worry about holding on to what he does not have, he says: "¿Qué honra tengo que perder? ¿De cuál crédito vendré a faltar?"[15] He does not covet the honors that Fortune has bestowed on some of his masters; indeed, he is glad to live free of the burdens and obligations that honorable status imposes: "¡Lo que carga el peso de la honra y cómo no hay metal que se le iguale! ¡A cuánto está obligado el desventurado que de ella hubiere de usar!"[16]

Like Lazarillo, Guzmán lashes out against the false honor that only deceptive appearances can sustain. He too has served a man whose pathetic sense of dignity bars him from working for a living. With no means to provide for himself, the Captain and Guzmanillo have tacitly agreed to operate in much the same way as the Squire and Lazarillo: Guzmanillo will support himself and the Captain without endangering the latter's reputation. Eventually, the ungrateful Captain abandons Guzmanillo, as the Squire had abandoned Lazarillo, and Guzmanillo is left with only himself to take care of.

The reformed Guzmán comments that true honor is the daughter of virtue, not of lineage, reputation, or appearances. Guzmanillo, however, is not yet wholly immune from these concerns. He suffers from the shame that idle, vicious gossip has imbedded in him. And even after he flees his home, he still worries about what his peers think of him. In one episode, for instances, a pig picks him up, carries him for several blocks, and finally deposits him in a heap of filth (a physical reflection of the moral degradation into which he has fallen). Humiliated, he considers himself the most miserable of men. What will he do?, he asks himself. Where will he go? What will become of him? How will he hide this shameful incident from the perked ears of his companions and fellow servants? How will he dissimulate so that he can escape the martyrdom of ridicule?:

> Levantando los ojos, casi con desesperación, dije: '¡Pobre miserable hombre! ¿Qué haré? ¿Dónde iré? ¿Qué será de mí? ¿Qué consejo tomaré para que los criados de mi amo y compañeros míos no sientan mis desgracias? ¿Cómo disimularé para que no me martiricen?'[17]

Guzmanillo's wounded pride heals in time, but the shame of his heritage still festers within him. Society reinforces his sense of shame, and he reacts by striving as best he can to maintain his independence from some of the values that society cherishes. Yet he needs to belong to the same world whose values he deplores, for only in belonging can he prosper. On the one hand, he rails against those who have trampled on his self-esteem. On the other, he must win their respect if he is to attain a modicum of self-respect.

When he is reborn as Guzmán, he is able to distinguish more clearly than ever between truth and falsity because he has arrived at the state of *desengaño*, the awareness of reality as it is and not as it seems.[18] As Guzmanillo, however, his perception of reality is limited and overriden by his ambition to thrive in a hostile world. In order to get ahead, he must assume new roles. With few exceptions, his role models, like Lazarillo's, have exemplified moral baseness. From parents to acquaintances, they have gambled, cheated, defrauded, stolen, and prostituted themselves. Masters of hypocrisy and dissimulation, they have betrayed the ideals and values they pretend to uphold, and they have betrayed Guzmanillo as well: the Italian branch of his family rejects him; the Captain deserts him; his "friend" Sayavedra[19] robs him; another companion, Soto, falsely accuses him of theft; and his mother and wife turn their backs on him at his trial.

Victimized, Guzmanillo victimizes others. Deceived, he deceives. And he is fully aware that evil breeds evil, a point he makes, in part, to justify himself. He tells us, for example, that he stole from an old man, something he never would have done, had Sayavedra not stolen from him.

Corruption permeates Guzmanillo's entire being. His experiences have exposed him to few examples of Christianity, and expediency has caused him to disregard his infrequent pangs of conscience. He reaches the depths of immorality in his relationship with his second wife. In an episode reminiscent of Lázaro's marital situation, he causes and consents to his wife's career as a prostitute. Although on other occasions he defends conjugal honor, it is evident that he will overlook his own dishonor when there is a profit to be made.

Lázaro benefited from immorality and fancied himself the luckiest of men. Guzmanillo, however, has accomplished less in the long run than he would have, had his means been lawful. He finds himself worse off than when he left home years before. Not only has he not permanently fulfilled any of his dreams, but he is a condemned prisoner, and he feels terribly alone.

His misfortunes prompt him to reconsider what he is and what has led him to such a disastrous end. Disappointed, dejected, *desengañado*, he begins to realize that the masks he donned, the wealth he at times amassed (and lost), and life itself are but an illusion. All the things men cherish—money, position, power, and happiness—are fleeting and deceptive, he acknowledges: "No hay cosa segura ni estado que permanezca, perfecto gusto ni contento verdadero: todo es fingido y vano."[20] Guzmanillo did not refuse the world's enticing offers, but the reborn Guzmán now scorns them because they lack true meaning. Guzmán differs from his predecessor Lázaro in that he sees through the veil of illusion and finally grasps the most important lesson disillusionment can teach him—that he who has been deceived not only deceives others but ultimately deceives himself: "Que todo miente y que todos nos mentimos."[21]

Literary critics have debated at great length Guzmán's so-called "conversion". Is he sincere or a hypocritical opportunist? Was his repentance simply a ploy on Alemán's part to guarantee the book's safe passage through the hazardous route of censorship?

Guzmán fervently proclaims his sincerity. He takes full responsibility for his actions and for the calamities that have beset him (although twentieth-century readers are apt to blame society for engulfing him in its wickedness). He trusts that grace, which he has accepted, will strengthen his resolve to eschew licentiousness. Nonetheless, his conversion does not signify instant saintliness. He will still, he admits, fall into occasional temptation, but he will find it easier to resist than before.

The one sad note in this otherwise happy ending is Guzmán's awareness that his acquaintances, and perhaps his readers, consider him a hypocrite. People who knew him as Guzmanillo will always suspect his good deeds and will wonder what evil lurks behind them. The heritage of infamy, which his misdeeds have compounded, will always haunt him:

> Siempre por lo de atrás mal indiciado, no me creyeron jamás. Que aquesto más malo tienen los malos, que vuelven sospechosas aun las buenas obras que hacen y casi con ellas escandalizan, porque la juzgan por hipocresía.[22]

It is quite probable that Mateo Alemán, a New Christian, saw the similarity between the sincere *Converso*'s plight and that of the reformed criminal. Neither could escape his past. Neither would fully fit into the mainstream of society, which would look down on them as inferior beings. As a result, both would experience moments of negative solitude and conflict. Regardless of their ancestry and their social inferiority, however, the *pícaro* and the *Converso* were born equal to their oppressors in the eyes of God. All men, victims and victimizers alike, carry the stain of original sin, and all men can steer their free will in the direction of redemption. God accepted an Alemán and forgave a Guzmán; society, most unfortunately, did not.

Guzmán's conversion is a logical consequence of his disenchantment with life. His hopes for a better earthly existence have repeatedly been destroyed. *Desengaño* reminds him of his mortality, and he fears that his sins may imperil his chance for salvation. Corruption has netted him nothing of substance; virtue, to the contrary, will surely pay off for him after he dies. His conversion, in effect, is a not untypical blend of sincerity, disillusionment, and a dash of pragmatism.

His practical approach toward morality has persuaded many of his readers that his "spiritual rebirth" is more a matter of self-preservation than of genuine repentance. Indeed, it immediately yields him significant dividends: it enables him to curry favor with the captain of the galley and, thereby, to forestall the hardship of enforced rowing. And then, as if by miracle, Soto's malice is discovered, and Guzmán awaits the official pardon that will make him a free man.

Readers who smirk at Guzmán's "repentance" justify their cynicism by citing the last sentence of the book. Guzmán promises to write a third and final part of his life story (a popular picaresque device, as the reader will note). To describe the remainder of his life, he uses the ambiguous verb "*gastar*", which means either "spend" or "waste": "La [vida] que después gasté todo el restante de ella verás en la tercera y última parte."[23] Detractors of Guzmán interpret this sentence to mean that he will tell us how he *wasted* his life. However, they fail to take into account the preceding sentence, in which he states that he put an *end* to his evil past: "Rematé la cuenta con mi mala vida."[24] That being the case, he would be less inclined to squander his future than to spend it in the pursuit of good.

PICARESQUE NOVELS OF SPANISH WRITERS IN EXILE

[Mateo Alemán and the author of *Lazarillo de Tormes* imply that the *pícaro* should not be expected to assume full responsibility for his antisocial and immoral acts, since his milieu has played a considerable role in shaping his values. These writers did not overtly inveigh against the hierarchical order of the world and the Church, foundations on which medieval and Golden Age society rested. Rather, they limited their criticism to individuals whose cancer-like corruption threatened to destroy the theoretically healthy organism of society and the integrity of its members.]

[margin note: It is implied, in the writings chosen for this paper]

Two authors, nevertheless, did dare to launch assaults on one institution in particular that fostered injustice and evil—the Spanish Inquisition. These novelists, Juan de Luna and Carlos García, left Spain because of their religious heritage and/or beliefs. Only when they were safely ensconced in France were they able to publish their picaresque novels. Only then could they attack the hypocrisy and the cruelty of a world that had forced them into exile.

Juan de Luna was a Protestant of possible *Converso* origin. His second part of *Lazarillo de Tormes* made its appearance in 1620. Luna's Lazarillo has tired of domesticity and longs for the freedom he relinquished when he married the Archpriest's mistress. He glorifies the carefreeness of the picaresque life-style, which he finds preferable to the regimentation and the dangers that fill the lives of distinguished mortals. Eager for adventure, he sets out to embark on an expedition against the Algerian pirates, but a series of misadventures thwarts his plans.

Lazarillo meets up with his third master, the Squire, who confesses that a greedy woman has reduced him to wearing tattered rags! She has deflated his pompous ego but has not improved his despicable character. Lazarillo, true to the compassionate nature he had displayed while serving the Squire in the original book, offers to share his bed with him, whereupon the Squire robs him and flees. Once again, the tables of their relationship are turned, and Lazarillo, poorer and disillusioned, returns to Toledo after a year's absence. To his dismay, his wife is about to give birth. Simple arithmetic tells him that he is not the father, and he is chagrined to learn that the Archpriest has interpreted so literally his request that he look after his wife as if she were his own. Lazarillo sues the lovers for adultery, only to discover that his wife's other child is also the Archpriest's. He cannot afford to meet his legal expenses, and the case dwindles to a halt. To add insult to injury, the lovers then sue Lazarillo for damages and have him banished forever from Toledo.

Defeated by injustice, Lazarillo eventually decides to end his few remaining days in a church, thereby sparing the priests the trouble of bringing him back to church for a funeral Mass once he dies.

Luna's book is stridently anticlerical. Through Lazarillo, Luna lashes out against Franciscans, whose hypocrisy and gluttony he despised. An *auto-da-fé* Lazarillo witnesses gives him the opportunity to unleash his anger at the Inquisition. After describing the convicted penitents, who were forced to wear muzzles as if they were vicious dogs, he comments with profound irony that the ministers of the Inquisition are as saintly and perfect as the justice they administer:

> Vi salir entre los otros penitentes a los tres pobres diablos, con mordazas en las bocas, como blasfemos que habían osado poner la lengua en los ministros de la Santa Inquisición, gente tan santa y perfecta como la justicia que administran.[25]

Lazarillo also mocks the airs of conceited Spaniards, like the Squire, who would sooner die of hunger than toil with their hands. Since they claim descent from the Visigoths (a euphemism connoting ancient lineage and "untainted" blood), they believe that manual labor is demeaning. This attitude explains why, in Lazarillo's (and Luna's) opinion, Spain has produced all too few good workingmen. ⌐

The message of Luna's sequel is clear: Spanish society has instilled injustice, duplicity, and arrogance in its members. Those who conform to the system damn themselves in the long run and make life miserable for those who do not or who cannot conform.

Carlos García, a *Converso* doctor, published his novel *La desordenada codicia de los bienes ajenos* in 1619. While he was imprisoned, García explains, he met the thief Andrés, who proceeded to tell him the story of his life.

Andrés differs from other rogues in that his parents were honorably born. Neither rich nor poor, they were honest, upright members of their community. But virtue does not guarantee immunity from injustice, a lesson Andrés would learn when the Inquisition wrongly accused his mother of sacrilege and sentenced her to death. Andrés then severed his ties with his past and became a *pícaro* and a thief. Apprehended by the law, he is in jail awaiting formal sentencing to a lifetime of rowing, and he whiles away the time conversing with the author.

Andrés tells García that the underworld of thieves to which he belongs is more just, lawful, and orderly than the overworld it distortedly reflects: "'No se hace entre nosotros cosa alguna que no esté reglada con razón, estatutos, leyes y premática.'"[26] The justice he has encountered among thieves contrasts markedly with the injustice of mainstream society, an injustice his mother's death exemplifies. Inordinate and disorder-producing agreed (*desordenada codicia*) for other people's goods (*bienes ajenos*) permeates the overworld as well as the underworld, Andrés asserts. The former, which ought to abide by the principles of justice and moderation, represents the opposite. Its members are thieves whose "respectability" cloaks their avarice. Druggists and butchers, for example, tamper with their scales—at the customers' expense. Grieving relatives pay a priest to say forty Masses for the dearly departed; he says four and pockets the change.

Society at large has taught Andrés to live by its unwritten law of greed. He is neither better nor worse than the druggist, the butcher, or the priest. Society has corrupted them all. Only Andrés, however, has been the victim of gross injustice, a circumstance the overworld does not view as mitigating.

A third Spanish writer in exile, Antonio Enríquez Gómez (whose suffering at the hands of the Inquisition the reader may recall), also penned a picaresque novel, *Vida de don Gregorio Guadaña*. Published in France in 1644, this book is less "picaresque" than the others we have examined so far. Neither ignominy nor injustice mars Gregorio's life, nor does he reach the level of depravity and criminality that we associate with other *pícaros*. He left home not to escape his heritage and to prosper but to further his formal education, a most uncharacteristically picaresque motivation.

Although Enríquez Gómez' book is thoroughly enjoyable, it does not recreate the conflicts between the individual and society that characterize the other picaresque works we have seen; nor does his novel contain the mordant social criticism that we identify with true picaresque novels. His dream of returning to Spain came true five years after he published his book; this fact might explain why he wrote a novel that would not arouse undue Inquisitorial concern.

EL BUSCÓN

One of the principal intellectual figures of the seventeenth century was Francisco de Quevedo. An essayist and poet of great repute, he also wrote one of the great picaresque novels, *Historia de la vida del Buscón, llamado don Pablos* (commonly called *El Buscón*), which appeared in 1626.

Pablos, the cheat and swindler (*buscón*) who narrates his story, shares with Lazarillo and Guzmanillo a growing cynicism

84

regarding society. He resembles Lazarillo in that he never repents his past. Quevedo, however, differs from the authors of *Lazarillo* and *Guzmán* (two works that influenced *El Buscón*) in one essential point: he shows little sympathy for his *pícaro* and portrays him as unfavorably as he does the world that has brought Pablos down to its level. Quevedo sentences Pablos to failure, a clear indication on the author's part that Pablos' ignominious relatives and his shame-ridden childhood could in no way excuse his audacious social aspirations and the deceitful measures he took in an attempt to fulfill them. ⌐

Pablos' parents were as base as Guzmanillo's. His mother, a *Conversa* who tried to convince the world that she was an Old Christian, practiced witchcraft. His brother was a common criminal, as was the man whom Pablos presumed to be his father. In time, Pablos learns that any one of several men could have fathered him, and he reacts to his dishonorable family with shame. Since the townspeople will always remind him of where he came from, he must hide his parents' notoriety if he is to follow the difficult path of honor and virtue: "Iba yo entre mí pensando en las muchas dificultades que tenía para profesar honra y virtud, pues había menester tapar primero la poca de mis padres."[27]

His first step toward a new beginning is to leave home. Soon, he befriends the noble Diego Coronel, who is studying at a school in Segovia, Pablos' hometown. Pablos agrees to serve him, and the two board in a house run by the miserly Licentiate Cabra, whom Quevedo modeled after the Priest in the second chapter of *Lazarillo de Tormes*. The Licentiate comes close to starving the lads to death. Unable to take any more of his sanctimonious niggardliness, they bid him farewell and move on to the famed University of Alcalá. There, Pablos becomes the butt of malicious ridicule and vicious pranks. Turning the other cheek has not improved his reputation, and so he resolves to win his tormentors' respect by outdoing them in cunning and knavery. After he succeeds in mastering the skills required of a full-fledged scoundrel, Pablos wins their acceptance. He must still, however, gain entrée into the world of his betters if he is to heal the crippling blows dealt his self-esteem through the years.

His interlude at Alcalá abruptly ends when his uncle, the hangman of Segovia, writes him calamitous news: he has had to execute Pablos' "father"; moreover, the Inquisition has sentenced Pablos' mother to death for witchcraft. The uncle bemoans the dishonor that the mother has brought to all her family and especially to him. After all, he arrogantly and uncompassionately points out to Pablos, he is the king's minister and can hardly afford to be linked to such scandal: "'Pésame que nos deshonra a todos, y a mí principalmente, que al fin soy ministro del rey y me están muy mal estos parentescos.'"[28]

More ashamed than ever, Pablos must hurry back to Segovia. He vows never to speak to his uncle and to leave the city for good, once he collects his inheritance: "Penséme morir de vergüenza. . . . y así, me aparté tan avergonzado, que a no depender de él [el tío] la cobranza de mi hacienda, no le hablara más en mi vida ni pareciera entre gentes."[29] He does settle his affairs and then departs for the second time. He cannot join Diego in Alcalá, however, for Diego's father has heard of Pablos' unsavory escapades and has compelled his son to sever his ties with his servant.

Despite this snub, Diego still personifies everything Pablos craves: noble status, wealth, and respect. Ambitious to emulate him, Pablos makes plans to journey to the court, where nobody will know who he is and who his parents were. Anonymity will assist him to rise from the depths of infamy and humiliation.

On the way, Pablos happens upon a squire, Don Toribio, who is even more cynical than his literary predecessor, Lazarillo's Squire. Toribio opens his hypocritical heart to Pablos and tells him that such impoverished squires as he have no recourse but to encounter *caballeros* to serve. How do squires endear themselves to cavaliers? They must feign the appearance of wealth. For example, Toribio explains, although squires can only afford to eat leeks, they should pretend that capon is the staple of their diet. Only by lying can they survive with comfort and dignity. They are, Toribio admits, living lies, and Toribio is no exception. He has little to eat except a few crumbs, which he carries in his pocket. But instead of nibbling them on the sly, he spreads them over his clothing and his beard so that people will think he has dined royally!

Pablos quickly absorbs Toribio's lessons in deception, for he knows that he will never achieve success unless he pretends to be what he is not. He will conform to what he sees around him: "'Haz como vieres', dice el refrán, y dice bien."[30] He will ingratiate himself with a world that would readily throw him out if it could penetrate his mask. What is more, he will beat the world at its own game. Integrity and conformity to fraud do not mix, and Pablos discards the virtue he once professed to admire. He is aware that life has offered him few examples of virtue, and he uses this fact, as did Guzmanillo, to rationalize his increasingly corrupt nature: "Decía a solas: 'Más se me ha de agradecer a mí, que no he tenido de quién aprender virtud, ni a quién parecer en ella, que al que la hereda de sus abuelos.'"[31]

Heeding Toribio's lessons, he gives himself the illustrious-sounding name of Don Álvaro de Córdoba, and he steals to live accordingly. His career as a "nobleman" comes to an unexpected halt, however, when he is jailed for theft. After his release, he again assumes a new identity, that of a rich cavalier. As fate—as well as the manipulative pen of Quevedo—would have it, his old "friend" Diego Coronel recognizes him and administers him a sound beating, a fitting way, he declares, for a baseborn *pícaro* to pay for his imposture: "¡Así pagan los pícaros embusteros mal nacidos!"[32] Pablos has tried to replace his old identity with new ones, and he has failed. To compound his woes, word of Diego's discovery leaks to Pablos' wealthy fiancée. She immediately terminates their engagement and, with it, his hope of a generous dowry.

Pablos has progressed, only to regress. He has gained nothing except a deceitful character. At the end of the book, he is about to embark for the Indies. Like Guzmán, he fails to carry out his promise to write of his further misadventures.

Quevedo's motives for writing *El Buscón* are not as shrouded in mystery as are those of Alemán and the author of *Lazarillo de Tormes*. The decadence and duplicity of Spanish society troubled Quevedo deeply, and he expressed these concerns not only in *El Buscón* but in other prose writings as well.

A favorite target of Quevedo's critical pen is worldly honor, which Spaniards so espoused that they would go to any foolish or illegal length to attain and maintain it. Quevedo recognized the evils that obsession with honor causes. People like Toribio destroy the truth and corrode society. Without the principle of truth to guide it, the orderly world Quevedo so ardently defended would soon crumble. Luna and García hinted that the very structure of society was corrupt. In Quevedo's opinion, corruption is not the result of an inherently perverse social order but of individual men and women whose wickedness brings disorder to an otherwise ordered world. These people disregard their consciences, heed only the calling of false honor, and set a poor example for unfortunate rogues, like Pablos, who are only too eager to imitate them.

Pablos is neither more nor less evil than the Licentiate and the Squire. Why, then, does Quevedo allow them to succeed while he dooms Pablos to failure? The answer lies in Quevedo's traditional approach to social change. He is unyielding in his defense of the status quo. Just as obsession with worldly honor tears at the moral fabric of society, so does an ignominious *pícaro's* social ascent jeopardize social stability. Quevedo punishes Pablos not only for his antisocial acts (which, he acknowledges, are a reflection of society's) but also for his social pretensions. Pablos has refused to recognize his place in the scheme of things and to assume the roles commensurate with his social status. Even worse, he has deluded himself into thinking that he could escape his heritage. Consequently, Quevedo must punish his every effort to become what he is not.

Female rogues also appear in Spanish picaresque novels, though not as frequently as their male counterparts. Indeed, a woman is the principal protagonist of one important precursor of the picaresque novel, *La Lozana andaluza*. Its author Francisco Delicado was a New Christian cleric who left Spain for Italy at the beginning of the sixteenth century. Whether his *Converso* heritage or his professional ambition precipitated his departure remains a mystery; for whatever the reason, he settled in Italy, where he published his book in 1528. He grew familiar with the sizable group of Spanish Jews and New Christians who lived in Rome, and their life-styles contribute to the framework of *La Lozana andaluza*.

The Andalucian Lozana's *Converso* ancestry is as tainted as Guzmanillo's and Pablos'. Her father was a pimp; her mother, a woman of dubious reputation. After their deaths, she leaves Córdoba in the company of a prosperous Italian merchant. The couple travels throughout the Mediterranean. She bears him two children, whom he entrusts to his parents' safekeeping. He promises to wed her, once they meet his mother and father in Marseilles. But upon the couple's arrival, the cruel father hires a boatman to kill the hapless Lozana in order to marry his son off to a more suitable woman. The boatman, however, takes pity on Lozana and ships her to Italy.

Astute, amoral, and resiliant, Lozana quickly recovers from her disappointment at losing her children and their father. Alone in the world, she must fend for herself. She soon learns to put her talents and wits to profitable use. Beginning as a courtesan, she broadens her professional horizons to include folk medicine, cosmetic saleswomanship, and sexual procurement.[33] Her many skills give Delicado the opportunity to describe sixteenth-century Rome, a city, he informs us, that was one large, venereal disease-infected brothel.

Delicado writes himself into the novel as the character "Author" and tries to guide Lozana toward the path of virtue. Lozana, however, is proud of the esteem in which her clients and fellow courtesans hold her.[34] If she were to follow the Author's advice, she would have to forsake the only honor she has a chance of possessing, the good reputation that results from professional expertise:

> Yo quiero de aquí adelante mirar por mi honra, . . . quiero que se diga que no fue otra que mejor lo hiciese que yo. ¿Qué vale a ninguno lo que sabe si no lo procura saber y hacer mejor que otro?[35]

As the book draws to a close, Lozana begins to pay attention to the Author's admonitions. Disillusioned at long last with the world of prostitutes, hustlers, and venereal disease, she yearns to end her tumultuous life in peace. She wisely reasons that it would be better for her to move from Rome while she is still in her professional prime than to wind up a faded, jaded has-been. Her reputation of excellence intact, she will settle on the island of Lipari and will experience a new beginning.

Although she fears the eternal damnation that would await her if she did not reform, she is not truly repentant of her past. Disappointment, fatigue, and common sense, not a contrite heart, persuade her to change her life. (Readers left unconvinced by Guzmán's "conversion" might easily draw a parallel between Lozana and Guzmán, who followed her by three quarters of a century.)[36]

Delicado's portrait of Lozana reveals less depth and development of character than we encounter in the great picaresque novels. Lozana loses her innocence at an early age and consistently displays an amoral, nonjudgmental attitude toward herself and the men, women, and values that constitute her milieu. Not until the conclusion of the book does the question of right and wrong seriously enter her mind.

Delicado's objective in writing La Lozana andaluza was to warn of the punishment God inflicts on those who transgress His laws. In this sense, Lozana is more fortunate than the Roman courtesans whom she leaves behind. Realizing that her soul and her body are imperiled, she willingly flees the temptations of the Eternal City. Her dissolute life has pitted her against God.

She has come close to selling her soul. Only when the desire for peace and salvation takes precedence over mundane considerations does she determine to right the wrongs of her past and to trade her old identity for a new one.

Lozana's sullied family history and the unfortunate circumstances that forced her to live by her wits are typically picaresque. What distinguishes her, however, from authentic *pícaros* is her relationship to her world. Unlike Lazarillo, Guzmanillo, and Pablos, she has achieved success and security in the environment she has always known, an environment that has never coerced her into sacrificing her sense of self. Furthermore, her concern for her reputation proves that she enjoyed a privileged position within society. While moralists anathematized courtesans like Lozana, most sectors of society, marginal and established, clearly tolerated their presence and regarded their activities as immoral, not necessarily as antisocial.

Pícaras, who make their appearance as principal characters in Spanish literature at the beginning of the seventeenth century, not only prostitute themselves but tend to be scheming, thieving, fly-by-nighters. They are antisocial as well as immoral. They crave money, freedom, and social prestige, not the kind of professional status that Lozana earned but rather the social position that only deceit can bring them.

These *pícaras* show no remorse for their wickedness and remain to the end blithely unconcerned about the state of their souls.

The first novel about a female rogue, *La pícara Justina*, was published in 1605. Its author is Francisco López de Úbeda, a courtier of probable *Converso* origin.

Justina spices her fascinating "autobiography" with witty observations of human behavior. One target of her satirical tongue is people who commission false genealogies. Since they embellish the truth to fit their social aspirations, she mockingly points out, they naturally suspect everyone else of doing the same. She too will make known her lineage, although her doubts about the veracity of other people's family trees suggest that we should not necessarily take her words at face value either:

> Mas, ¿qué hago? ¿Historia de linaje, y linaje propio, he de escribir? ¿Quién creerá que no he de decir más mentiras que letras? . . . el hacerse uno honrado, que es cosa tan pretendida, ¿quién habrá que no la ajuste con su gusto, aunque sea necesario desbaratar la verdad para que venga al justo?[37]

Justina's father and her New Christian mother were quick-fingered innkeepers who pilfered from their guests. Like Guzmanillo and Pablos, she emphasizes the good and evil qualities children inherit from their parents—and even from their nursemaids. She claims to believe that her parents' behavior and attitudes have predisposed her to follow in their footsteps. That she emulates them confirms the atavism that seems to direct the course of her life. She has learned to steal from watching her mother at work, and it is inevitable that she should also have acquired her mother's talents. Yet we wonder whether Justina's references to heredity and negative role models are simply an excuse for her to justify her own self-centeredness.

Justina's parents die, and her selfish brothers lock her out of the house. Rejection, however, does not dishearten her, and her happy-go-lucky nature carries her through this and many other vicissitudes that life has in store for her. She first dons the garb of a pilgrim, then that of a beggar; these disguises afford her the opportunity to rob and defraud the people whom she encounters in her travels.

Throughout her story, Justina criticizes hypocrites, especially social climbers and arrogant, impoverished noblemen. True to her picaresque nature, however, she is what she deplores in others. She knows perfectly well, for example, that her ancestry is clouded and that, notwithstanding her efforts to pretend otherwise, her mother was of New Christian stock. Nevertheless, Justina passes herself off as an Old Christian, for only by lying can she fulfill her ambition to rise socially.

Justina seizes the opportunity to leave the nothingness in which she grew up, she tells us, when she meets and marries her first husband, the *hidalgo* Lozano: "Mi presunción no era poca, pues casando con hijo de algo, había de salir de la nada en que me crié."[38] Lozano epitomizes the *hidalgo*-squire type with whom we have become familiar. He is so poor, Justina laments, that his pedigree would have been long buried in the grave of oblivion, had he not boasted so much about it:

> Era mi marido Lozana en el hecho y en el nombre pariente de algo e hijo de algo. Y preciábase tanto de serlo, que nunca escupí sin encontrar con su hidalguía. Podía ser que lo hiciese de temor que no se olvidase de que era hidalgo, y no le faltaba razón, porque su pobreza era bastante a enterrar en la huesa del olvido más hidalguía que hay en Vizcaya.[39]

Justina married into the nobility, but she must pay the substantial price of supporting herself and Lozano and of satisfying his considerable gambling debts. Only López de Úbeda knew how she would extricate herself from the pompous spendthrift whom she wed.

At the end of the book, Justina promises to write a second installment of her story, one in which she will reveal how she has come to be happily married to her third husband Guzmán de Alfarache! Unfortunately, López de Úbeda never published this sequel, although it seems likely that he did plan to write it.

La pícara Justina is a book that bridges the picaresque masterpieces and the later pseudopicaresque novels. It resembles *Lazarillo de Tormes, Guzmán de Alfarache,* and *El Buscón* in its criticism of hypocrisy and in its satire of social types and practices. Yet it differs from those works in that Justina does not evolve into a *pícara*; rather, as she herself notes, she has been a *pícara* from the beginning—ab initio: "Yo mostraré cómo soy pícara desde la abinición."[40] This lack of character development or change sets the pseudopicaresque stories apart from their literary predecessors.

Alonso Jerónimo de Salas Barbadillo and Alonso de Castillo

Solórzano were two popular authors of seventeenth-century pseudopicaresque tales. Their female protagonists, like Justina, were born con artists and thieves; therefore, the external factors that incline true *pícaros* toward a life of corruption are extraneous and irrelevant in the case of these *pícaras*. As their parents were, they are and will be. They would not have been able to avoid their fate even if they had been willing to do so.

Elena, the lead character of Salas Barbadillo's *La hija de Celestina*,[41] is the daughter (*hija*) of a Moorish witch whose diabolical and sexual activities reminded those who knew her of the famed Celestina's. When Elena is still a girl, her mother prostitutes her. Following the mother's death, Elena sets out with Montúfar, a despicable young thug, in order to see more of the world than the inside of a whorehouse. Like Justina, the couple poses as pilgrims and, in the course of their travels throughout Spain, dupes numerous innocent victims. The two marry, and Montúfar agrees that Elena should resume her career as a prostitute, provided that she split the proceeds with him. She takes a lover; Montúfar then beats her in a fit of jealousy, and she and her lover are executed after the latter murders her husband.

Since Salas Barbadillo wrote his tale in the third person, he interjects his own judgmental comments concerning Elena's life. He treats her harshly and shows not a trace of compassion for the girl whose mother corrupted her. Her destiny would not have been any different, he implies, had the mother not compelled her to become a prostitute. Perversity had run in the family for generations, and Elena never would have been able to escape its grip.

Castillo Solórzano wrote a pair of novels about *pícaras*. His female rogues differ from most of the *pícaros* and *pícaras* whom we have seen so far in that no Jewish or Moslem blood "contaminates" them. They have, nonetheless, inherited their parents' propensity toward immorality. They resemble Justina in that they are social climbers and opportunists. At the conclusion of these tales, the author assures us that sequels are forthcoming, although to date they have never come forth.

Teresa, the protagonist of *La niña de los embustes, Teresa de Manzanares*, lives by her wits and the tricks (*embustes*) she plays on her victims. The trickster is herself tricked, however, when her fourth husband, a miserly merchant, weds her for her money.

Rufina plays the principal role in Castillo Solórzano's *La garduña de Sevilla y anzuelo de bolsas*.[42] Her father forces her to marry a rich old man. She consoles herself with a lover, and shortly thereafter both her father and her husband die. Although she must relinquish her inheritance to pay off her late husband's debts, she does not relinquish her inherited taste for the illegal, and she becomes a skillful sneak thief (*garduña*) and purse snatcher (*anzuelo de bolsas*). She teams up with a succession of male thieves, the third of whom she weds. She and her husband manage to flee Madrid, where the bailiffs are hot on their heels. With the money they have fleeced during their lucrative time together, they settle in Zaragoza and open a silk-goods store. They seem to the world to exemplify respectability; the author, however, indicates that Rufina's heart remains as corrupt as ever.

Salas Barbadillo's and Castillo Solórzano's stories are amusing and entertaining, to be sure, but they fall short of the great picaresque novels because it is difficult for the reader to empathize or sympathize with an Elena, a Teresa, or a Rufina. These *pícaras* are not portrayed as individuals whose immoral, antisocial life-styles are, at least in part, the result of the wrongs that society has inflicted on them. To the contrary, they are depicted as inherently base, a characterization that purposely evokes little understanding or feeling in the reader.

ENDNOTES

[1] The authentic *pícaro*, like Lazarillo de Tormes, Guzmán de Alfarache, and Pablos (*el Buscón*), reveals depth and evolution of character; his plight reflects the hollowness and corruption of the world around him. I distinguish these authentic *pícaros* from the so-called "decadent" pseudo*pícaros*, who are portrayed as corrupt from birth and therefore show no character development.

[2] Cervantes gives us a most detailed description of the *hampa* in his short "exemplary" novel "Rinconete y Cortadillo". He implies that the members of the *hampa* are no more immoral, criminal, or hypocritical than many of their "respectable" counterparts in established society. What is more, the *hampa* provides these marginal men and women with a sense of identity and belonging, which they could seldom find in mainstream society.

[3] See J.A. Maravall, "Relaciones de dependencia e integración social: Criados, graciosos y pícaros."

[4] "Half-outsider" is a term that C. Guillén uses to describe those *pícaros* who fully belong neither to the world of their birth nor to the world of their aspirations; see C. Guillén, "Toward a Definition of the Picaresque."

[5] Francisco Santos, *Periquillo el de las gallineras*, Ch. xvii, in *La novela picaresca española*, ed. A. Valbuena Prat, 6th ed. (Madrid: Aguilar, 1968), p. 1915.

[6] One *pícaro* who is the real author of his autobiography is Estebanillo González. His *Vida y hechos de Estebanillo González, hombre de buen humor* reveals that he was a cowardly, opportunistic buffoon who willingly sacrificed his dignity in return for the material tokens of his amused masters' appreciation.

[7] One anonymous sequel appeared in 1555; another continuation, which we shall examine in this chapter, was published in 1620 by Juan de Luna.

[8] *La vida de Lazarillo de Tormes y de sus fortunas y adversidades*, Ch. iii, in *Nov. pic. esp.*, p. 100.

[9] Ibid., p. 101.

[10] Ibid., p. 99.

[11] Ibid., Ch. i, p. 86.

[12] Ibid., Prologue, p. 84.

[13] Ibid., Ch. vii, p. 111.

[14] Mateo Alemán, *Guzmán de Alfarache*, Pt. I, Bk. I, Ch. vi, in *Nov. pic. esp.*, p. 269.

[15] Ibid., Pt. II, Bk. I, Ch. vii, p. 421.

[16] Ibid., Pt. I, Bk. II, Ch. ii, p. 301.

[17] Ibid., Pt. II, Bk. I, Ch. vi, p. 418.

[18] Guzmán's pessimistic view of human nature is reminiscent of Critilo's in Baltasar Gracián's *El criticón*, a work we will examine in Ch. 9.

[19] Mateo Luján de Sayavedra robbed Alemán of his character Guzmán in his spurious sequel; in revenge, Alemán named his robber character "Sayavedra" in his true sequel.

[20] *Guzmán*, Pt. I, Bk. I, Ch. vii, p. 269.

[21] Ibid., Pt. II, Bk. I, Ch. vii, p. 422.

[22] Ibid., Pt. II, Bk. III, Ch. viii, p. 570.

[23] Ibid., Ch. ix, p. 577.

[24] Ibid.

[25] Juan de Luna, 2nd part of *Lazarillo de Tormes*, Ch. xii, in *Nov. pic. esp.*, pp. 135–136.

[26] Carlos García, *La desordenada codicia de los bienes ajenos*, Ch. xiii, in *Nov. pic. esp*, p. 1193.

[27] Francisco de Quevedo, *Historia de la vida del Buscón, llamado don Pablos*, Bk. II, Ch. ii, in *Nov. pic. esp.*, p. 1114.

[28] Ibid., Bk. I, Ch. vii, p. 1111.

[29] Ibid., Bk. II, Ch. iii, p. 1120.

[30] Ibid., Bk. I, Ch. vi, p. 1106.

[31] Ibid., Bk. II, Ch. ii, p. 1114.

[32] Ibid., Bk. III, Ch. vii, p. 1144.

[33] Lozana's sexual activities are reminiscent of the bawd's in Fernando de Rojas' *La Celestina*, a book that influenced Delicado.

[34] Celestina is also proud of her professional reputation, another point of contact between her and Lozana.

[35] Francisco Delicado, *La Lozana andaluza*, Ch. xli (Barcelona: Zeus, 1968), pp. 156–157.

[36] In his "El mundo converso de '*La Lozana andaluza*'," F. Márquez Villanueva believes that Lozana's attitude concerning her "conversion" is symptomatic of her *Converso* ancestry.

[37] Francisco López de Úbeda, *La pícara Justina*, Bk. I, Ch. ii, in *Nov. pic. esp.*, p. 730.

[38] Ibid., Bk. IV, Ch. iv, p. 880.

[39] Ibid., p. 878.

[40] Ibid., Bk. I, Ch. ii, p. 731.

[41] *La hija de Celestina* was published in 1612; an amplified edition entitled *La ingeniosa Elena* appeared in 1614.

[42] *La garduña de Sevilla* is a continuation of a story Castillo Solórzano wrote about the *pícaro* Trapaza, entitled *Aventuras del bachiller Trapaza*.

III

The Reality of Estate Society

5

Wealth, Appearances, and the Impoverished Nobleman

Spanish literary works of the twelfth through the seventeenth centuries afford us a view of established society as it was in theory: a static, stratified world, which repulsed as best it could the efforts of marginal men and women to secure a foothold in it. Literature also echoes the social reality of the late Middle and the Golden Ages—that the notion of noble status defined by lineage was beginning to evolve into the modern concept of class determined by wealth. A member of the aristocracy, as we have noted with regard to the picaresque, would find it increasingly more difficult to rest solely on his inherited laurels and his "pure" blood, for his peers would likely take into account his financial state as a measure of his worth.

To appreciate the importance society attached to wealth, we should understand the relationship between monarchy and nobility. Theirs was one of mutual dependence, which enabled both to thrive. Kings demanded of their nobles loyalty as well as military and monetary services, in return for which the nobles were granted the privileges they coveted, privileges that only monarchs could confer. Nobles defended the monarchy since it was essential to their well-being and to the very existence of their estate. To ensure its own preservation, the monarchy promoted the interests of the nobility and safeguarded a system that permitted it to prosper. Consequently, the honors system benefited kings and aristocrats alike, and it strengthened the bonds between them.

A nobleman's power and prestige derived more from wealth than from an illustrious pedigree. His wealth, in turn, derived from honors bestowed on him by the king, a point that the sixteenth-century dramatist Francisco Agustín Tárrega makes in his *La sangre leal de los montañeses de Navarra*. This play attests to the diminishing importance of a noble's bloodline (*sangre*) and to the king's significance as the source of all honors. The female protagonist, Doña Lambra, reminds King García of Navarre that her ancestral nobility is ancient in origin and therefore predates the honors he has conferred on her loyal (*leal*), mountain-dwelling (*montañeses*) family. Likening the King to a silversmith, she denies that he has "created" her nobility; rather, he has merely "adorned" it:

> Mira tú que en mi lugar,
> Nobleza siempre he tenido;
> Era una pobre vasalla,
> Sangre tuve sin riqueza,
> Y tu poder, por honralla,
> No me ha dado la nobleza,
> Sí me dio con que adornalla,
> . . .
> Dísteme hacienda y provecho,
> Mi linaje has levantado,
> Y así eres en mi pecho
> Platero que me has limpiado,
> No platero que me has hecho.[1]

The King, however, replies that her nobility would have remained invisible, had he not given it luster. Indeed, he argues, he *did* create it since, unseen, it would have been worthless: "Que yo hice esa nobleza, / Pues que no vista era nada."[2]

Ideally, monarchs were to grant privileges on the basis of virtue and merit. In reality, nevertheless, the recipients of their recognition were not always as honorable as Doña Lambra and her kinsfolk. We have already seen that many merchants and *Conversos* not only falsified documents but also used their wealth in order to attain titles of nobility. The fact that money was weakening the fiber of the aristocracy alarmed conservative

102

noblemen, like Francisco de Quevedo, who feared a drastic change in the estate system they ardently defended.

Wealth had long been a subject that authors treated with ambivalence. Medieval and Golden Age writers were wont to lash out against the power it gave to obtain social status and positions of prestige, and diatribes against the evils of money appear in literary works written as early as the fourteenth century.

In one poem of that century, the pessimistic *Libro de miseria de omne*, the anonymous author condemns the "wisdom" with which wealth automatically imbues a person. No one, the poet laments, listens to the cries of a poor man (*omne; "hombre"* in modern Spanish), while all heed the voice of a rich one:

> Onde el pobre y el mezquino siempre han de llorar
> Ca maguer llame su cuita no lo quiere escuchar
> Mas si viniere el rico que no sabe razonar
> Todos los que conocen la su voz van tomar.[3]

Juan Ruiz, the Archpriest of Hita, has much to say about the properties of money in his fourteenth-century masterpiece *Libro de buen amor* (*Book of Good Love*). As serious as the author of *Libro de miseria de omne*, though more jocular in tone, Ruiz likewise reminds us that money buys respect and blinds a wealthy man's acquaintances to his true character. A foolish, crude, but prosperous man, Ruiz notes, is taken for a knowledgeable *hidalgo;* the more he has, the more worthy he is deemed: "Sea un hombre necio y rudo labrador, / Los dineros le hacen hidalgo y sabidor, / Cuanto más algo tiene, tanto es de más valor."[4]

Blurring the distinction between truth and falsehood, Ruiz complains, money opens doors for the unqualified of society. It has made priors, bishops, abbots, archbishops, doctors, patriarchs, potentates, clerics, priests, monks, and nuns, and it has transformed many a foolish clergyman into a dignitary; in effect, it has enabled ignorant men and women to buy their way into the clergy, an estate from which similarly uneducated but poor people have often been barred:

[El dinero] hacía muchos priores, obispos y abades,
Arzobispos, doctores, patriarcas, potestades,
A muchos clérigos necios dábales dignidades,
Hacía verdad mentiras y mentiras verdades.
Hacía muchos clérigos y muchos ordenados,
Muchos monjes y monjas, religiosos sagrados:
El dinero les daba por bien examinados;
A los pobres decían que no eran letrados.[5]

Ruiz, a realist, satirizes a world that is awed by riches. At the same time, however, he recognizes the one chief virtue of money—that it allows a man to be his own master: "El que no ha dineros, no es de sí señor."[6] By the Golden Age, as the picaresque novels reveal, society would come to apprize money for being an essential ingredient not only of self-esteem and independence but of worldly honor. The medieval principle of honor grounded solely in lineage would be relegated to the realm of theory, and reality would impose with increased vigor its own message—that a nobleman should manifest a life-style befitting his elevated rank. If he lacked wealth (as did, for example, Lazarillo's Squire and Justina's *hidalgo* husband), he should at least *seem* to the world to possess it, for only if he appeared wealthy could he win his peers' respect.

Dr. Juan Huarte de San Juan, a prominent sixteenth-century observer of human nature, provides us in his famed treatise on wit and talent, *Examen de ingenios para las ciencias*, with a detailed analysis of the various attributes that comprise a man of honor. Such a man, in Huarte's estimation, must be of good character; his profession, worthy of respect (he must not engage in a mechanical trade). Although a good family name is the sine qua non of an enviable reputation, Huarte remarks, it means little if not accompanied with riches: "Ser bien nacido y de claro linaje es una joya muy estimada. Pero tiene una falta muy grande: que sola por sí es de muy poco provecho, . . . Pero, junta con la riqueza, no hay punta de honra que se le iguale."[7]

Unhappily for the poor aristocrat, however, wealth and noble status did not always go hand in hand. The customs of primogeniture and entailment made it difficult for all but firstborn sons to inherit their fathers' lands (although younger brothers and sisters could inherit money and family treasures). Provided that they did not squander their inheritances, firstborn sons, therefore, generally fared better economically than their legitimate siblings. Illegitimate offspring, unless formally recognized, could not hope to share in any part of their fathers' possessions. The financial hardships and the ensuing conflicts and emotional distress of these dispossessed nobles (legitimate and illegitimate) are common motifs in Spanish medieval and Golden Age literature.

If wealth brought a man honor and power, poverty subjected him to the derision and rejection of his peers, a plight that the fifteenth-century poet Ruy Páez de Ribera most eloquently evokes. The poor man's only companion, he laments, is solitude. His family and friends have abandoned him, not for any misdeed on his part but only because he has fallen on hard times; moreover, they conveniently overlook any good deed he or his forefathers might have done them:

> El pobre no tiene parientes ni amigos,
> Donaire ni seso, esfuerzo y sentido,
> Y por la pobreza le son enemigos
> Los suyos mismos por verlo caído;
> Todos lo tienen por desconocido
> Y no se les miembra del tiempo pasado,
> Si algún beneficio hubieron cobrado
> De aquellos de quien él ha descendido.[8]

Alienated from his world, the impoverished nobleman feels vulnerable, even impotent, in the face of circumstances seemingly beyond his control. How can he right the feeling of shame that envelops him? How can he avoid the fate that befalls other poor aristocrats, like Lazarillo's and Pablos' squires, who must find wealthy nobles to serve? One way is for him to sacrifice his integrity on the altar of ambition, a theme that permeates many Golden Age plays. The poverty-stricken but noble *galán* 'gallant' of these works tries to alleviate his financial dilemma by marrying a young lady of means. He hopes that an advantageous marriage will represent only the beginning of a prosperous future. Wealth will make it possible for him to rise in court circles and will place him in a position where he will be able to vie for the king's favors. Although most *galanes* end up falling genuinely in love with their *damas* 'ladies', some are thoroughly unscrupulous opportunists who wed solely for convenience.

The male protagonists in several plays of the Golden Age playwright Guillén de Castro are particularly ambitious; they realize success in spite of the honesty and merit they lack.

One of these unsavory characters is Don Diego, the destitute and loathsome aristocrat of *La verdad averiguada y engañoso casamiento*. Driven by greed, he marries the wealthy *Conversa* Leonor and passes from rags to undeserved riches. Shortly thereafter, Leonor is falsely accused of having an affair with another man. Believing the news, Diego deserts her. He then takes up with Hipólita and enters into a fraudulent marriage (*engañoso casamiento*) with her to save her reputation, which their relationship has tarnished. While Diego may seem to be concerned with the demands of honor, such considerations disappear in the face of Hipólita's poverty. Encouraging her to extract money from Don Rodrigo, her admirer, Diego justifies his immoral behavior on the grounds that he must relinquish honor-virtue if he is to advance economically: ". . . importa perder honor, / Si quiere ganar dinero."[9] Leonor, in the meantime, sets about to restore her honor, which slander and abandonment have sullied. She convinces her detractor to confess that he lied about her. Once the truth is revealed (*verdad averiguada*), Diego gladly leaves Hipólita for Leonor and resumes the opulent life-style he had previously enjoyed. We may wonder how Leonor can stand the sight of her bigamist husband, to say nothing of his embrace. Unfortunately, she has no other choice. Only he can return what he stole and what she cherishes most—her honor. Unusual indeed is the fact that Rodrigo marries Hipólita; a virgin, after all, she is not. But Rodrigo, a man of extraordinary understanding, does not consider her a fallen woman, since Diego deceived her about the validity of their union.

Tirso de Molina also writes about ambition in many of his plays. What distinguishes several of Tirso's leading male characters from Guillén's, however, is what they would willingly discard in order to climb the ladder of success: Guillén's would sacrifice integrity; Tirso's, integrity—and love.

Don Rodrigo, the pathetic *galán* of Tirso's *El castigo del pensequé*, at first arouses our sympathy as he bemoans the predicament of the secondborn son. His rich, older brother has treated him miserly and meanly, and poor Rodrigo has had to put up with his numerous follies as well. Hoping to improve his condition, Rodrigo sets out for Flanders, where he pretends to be the long-lost son of a wealthy nobleman. He meets the Countess, who appoints him her secretary and whets his appetite for greater things to come. What he has not counted on is falling in love with his "sister", the nobleman's daughter. If he brings to light his true identity, he might win her hand, but he also might forfeit what he desires even more—marriage to the Countess (whose ambivalence toward her social unequal reminds us of the Countess' in Lope's *El perro del hortelano*). As it turns out, he winds up with neither woman because of a foolish error of judgment, and the Countess banishes him from Flanders.

In the second part of the play, *Quien calla, otorga*, Rodrigo has learned his lesson well: he will keep his eyes and ears open to anything and everything that may promote his self-interest. The same pattern repeats itself: the Marchioness appoints him her majordomo and discreetly signals him of her amorous intentions. Although he loves her sister, he vows not to miss this chance for the marriage of his dreams. Consequently, he renounces his true love but wins the hand of his Marchioness.[10]

Not all impoverished *galanes* of Golden Age theater, however, are ambitious fortune hunters. Some become sincerely enamored *before* they discover the magnitude of their ladyloves' dowries. But winning a *dama*'s heart and winning her hand are two entirely different matters. If he is to marry her, the *galán* must on occasion appear to be a man of means himself. That he courts her under false pretenses usually pays off for him in

107

the end. Acquiescing to the demands of superficiality that his society imposes on him, he is rewarded with her hand and with the dowry it presupposes.

The protagonist of Lope de Vega's *Servir a señor discreto*, Don Pedro, exemplifies the poor cavalier who has depleted his meager resources in order to woo the woman of his dreams. Initially, the haughty Doña Leonor rejects him, but the thought of marrying another suitor causes her to change her mind; besides, the wealth that Pedro feigns impresses her and her father immensely. Just as Pedro is about to spend the last of his reserves, the discreet Count of Palma hires him as his secretary and generously lends him a splendid home to call his own. Leonor's father eventually learns the truth about Pedro but consents to their marriage, nonetheless; he would rather a poor, humble son-in-law, he concedes, than a rich, arrogant one. Pedro is a likable and honorable suitor whose motives are unselfish. He has practiced deception to win only Leonor's love, not her riches, and luckily winds up with both.

The gallants of the seventeenth-century dramatist Agustín Moreto resemble Lope's Don Pedro in that love and honor moderate their ambition. They behave with a considerable degree of virtue, in marked contrast to the hollow and devious characters who surround them. In the hilarious *Trampa adelante*, for example, the impoverished Don Juan and the rich Doña Leonor are in love. She has been forced into a betrothal of convenience to the greedy Don Diego, whose sister, the wily Doña Ana, also loves Juan. Ana steals from Diego in order to bribe Juan's servant, whose intercession, she believes, is crucial if she is to snare Juan. But her tricky plan (*trampa*) backfires when Juan marries Leonor. Thanks not only to Leonor's dowry but to the money his servant has conned out of Ana, Juan's fortune is considerable. He rejoices at his new-found happiness, and we rejoice that Diego and Ana have little to comfort them.

Poverty condemned the aristocrat like Don Juan to subsist on the fringes of a world that would have welcomed him with open arms, had his circumstances been more favorable. For society to admit him fully, he must capitulate to its expectation that his life-style befit his pedigree. Marriage to a wealthy woman provides the means for the social acceptance he desires. It restores him to his rightful place in the world and wins him his peers' respect. Having become a "man of honor", he eagerly awaits the recognition of the king, on whom his dream of future honors rests.

The dramatist who most harshly criticizes the materialism and superficiality of Golden Age society is Juan Ruiz de Alarcón. In several of his plays, he presents two noblemen whose ways of life are diametrically opposed. The protagonist is poor but virtuous; integrity forms the basis of his honor. The antagonist cares not to discern between essentials and externals, between substance and appearance. He reflects society in that he has debased the concept of honor by equating it with pedigree, money, and influence.

Ruiz de Alarcón is a firm proponent of noblesse oblige. A nobleman, in his view, should live in accordance with the obligations inherent in his title. If he carries out his duties truthfully and justly, he will add luster to his ancestral name; if, to the contrary, he behaves with deceit and malice, he will tarnish it.

Two of Ruiz de Alarcón's most famous plays, *Las paredes oyen* and *La verdad sospechosa*, involve characters who personify the falsity their creator deplored. Their moral defects are antithetical to true honor and lead them to their downfall. Had Guillén de Castro written these plays, the characters might have succeeded in attaining their goals, and their success would have served to underscore the milieu of hypocrisy in which they live. Ruiz de Alarcón, however, does not permit duplicity to triumph and consequently punishes his characters.

Don Mendo, the antagonist of *Las paredes oyen*, is a slanderer. He and Don Juan both court the beautiful Doña Ana, who prefers Mendo until she overhears him tell another suitor that she is ugly. She finally sees Mendo as he really is, dismisses him, and determines to love Juan, who has never spoken ill of her. The moral of the play, of course, is that even walls have ears (*las paredes oyen*). Don García, the antihero of *La verdad sospechosa*, is a chronic liar. In the end, he also loses the woman whom he loves; even worse, he must marry a woman whose reputation he defamed while wooing his truelove.[11]

Straightforwardness is a virtue that Ruiz de Alarcón prizes highly, for it represents the opposite of slander, lies, and superficiality. Indeed, the hero in another well-known play of his, *No hay mal que por bien no venga; Don Domingo de don Blas*,[12] embodies straightforwardness and, as such, is one of the few true eccentrics of Golden Age theater. He defies the absurd conventions of appearance-ridden, courtly society. What is more, he is a creature of comfort. He deigns not to follow the dictates of fashion, and he refuses to wear anything that might cause him the slightest discomfort. He courts the conventional Doña Leonor in his own uncourtly way, and his ungallantry appalls her. An early-to-bedder, he cannot fathom the idea of serenading her during the wee hours of the night. Since he refuses to risk his life needlessly in order to impress her, he would never consider dueling with another suitor or fighting a bull. Don Domingo, however, is honorable in the true sense of the word. When principles, not foolishness, are at stake, he displays courage and loyalty. As for Leonor, she chooses a more gallant suitor, and he marries a woman who accepts him for what he is—a thoroughly sensible and delightful nonconformist.

Unlike the courtly society he portrays, Ruiz de Alarcón deals harshly with perverters of honor and truth. And when an unscrupulous antagonist is pitted against a virtuous protagonist for the love of a woman, he rewards his upright character with love.

The path of integrity, however, is not always an easy one to follow, as Don García, the poor but honorable hero of Ruiz de Alarcón's *Los favores del mundo*, discovers. He and Doña Anarda are in love, and his hopes for a bright future seem to come true when the Prince names him his royal counselor. But García's rising star is about to plummet when he finds out that the Prince is also smitten with Anarda. García must make the choice between love and ambition. He courageously forsakes the favors of the world (*favores del mundo*) for Anarda and a life of obscurity.

Don García typifies many of Ruiz de Alarcón's male characters in his adherence to true honor and in his rejection of false societal values. As for his female lead characters, Ruiz depicts them in a less favorable light. Like Doña Ana, the heroine of *Las paredes oyen*, they tend at first toward frivolity and shallowness, although as the plays progress, they begin to distinguish between essentials and nonessentials. Doña Ana, for instance, initially feels repelled by Don Juan's ugliness. She judges the proverbial book by its cover. To her credit, however, she eventually learns that one man's integrity means more than another's good looks, and she turns Mendo down in favor of Juan.

Ruiz de Alarcón's *damas* resemble most of their counterparts of Golden Age theater in their fear for their reputations, but they surpass the other young female characters in their undue concern for the external aspects of honor. Not only do Ruiz's *damas* safeguard their chastity, on which any young woman's good name hinges; they also go to great lengths to determine the quality of their suitors' reputations. The criteria they use in accepting or rejecting a *galán* reveal the superficiality of society. The eccentric Don Domingo's first love, for example, is horrified at his uncourtly ways and bestows the pleasure of her company on Don Juan. But theirs is a stormy romance. What attracted her to Juan was his apparent wealth. Once he has spent what was left of it, she has nothing to do with him. He has fallen on hard times and, to compound his dilemma, has acquired the unenviable reputation of a squanderer. If she were to marry a man who neglects his good name, her own would suffer, and even *he* would cease to respect her, she tells him:

> Teniendo yo por marido
> A quien tanto la [opinión] ha perdido,
> ¿Mereciera estimación
> Ni aun de vos? No soy tan necia,
> Que quiera darme a entender

111

Que estimará a su mujer
Quien su mismo honor desprecia.[13]

Only when Juan mends his ways and recovers his reputation does she consent to wed him.

Another factor that Ruiz de Alarcón's *damas* take very seriously is their beaux' bloodlines. A *dama* will refuse her *galán*'s proposal of marriage until he proves that his ancestry is not "tainted", for nothing besmirches a man's reputation and, by extension, his prospective fiancée's more than the hint of *Converso* blood. Ruiz's young female characters usually learn to overlook ugliness, ungallantry, and even poverty in their suitors, but they are steadfast in their intolerance of anything that may seriously jeopardize the good esteem in which society holds them.

What we know of Ruiz de Alarcón's life sheds some light on why he took society to task for worshiping with such devotion the false idols of wealth and appearances. Ruiz was born in Mexico of a noble family. He moved to Spain, where he studied and practiced law. The fact that he used the title "don" before his name subjected him to the derision of those who considered his noble status suspect. In addition, the world ridiculed a physical deformity that had afflicted him from birth. Like many of his characters, Ruiz was not a wealthy man. He hoped, nevertheless, that his integrity and abilities would merit for him a position in the government (a hope he shared, the reader may recall, with Cervantes). He was finally granted a position after many long years of waiting, during which time he undoubtedly witnessed the rise of other aspiring bureaucrats who were far less qualified morally and intellectually than he.

Ridicule and disillusionment alienated Ruiz de Alarcón from the society that refused to accept him for what he was—gifted—and that insisted on judging him for what he appeared to be—pretentious and deformed. It is understandable why he in turn ridiculed society in his plays and why he created heroes who win the vindication that always eluded him.

ENDNOTES

[1] Francisco Agustín Tárrega, *La sangre leal de los montañeses de Navarra*, Act I, in *Poetas dramáticos valencianos*, ed. E. Juliá Martínez (Madrid: R.A.E.; BSCE, 1929), I, 346.

[2] Ibid.

[3] *Libro de miseria de omne*, st. cclxviii, ed. M. Artigas, in *BBMP*, 2 (1920), 43.

[4] Juan Ruiz, Archpriest of Hita, *Libro de buen amor*, st. cdxci, ed. J. Cejador y Frauca, 9th ed. (Madrid: Espasa-Calpe; CC, 1963), I, 182.

[5] Ibid., sts. cdxciv-cdxcv, p. 183.

[6] Ibid., st. cdxci, p. 182.

[7] Juan Huarte de San Juan, *Examen de ingenios para las ciencias*, ed. E. Torre (Madrid: Editora Nacional, 1977), p. 277.

[8] Ruy Páez de Ribera, "Decir sobre la Fortuna," in *Cancionero de Juan Alfonso de Baena*, ed. J. M. Azáceta (Madrid: C.S.I.C., 1966), II, 606.

[9] Guillén de Castro, *La verdad averiguada y engañoso casamiento*, Act III, in *Obras*, ed. E. Juliá Martínez (Madrid: R.A.E.; BSCE, 1926), II, 284.

[10] Agustín Moreto borrowed from Tirso's *El castigo del penséque* to create one of the most memorable Spanish plays of mistaken identity, *El parecido en la corte*. Unlike Rodrigo, however, the hero of Moreto's play does not sacrifice his truelove in order to fulfill his ambitions.

[11] Ruiz de Alarcón's *La verdad sospechosa* was the source for Pierre Corneille's *Le Menteur*, a play that in turn served as a model for Carlo Goldoni's *Il Bugiardo*.

[12] The title of this play derives from a Spanish proverb that means "there is no evil that may not come from good".

[13] Juan Ruiz de Alarcón, *No hay mal que por bien no venga; Don Domingo de don Blas*, Act II, in BAE, XX, 186.

The Plight of the Destitute, Oppressed Commoner

If wealth signified dignity and social security (in the true sense of the word), poverty, to the contrary, spelled conflict, pain and ostracism. Impoverished aristocrats might try to hide their misfortune or to right it with a profitable marriage, but destitute and oppressed commoners could avail themselves of few alternatives to the suffering that characterized their existences.

Fleeing starvation, some have-nots descended to the world of prostitutes, vagabonds, *pícaros*, and thieves, whose ways of life, as we have noted, were marginal to established society. Others chose not to engage in disreputable professions for moral and/or social reasons, and their decision placed them at the mercy of the uncaring and filled their lives with despair.

The plight of the poor common folk who lived during the late Middle and the Golden Ages bears a direct relationship to events that took place in the fourteenth century. During that period of Spanish history, a succession of plagues brought about a sharp decrease in the number of farm laborers. Inflation mounted, poverty and hunger increased, and multitudes of the destitute flocked to cities and large towns in the hope of improving their condition. These critical factors produced great social instability, to which the satirical poetry of protest that arose at that time bears witness. In bitter and gloomy terms, fourteenth-century poets express the insecurity of the individual who must cope with a rapidly changing world, a world that at any moment could prove hostile.

Avarice and poverty are the predominant themes of this poetry. Greed is the root of great evil and suffering, for it drives the rich to become richer and more powerful at the expense of the poor. We should not, however, interpret these poems as necessarily critical of the medieval social order. Rather, poets condemn only the wealthy and the mighty who abuse their privileges and who, in doing so, unwittingly risk undermining the very estate system they are obligated to safeguard.

The rabbi Sem Tob is one of several poets who treat the sin of avarice. His *Proverbios morales*, a collection of moral proverbs concerning the "ways of the world", reflects a society in which no member is satisfied with what he has. Greed motivates all men, rich and poor alike:

> En el mundo hallé
> Dos hombres y no más,
> Y nunca alcancé
> El tercero jamás.
> . . .
> Ca no hay pobre hombre
> Si no el codicioso;
> Ni rico si no hombre
> Con lo que tiene gozoso.
> Quien lo que le cumple quiere,
> Poco le bastará:
> Al que sobras quisiere,
> El mundo no le cabrá.[1]

Sem Tob's formula for peace of mind is quite simple: shun greed at all costs: "Guárdese de codicia, / Que es lo que más le daña."[2]

Other poets show more compassion for the poor man than does Sem Tob. Juan Ruiz, for example, lashes out in his *Libro de buen amor* against arrogant nobles who crush the less fortunate in the same way they would a dry sardine:

> El derecho del pobre piérdese muy aína,
> Al pobre, al menguado, a la pobre mezquina
> El rico los quebranta, soberbia los inclina;
> No son end' más preciados que la seca sardina.[3]

And in his *Rimado de palacio*, a harsh commentary on palace life,

Pero López de Ayala deplores the victimization of orphans and widows at the hands of noblemen who, instead of protecting them, turn a deaf ear to their cries and who force them to pay even more burdensome taxes:

> Los huérfanos y viudas, que Dios quiso guardar
> En su gran encomienda, véoles voces dar:
> Acórrenos, Señor; no podemos durar
> Los pechos y tributos que nos hacen pagar.
> De cada día veo asacar nuevos pechos
> Que demandan señores demás de sus derechos.[4]

Protest poetry of the fifteenth century continues to denounce the powerful who amass their fortunes with little regard for the poor. A passage in the famed poet Juan de Mena's *Laberinto de fortuna* exemplifies the righteous indignation that many poets felt toward avaricious clergymen, in particular. Neglecting to minister to the needs of their flocks, the poet maintains, these nonexemplary priests collect tithes and other monies from them in order to support their own "vile habits":

> ¿Quién asimismo decir no podría
> De cómo las cosas sagradas se venden,
> Y los viles usos en que se despienden
> Los diezmos ofertos a Santa María?[5]

Another poet of that era, Fernán Pérez de Guzmán, confesses in his "Confesión rimada" that he himself was guilty of oppressing the poor. He finds himself as much at fault as those whose opulent life-styles he then proceeds to condemn in the harshest of terms. He accuses prelates, who are the treasurers of Christ's patrimony, of spending on falcons, hunting dogs, wars, and other godless pursuits what they should have given to the poor. As for noblemen, the money they spend on the silk adorning one of their horses alone could clothe a hundred poor folk, and the coats of arms bedecking one of their mules could be sold to clothe several naked men:

> Acordarme debo que a pobres tomé
> Todo aquello de que estoy guarnido.
> . . .

116

Los grandes prelados, que son tesoreros
Del patrimonio del Crucificado,
Con aves de caza y canes monteros,
Y lo que es más grave, en guerras gastado,
El tercio que a pobres debiera ser dado,
Gastándolo en usos de Dios prohibidos.
Creo que suspiros, voces y gemidos
Llegan a los cielos del pobre cuitado.
Los grandes señores y los caballeros
Traen sus caballos emparamentados
De paños de seda y muy bien obrados,
Y a sus acémilas tales reposteros,
Que podrían por cierto con tantos dineros
A algunos pobres desnudos vestir:
En lo que un caballo cuesta cubrir
Se podrían vestir cien pobres enteros.[6]

The fifteenth century was indeed a tumultuous period. Noblemen fought among themselves. Struggling to retain their privileges, all too many of them ignored the pleas of those around them. Out of this havoc emerged the figure of the *privado* 'royal favorite'. Needless to say, the nobility envied him the influence he succeeded in wielding over the monarch. Nor did the *privado*'s presence please the underdogs of society, who had little reason to hope that he would intercede on their behalf. The *privados'* ambitions gave rise to sharp political criticism, which takes two forms: traditional satire directed against the powerful in general who abuse their rights, and invectives leveled at specific individuals.[7]

Álvaro de Luna served as the favorite of King Juan (John) II of Castile, who ruled during the first half of the fifteenth century. Although Luna enjoyed the support of certain nobles, others rebelled against him because they feared that his influence would diminish their power and would strengthen the monarch's authority. Luna became the target of caustic invectives. In the *Doctrinal de privados*, for example, which his archenemy, the Marquess of Santillana, composed after Luna's death, Luna "confesses" to numerous sins against the poor, the captives, the sick, and even the dead:

Los menguados no harté:
Alguno, si me pidió
De vestir, no lo halló,
Ni los pobres recepté,
Cautivos no los saqué,
Ni los enfermos cuitados
Fueron por mí visitados,
Ni los muertos sepulté.[8]

Unlike his father Juan II, the weak and decadent Enrique (Henry) IV was himself the object of bitter attacks. Anonymous ballads written during his reign express the sentiments of the downtrodden and depict him as the "shepherd" who neglects his "sheep" as he drunkenly chases after his young, male "shepherd's helpers":

Ándase tras los zagales
Por estos andurriales
Todo el día embebecido,
Holgazando sin sentido,
Que no mira nuestros males.[9]

Lament as they did the tribulations of their victimized brethren, poets foresaw little that would mitigate their suffering. In the final analysis, the poor and the subjugated were bound to a system in which social barriers inevitably bred injustice and a radically unequal distribution of wealth.

The fifteenth-century Ferrán Sánchez de Calavera is one of the few poets who dare to question the inequities of the world. Unable to find a satisfactory answer to the poverty, suffering, worries, burdens, and sadness he sees about him, he can only conclude that God, for reasons known only to Him, has preordained the social order to be as it is, and he begs God to illuminate him in His mysterious ways:

Señor, yo veo que a mí no fallecen
Pérdidas y daños viviendo en pobreza,
Dolencias, cuidados, pesares, tristeza;
Y veo a otros que nunca adolecen,
. . .

Y pues que notorio y sobre natura,
Señor, es el vuestro absoluto poder,
Hacedme por vuestra merced entender
Aquesta ordenanza que tanto es oscura.[10]

Criticism of nobles who abuse common folk appears in fifteenth-century fiction as well as in poetry. One character who protests the victimization of the poor at the hands of the rich is Areusa, the independent and strong-willed prostitute, the reader may recall, of Fernando de Rojas' *La Celestina*. Speaking to the procuress Celestina, Areusa unleashes her anger at wealthy noblewomen who defame, mistreat, and subjugate their humble serving girls: "Denostadas, maltratadas las traen, contino sojuzgadas."[11] These mistresses falsely accuse the poor girls of sneaking men into their homes or of stealing. Furthermore, they take pleasure in raising their voices at them, and they glory in berating them. The better the quality of the girls' work, the less content they are. For this reason, Areusa explains, she has always wanted to live free and to be her own mistress in her own little house rather than endure subjugation and captivity in other people's opulent palaces:

Su placer es dar voces, su gloria es reñir. De lo mejor hecho menos contentamiento muestran. Por esto, . . . he querido más vivir en mi pequeña casa, exenta y señora, que no en sus ricos palacios sojuzgada y cautiva.[12]

Areusa has learned at a tender age that kindness is a virtue few of her social superiors practice. While she may be accused of distorting reality to justify her own way of life, the words and deeds of the servant characters in *La Celestina* also bring to light the self-interest that was eroding the bonds of responsibility and respect, bonds that ideally linked the noble and the affluent with the humble and the poor.

Complain as they did, the downtrodden of society had no

119

choice but to resign themselves to the inequities of human existence. Their only consolation was the fact that death renders mankind biologically equal as it reduces the lowly and the mighty alike to ashes. Indeed, the theme of Death, the Great Leveler, emerged in the fourteenth century as a logical consequence not only of pestilence but also of social and economic inequality. The destitute and the oppressed who despaired of earthly justice placed their faith in the promise of divine justice, in the promise that God judges all men, irrespective of birth, wealth, or position, according to how virtuously they have acted out their roles on earth.

The "Great Leveler" theme appears in the *danse macabre* 'dance of death', which was a popular motif of fourteenth- and fifteenth-century European literature. The *Danza de la Muerte*, an anonymous, early fifteenth-century Castilian variant of the *danse,* is a biting satire of social types representing the three estates as well as Jews and Moslems. Death (*Muerte*) invites all men to her dance: "A la danza mortal venid los nacidos / Que en el mundo sois de cualquiera estado."[13] Exposing their vices and weaknesses, she deals severely with the highest members of society—the Pope and the Emperor—who have used their power wrongly. On the other hand, she treats the lowest with compassion. The Farmer, she tells him, may look forward to salvation, provided that he never stole from another; and the Hermit who has led a life of self-deprivation may also expect his just reward, as may the rule-abiding Benedictine monk.

Later in the same century, Juan de Mena wrote his "Razonamiento con la Muerte", a poem in which he also availed himself of the "Great Leveler" theme to assure us that Death makes the rich and powerful the equals of the poor:

> Padre Santo, emperadores
> Cardenales, arzobispos,
> Patriarcas y obispos,
> Reyes, duques, y señores,
> Los maestros y priores,
> Los sabios colegiales,

> Tú [la muerte] los haces ser iguales
> Con los simples labradores.[14]

Playwrights of the sixteenth century continued to make use of this theme for its dramatic potential. Death is a particularly Grim Reaper in Sebastián de Horozco's *Coloquio de la Muerte con todas las edades y estados*, for it transforms mankind, from the loftiest to the lowliest, into maggots:

> Grandes, menores, medianos,
> Altos, bajos y más chicos,
> Han de ser pobres y ricos
> Convertidos en gusanos.[15]

The image of Death, the Great Leveler, reappears in the seventeenth century with Pedro Calderón de la Barca's sacramental play (*auto sacramental*), *El gran teatro del mundo*.[16] The theater is a metaphor of the world, of earthly life. God, the author of the play, assigns different roles to his actors, the men and women who comprise society. Man's ultimate destiny is eternal life, compared to which his temporal life is as ephemeral as the performance of a play. Yet the moral quality of his fleeting, earthly existence determines the final outcome of his soul. What matters is not whether he is a pope, an emperor, or a farmer but how he has fulfilled his preordained role.

The Poor Man is the key to the theology of *El gran teatro*. The humblest member of society, he acknowledges that he is the scum of the earth. He relies on the charity of others and mistakenly believes that they have no use for him, that he has no productive part to play in the world. The others learn too late that they will be judged on the degree of compassion with which they have treated the Poor Man. His role, then, is to provide them with an opportunity to practice charity. As in *La vida es sueño* (which we will analyze in Ch. 9), the lesson Calderón dramatizes is that we should not contemplate eternal reward unless we interact selflessly with our fellowman. Altruistic behavior in society is the key to the individual's salvation; egotism, to his perdition.[17]

With the exception of Calderón's *El gran teatro del mundo* and of other *autos sacramentales*, Golden Age theater does not place as much emphasis on destitution as does the novel. What is more, the rare commoner who attempts to flee poverty usually meets with conflict and disaster, for he has refused to resign himself to his lot in life. Instead of accepting the inevitable, like the Poor Man in Calderón's *auto*, he has tried to change it by using the only means at his disposal: fraud and theft. Society deals as harshly with this upstart individual as it did with the *pícaro* because, unlike the Poor Man, he has momentarily disrupted its sense of order and its status quo.

What Golden Age theater does not usually expect a commoner to suffer is oppression—in particular, a nobleman's sexual abuse of a peasant's fiancée, daughter, or wife (motifs we will examine in Pt. V). This commoner type who challenges a lusty noble, however, differs radically from the *pícaro* in that he has not reached the depths of poverty, he is generally content with his traditional way of life, and he is innately virtuous and honorable. Since he embodies the same personal and societal ideals as an exemplary nobleman, he is allowed the right to win retribution for the injustice with which the nonexemplary nobleman has treated him.

ENDNOTES

[1] Rabbi Sem Tob, *Proverbios morales*, sts. ccxi, ccxiv-ccxv, in BAE, LVII, 344–345.

[2] Ibid., st. cxcviii, p. 344.

[3] Juan Ruiz, Archpriest of Hita, *Libro de buen amor*, st. dcccxx, ed. J. Cejador y Frauca, 9th ed. (Madrid: Espasa-Calpe; CC, 1963), I, 278.

[4] Pero López de Ayala, *Rimado de palacio*, sts. ccxli-ccxlii, in BAE, LVII, 432.

[5] Juan de Mena, *Laberinto de fortuna o las trescientas*, st. xcv, ed. J.M. Blecua (Madrid: Espasa-Calpe; CC, 1960), p. 54.

[6] Fernán Pérez de Guzmán, "Confesión rimada," sts. cxlii, cxlvi-cxlvii, in NBAE, XIX, 645.

[7] See K.R. Scholberg, *Sátira e invectiva en la España medieval*, espec. p. 300. During the seventeenth century, this penchant for writing invectives flourished once again.

[8] Marquess of Santillana, *Doctrinal de privados*, st. xlvii, in *Obras*, ed. A. Cortina, 3rd ed. (Madrid: Espasa-Calpe; Austral, 1964), p. 96.

[9] *Coplas de Mingo Revulgo*, st. iii, in *Coplas satíricas y dramáticas de la Edad Media*, ed. E. Rincón (Madrid: Alianza, 1968), p. 36. This metaphor of the neglectful shepherd also appears in the anonymous *Coplas hechas al rey don Enrique*.

[10] Ferrán Sánchez de Calavera, "Pregunta," in *Cancionero de Juan Alfonso de Baena*, ed. J.M. Azáceta (Madrid: C.S.I.C., 1966), III, 1068, 1070.

[11] Fernando de Rojas, *La Celestina*, Act IX, ed. J. Cejador y Frauca, 9th ed. (Madrid: Espasa-Calpe; CC, 1968), II, 41.

[12] Ibid., p. 43.

[13] *La Danza de la Muerte*, in BAE, LVII, 380.

[14] Juan de Mena, "Razonamiento con la Muerte," in NBAE, XIX, 207.

[15] Sebastián de Horozco, "Coloquio de la Muerte con todas las edades y estados," in his *Cancionero* (Seville: Sociedad de Bibliófilos Andaluces, 1874), pp. 187–188.

[16] The theme of Death, the Great Leveler, also appears in Cervantes' *Don Quijote*, Pt. II, Chs. xi–xii.

[17] See A.A. Parker, "'El gran teatro del mundo'."

IV

The Pursuits of Individuality, Freedom, and Eternity

Positive Solitude and Freedom

Spanish medieval and Golden Age literature bears ample witness to the painful states of conflict and negative solitude into which an individual is cast when his religious, social, or financial status alienates him from the world of his aspirations or of his birth. Literary works also treat the theme of positive solitude, the voluntary estrangement from the same materialistic, appearance-ridden, courtly milieu that *Conversos*, *pícaros*, and impoverished noblemen hoped to call their own. The men and women who crave solitude seek freedom as well, for they want nothing to do with the ungodliness that imprisons other individuals in search of society's acceptance.

The writers and characters whom we will examine typify men and women of all ages, including our own, who yearn to flee the physical and moral pollutants of urban life. In particular, they shun the ambience of the royal court, which from the second half of the sixteenth century was permanently situated in Madrid. The following century signaled the moral decline of the court, and Madrid came to be synonymous with intrigue, pretense, greed, and sexual license.

These individuals who wish to avoid the court desire the freedom to live as they want, uninvolved in devious machinations and the rituals of etiquette. They will encounter this freedom only in the countryside, where they will live far removed from the corruption and artifice that enslave the wealthy, the powerful, and the ambitious.

The men and women who extol the virtues of rural life treasure peace. They wish for nothing that might distract them from savoring the joys of nature and the simple, essential pleasures of life. They welcome the solitary mode of existence. Their solitude is not negative, for it has not been forced on them from without; rather, it is positive since they have willed it on themselves.

The so-called "decadent" pseudopicaresque offers several examples of "*pícaros*" who have tired of striving to survive and to rise in a corrupt world. Instead of continuing their uphill struggle any longer, they withdraw from the world and seek out the serenity of solitude. These literary characters differ from authentic *pícaros* like Lazarillo, Guzmanillo, and Pablos in two important points: their parents were respectable, and they themselves are not inclined toward evil.

One such pseudo*pícaro* is Alonso, the protagonist of Jerónimo de Alcalá Yáñez' *El donado hablador Alonso, mozo de muchos amos*. Once his mother and father die, Alonso must fend for himself, and he becomes a servant. He is loquacious (*hablador*), an attribute that his honest and kind nature more than offsets. Nonetheless, his masters treat him miserably. His wretched existence culminates when he is seized by pirates and carried off to Algiers. Ransomed at last, he retires to the solitude of a hermitage, where he intends to spend the rest of his life as a lay brother (*donado*).

Periquillo, the "*pícaro*" of Francisco Santos' *Periquillo el de las gallineras*, craves solitude even as a young boy, a trait he inherited from his adoptive father. The world, the father laments, is an unfortunate, sad, and greedy place where perpetual strife reigns supreme: "[El mundo es] tan desdichado, tan triste y avariento, donde todo es guerra perpetua: . . . todo él se compone de contrarios."[1] When circumstances reduce his parents to poverty, Periquillo leaves home and begins his career as a servant to numerous masters and mistresses, including a chicken dealer (*gallinera*). In order to survive, he has no recourse but to live in the society he abhors. He does not desire to change the world, which he believes has turned topsy-turvy; he simply wants to put it well behind him. Nor does ambition whet his appetite; he only cares to survive until he dies. He yearns to escape the enslaving atmosphere of the court, a reflection of Hell, and to end his days in the country, a prelude to Heaven:

> ¿Quién es el que no ama la soledad, pudiendo pasar en ella? ¿Hay mayor esclavitud que la vida de corte? . . . Las soledades del campo no te alabaré, ni pintaré su quieta habitación; sólo diré que es un remedo de la gloria y el bullicio de las cortes un dechado del infierno.[2]

One of the most famous Spanish Golden Age discourses on the shortcomings of the court and the virtues of the country is a treatise entitled *Menosprecio de corte y alabanza de aldea*. Its author is Fray Antonio de Guevara, a reknowned sixteenth-century courtier and intellectual. Guevara complains that a man is esteemed at the court for what he has, not for what he is: "Ninguno es servido y acatado por lo que vale, sino por lo que tiene."[3] Guevara stresses the freedom a man forsakes once he becomes a courtier. There is nothing in the world that can compare to freedom, he asserts. In the country, a man can go anywhere he pleases, notwithstanding his obligations. A courtier also has responsibilities, but he has neither the time nor the freedom to do what he wants to do, for even his pastimes are prescribed for him:

> No hay en el mundo otra igual vida sino levantarse hombre con libertad e ir do quiere y hacer lo que debe. Muchos son los cortesanos que hacen en la corte lo que deben y muy poquitos hacen lo que quieren; porque para sus negocios y aun pasatiempos tienen voluntad, mas no libertad.[4]

What factors cause a courtier to relinquish his freedom? His ambition entraps him, for one thing; for another, he becomes a slave to the vicious gossip of ill-intentioned people, to ¿qué dirán?. In the words of another sixteenth-century prose writer, Cristóbal de Villalón, what people (*vulgo*) say or think about a man obliges him to do many things against his will and better judgment, things that might prove disadvantageous for him.

And if he does not heed people's constant comments, he exposes himself to their indignation, for they never dissimulate or forgive anything: "Obligados somos a hacer muchas cosas contra nuestra voluntad y provecho por cumplir con el vulgo, el cual jamás disimula ni perdona cosa ninguna."[5] As it is very possible that Villalón was a *Converso*, his words take on a special and personal significance.

Literary works in praise of rustic life have figured prominently in Europe for more than two millennia. This theme, called *"Beatus ille"* (*"Dichoso aquél"* in Spanish; "Happy is the man" in English), derives from the first line of the Latin poet Horace's second *Epode*. Horace extols country life and expresses envy of the man who is not aroused by the enticements of money and power; rather, this happy man is content to look after his cattle, shear his sheep, and tend his vines and trees.

Horace's *Epode* circulated widely in Spain during the sixteenth century. So many Golden Age poets translated or imitated it that it became a hollow literary convention. Nevertheless, the fact that the *Beatus ille* theme enjoyed such popularity attests to the stifling, artificial atmosphere of sixteenth- and, in particular, seventeenth-century courtly society, an ambience that undoubtedly wearied many of the courtiers, aspirers, and hangers-on who read this bucolic literature.

Garcilaso de la Vega, the foremost Spanish poet of the first half of the sixteenth century, sings his song of praise for the countryside in his second *Égloga*, a poem intentionally reminiscent of Horace's second *Epode*. How happy, Garcilaso writes, is the man who lives carefree of the things that can harm his soul! He witnesses neither the teeming plaza of commerce, nor the haughty doors of the great lords, nor the adulators whom hunger for royal favor awakens; and he will not have to beg, pretend, fear, or be querulous:

> ¡Cuán bienaventurado
> Aquél puede llamarse
> Que con la dulce soledad se abraza,
> Y vive descuidado,
> Y lejos de empacharse

En lo que al alma impide y embaraza!
No ve la llena plaza
Ni la soberbia puerta
De los grandes señores,
Ni los aduladores
A quien la hambre del favor despierta;
No le será forzoso
Rogar, fingir, temer, y estar quejoso.[6]

Solitude is also a favorite motif of Lope de Vega, who was not only the father of the *Comedia nueva* but one of the leading lyric poets of his time as well.

In one poem entitled "A mis soledades voy", Lope reveals that he is perfectly content to come and go in solitude (*soledades*) since he needs no other company than his thoughts:

A mis soledades voy,
De mis soledades vengo,
Porque para andar conmigo
Me bastan mis pensamientos.[7]

In another poem, Lope glorifies the freedom of rustic life, which is more precious than gold and all the other goods of the earth. Let the courtier, Lope says, look for a soft bed and better sustenance; let him kiss the ungrateful hand of an unjust, powerful man; let him build towers of hope in the wind; let him live and die thirsting for an honorable position. Meanwhile, Lope will enjoy the soil, the air, the sun, and the ice. When all is said and done, Lope concludes, poverty amid peace is worth far more than wealth amid strife:

¡Oh libertad preciosa,
No comparada al oro
Ni al bien mayor de la espaciosa tierra!
. . .
Estése el cortesano
Procurando a su gusto
La blanda cama y el mejor sustento;
Bese la ingrata mano
Del poderoso injusto,

Formando torres de esperanza al viento;
Viva y muera sediento
Por el honroso oficio,
Y goce yo del suelo
Al aire, al sol, y al hielo,
Ocupado en mi rústico ejercicio;
Que más vale pobreza
En paz que en guerra mísera riqueza.[8]

Another Golden Age poet whom readers may identify with the themes of solitude and *Beatus ille* is Luis de Góngora y Argote. In the first part of his Baroque masterpiece *Soledades*, Góngora contrasts the naturalness of a rural lodge (*albergue*) with the artifice of the court. Neither ambition, nor thirst for fame, nor envy dwells in the rustic retreat he eloquently addresses:

¡Oh bienaventurado
Albergue a cualquier hora!
No en ti la ambición mora
Hidrópica de viento,
Ni la que su alimento
El áspid es gitano.[9]

Góngora also wrote a light-hearted variant of the *Beatus ille* theme. This poem is a gloss of the familiar Spanish proverb "Ándeme yo caliente y ríase la gente" ("As long as I'm warm, I don't care if people laugh at me"). Góngora waxes poetic about the epicurean delights of solitude. Let everyone else handle matters of state, he exclaims; let the prince eat off golden dishes. As long as Góngora has sausages hot off the grill and soft bread with butter to eat, and orange juice and spirits to drink, he is happy. If people laugh at his simple pleasures, pity them, for they do not know what they are missing:

Traten otros del gobierno
Del mundo y sus monarquías,
Mientras gobiernan mis días
Mantequilla y pan tierno
Y las mañanas de Invierno
Naranjada y aguardiente,

Y ríase la gente.
Coma en dorada vajilla
El Príncipe mil cuidados;
Como píldoras dorados;
Que yo en mi pobre mesilla
Quiero más una morcilla
Que en el asador reviente
Y ríase la gente.[10]

Variations on the theme of *Beatus ille* recur so often in Golden Age poetry that it seems to have formed an obligatory part of most poets' repertoires. This theme, however, becomes especially meaningful when we discover that a poet has been victimized (or believes he has been) by the evils of the society he criticizes in his poems. For these writers, solitude represents release from oppression. Their verses ring of sincerity when we can relate the solitude they crave to the conflict and suffering they have undergone.

Fray Luis de León, the reader may recall, endured many a trial (real and figurative) and tribulation during the course of his life. Yet, even as a young man, he sought the peace that only solitude could bring him. Did he hope to avoid the vicious tongues that might have whispered about his *Converso* status and the envious eyes that would have watched his every move and that might have read more into a word than was intended? Quite possibly. Moreover, Fray Luis spent much of his adult life embroiled in a series of disputes with his fellow theologians. His outspokenness certainly did not endear him to his colleagues, who later denounced him to the Inquisition. As he did not neatly fit into the Old Christian scholastic mold, his longing for peace of mind is particularly understandable.

One of Fray Luis's earliest and most famous poems is entitled "Vida retirada". How restful, Fray Luis exclaims, is the life (*vida*) of a man who retires (*retirada*) from the commotion of the world to follow the hidden path along which have gone the few wise men the world has known:

¡Qué descansada vida
La del que huye del mundanal ruïdo,
Y sigue la escondida
Senda por donde han ido
Los pocos sabios que en el mundo han sido![11]

There, at the end of the path, neither envy nor lust darkens his soul. There, a man needs not concern himself with fame, nor must he give or receive false flattery. Fray Luis uses the metaphors of the ship (*navío, leño*) and the sea (*mar*) to signify life and the world, respectively. He realizes that his ship is almost wrecked, and he flees the tempestuous sea for the repose that the mountain, the stream, the river, and the sweet, safe haven offer him:

¡Oh monte, oh fuente, oh río,
Oh secreto seguro deleitoso!
Roto casi el navío
A vuestro almo reposo
Huyo de aqueste mar tempestuoso.[12]

Let others who place their trust in a flimsy ship have their treasure: "Ténganse su tesoro / Los que de un falso leño se confían."[13] While they are miserably burning with an insatiable thirst for dangerous power, he will be lying in the shade and singing:

Y mientras miserable-
Mente se están los otros abrasando
Con sed insaciable
Del peligroso mando,
Tendido yo a la sombra esté cantando.[14]

Fray Luis composed "Vida retirada" years before his imprisonment, and his desire for positive solitude would never fade. Indeed, the negative solitude he was forced to suffer in jail heightened his wish to withdraw voluntarily from the world.

In one poem entitled "Al salir de la cárcel", which Fray Luis

134

wrote upon leaving (*salir*) prison (*cárcel*), he tells us that envy and lies kept him locked behind bars. Fortunate, he says, is the man who has the wisdom and the foresight to retire from this wicked world to the delightful countryside. There, at a humble table in a humble cottage, he has only God to direct the course of his life. There, neither envied nor envious, he can live alone:

> Aquí la envidia y mentira
> Me tuvieron encerrado.
> Dichoso el humilde estado
> Del sabio que se retira
> De aqueste mundo malvado,
> Y con pobre mesa y casa
> En el campo deleitoso
> Con solo Dios se compasa,
> Y a solas su vida pasa
> Ni envidiado ni envidioso.[15]

Fray Luis experienced injustice and the curtailment of his intellectual freedom, and his rivals imposed on him negative solitude. Only in self-imposed positive solitude would he find peace. And only in peace would he be able to journey along the hidden path toward oneness with God.[16]

Several prominent Golden Age courtier-poets were sent into exile for political reasons. One poet, Don Juan de Tassis y Peralta, the Count of Villamediana, found his banishment from the turmoil of the court quite gratifying. Exiled during the reign of Felipe III for writing verses satirical of courtly life, Villamediana transformed his enforced solitude into a beneficial experience, and he writes of the contentment he has discovered. No longer must be breathe the air of the court, which idolatry, disdain, wrath, fraud, ambition, lies, and deceit have fouled:

> Aquí la idolatría
> Ni conoce lugar ni tiene día,
> El desdén y la ira,
> Desvelados custodes de la puerta

A las fraudes abierta,
No dan leche ambiciosa a la mentira;
Aquí no es alimento
Hacer arte y oficio del engaño,
. . .
El aire cortesano
Acá no llega; . . .[17]

Eventually, the Count's term of banishment ended, and he came back to the court. He should never have chosen to leave the wholesome air of the country, for he was murdered shortly after his return; mystery has shrouded the circumstances of his death even to this day.[18]

Like the Count of Villamediana, Francisco de Quevedo was also sent into exile from the court of Felipe III. Nor did his troubles end once his banishment was lifted, for among his many enemies figured the Count-Duke of Olivares, the powerful favorite and minister of Felipe IV. Quevedo had attacked Olivares and the corruption that permeated the court. In revenge, Olivares sentenced Quevedo to a prison term of four years. A short time after he was freed, Quevedo died.

In addition to the picaresque *El Buscón*, Quevedo penned numerous essays, treatises, and poems. He was not afraid to unleash his indignation at the hypocrisy of courtly society, a milieu he thoroughly despised, for it signified the antithesis of simple, rustic life. In one poem addressed to a friend, Quevedo extols country living. How lucky is this friend, Quevedo exclaims. He has known the happiness of spending his youth and old age in a little cabin and of breathing the gentle breeze of pure air. His harvests, not the succession of rulers, mark the passing of the years, and he treads his world without deceit. He benefits from what he does not know, and he neither yearns for reward nor suffers injuries:

No cuentas por los cónsules los años,
Hacen tu calendario tus cosechas,
Pisas todo tu mundo sin engaños,
De todo lo que ignoras te aprovechas,
Ni anhelas premio, ni padeces daños.[19]

Another victim of courtly intrigue was the aforementioned poet, dramatist, and novelist Antonio Enríquez Gómez. He writes in one poem that he feels secure and content living at the foot of a cedar-covered mountain, and he contrasts the serenity of the countryside with the confusing din of Babel, of cities:

> Fabricio, si la vida
> En la santa quietud está cifrada,
> Al pie de esta lucida
> Montaña, de altos cedros coronada,
> La gozo más seguro
> Que en el Babel de ese confuso muro.
> . . .
> En estas soledades
> Vivo contento, alegre y descansado,
> No, como en las ciudades,
> Al bullicio sujeto del estado.[20]

Enríquez Gómez, the reader may remember, subsequently fled to France. Upon returning to Spain, he was persecuted and sentenced to death for his alleged crypto-Judaism. He shared with Villamediana and Quevedo a particularly lamentable kind of death: Villamediana met his destiny at the hands of an assassin; Quevedo and Enríquez Gómez in all probability succumbed to the indignities of incarceration.

Many poets yearned for the tranquil, rustic way of life. The luckier among them who owned country homes could convert their dreams into reality and could take periodic respites from the turbulence of the city and the court. For the most part, however, these poets were not born and bred in the country. As much as they criticized the court, it was still the milieu they knew best. Since it was the place where their fellow writers, literary patrons, and readers resided, they almost invariably returned to it after pleasant sojourns of solitude.[21]

Not able or willing to make a permanent break from the restrictive social conventions and from the atmosphere of intrigue that typified courtly life, certain writers expressed envy of the shepherd, whose life-style was diametrically opposed to their own. Birth has blessed the shepherd with a simple, unencumbered, solitary existence. He epitomizes freedom because he is his own master and can lead his sheep without restraint. Moreover, as he is far removed from the venal and carnal temptations surrounding the courtier, he does not live in conflict with established society. His only concern, writes the sixteenth-century poet Francisco de Aldana, is to tend his sheep. And nothing can deflect him from following the path of happiness (*ventura*, a word Aldana repeats for greater emphasis):

> Dichoso aquel pastor que a su ganado,
> Con dulce soledad blanda y segura
> Del dulce soto al fresco arroyo helado,
> Sólo apacienta y harta de verdura;
> Dichoso tú, pastor, que en monte o prado
> O donde va tu pie tras tu ventura,
> Lejos del mal que el bien pueda estorbarte,
> No hay quien tu pie de tu ventura aparte.[22]

The shepherd plays a leading role in the numerous pastoral romances written during the sixteenth century. These romances represent the renaissance of pastoral literature, a tradition dating back to the *Bucolics* of the third-century B.C. Greek poet Theocritus. Two centuries later, Virgil composed his *Bucolics* (also known as *Eclogues*), the earliest known example of Latin pastoral poetry. Virgil's *Bucolics*, like Horace's second *Epode*, enjoyed great popularity during the Renaissance and inspired so many Spanish authors to try their hand at penning a pastoral work that this kind of literature, like the *Beatus ille* poetry, became a literary commonplace.

The shepherds and shepherdesses in these romances are as unreal as the knights in romances of chivalry. They are not real-life, rustic shepherds but refined, erudite men and women. Their manner of speaking gives them the appearance of courtiers transported to a bucolic setting.

These fictional shepherds and shepherdesses eschew organized, hierarchical society. Although they crave solitude, they are not hermits. They prefer small, intimate groups to large ones, and they tend to pair off with each other in close bonds of love and friendship. The dialogue form in which many of these novels are written underscores the interpersonal nature of the shepherds' relationships.

The pastoral characters of these romances are subject to few social dictates, but they are generally neither immoral nor amoral. They do not equate freedom with license, and the tone of these works is neoplatonic rather than orgiastic.

What do a shepherd and a shepherdess do all day? Very little, which partially explains why these tales would hardly appear on a twentieth-century best-seller list. Their only responsibility is to take care of their sheep, a comparatively easy task that gives them ample time to contemplate the delights of nature. Alone with their thoughts, they also lament incessantly about their ill-fated love affairs, which have robbed them of their freedom and, therefore, of their happiness. Solitude only magnifies their anguish, and not even their idyllic surroundings can assuage their misery.

Knowing that love poses a hazard to their freedom and their well-being, shepherds and shepherdesses often strive to stay clear of Cupid's arrows, which, notwithstanding the efforts of these men and women to the contrary, usually hit their targets.

One very famous fictional shepherdess who does succeed in maintaining her independence from love and marriage is Marcela, a character in Cervantes' *Don Quijote*. Marcela suddenly appears before a group of goatherds, to whom Don Quijote is discoursing at great length. One of them relates to Don Quijote the story of Marcela's suitor Grisóstomo, who fell so madly in love with her that he died of grief after she spurned him. The goatherds blame Marcela for Grisóstomo's death, and she defends herself in an impassioned plea for society to respect the freedom inherent in every man—and every woman. She comes to them, she says, to tell them how unreasonable they are to believe that she is guilty: "No vengo . . . sino a volver por mí misma, y a dar a entender cuán fuera de razón van todos aquéllos que de sus penas y de la muerte de Grisóstomo me culpan."[23] She was born free, she asserts. In order to live perpetually free, she has chosen the solitude of the countryside. She communicates her thoughts to the mountain trees, her companions, and her beauty to the clear streams, her mirrors. She is wealthy in her own right and does not covet what is not hers. Since she embodies freedom, she will not subject herself to another person's will:

> Yo nací libre, y para poder vivir libre escogí la soledad de los compos: los árboles de estas montañas son mi compañía; las claras aguas de estos arroyos, mis espejos; con los árboles y con las aguas comunico mis pensamientos y hermosuras. . . . la mía [intención] era vivir en perpetua soledad, . . . Yo, como sabéis, tengo riquezas propias, y no codicio las ajenas; tengo libre condición, y no gusto de sujetarme.[24]

She will live as she chooses, and she will not be pressured into changing her life. Neither parental coercion nor the fear that a rejected suitor might die of a broken heart could ever justify her marrying against her will.

Her plea for tolerance and understanding wins Don Quijote—but not the goatherds—over to her side. Don Quijote recognizes in Marcela a kindred spirit. He too, as we shall see, defies convention; he too has chosen to lead his life as he sees fit, not as society has prescribed for him.[25]

Cervantes allows Marcela to resume her independent lifestyle because she has not challenged any religious or societal norm. She is not a criminal, and she is not immoral or amoral (despite the goatherds' opinion of her). In refusing to be forced against her will, she in fact upholds one of the fundamental tenets of Christianity, freedom from coercion.

In the rustic pastoral world, men and women are free to direct the course of their lives (provided, of course, that passionate love does not hold them in its grasp!). They live without artifice and are not hampered by the conventions of organized society. We should bear in mind, however, that the idyllic settings authors portray are fictional and dreamlike. They never allude to the harsh realities of country life. They never mention the tor-

140

rential rains, the droughts, and the diseases that can devastate a farmer's or a shepherd's source of livelihood. Instead, they project an idealized image of bucolic life, one that reflects their own wishful thinking as well as their readership's.

The Golden Age shepherd resembles the modern-day cowboy in that both figures epitomize freedom. They roam the hills and dales with their flocks, and they answer to no man. Pastoral romances were popular four hundred years ago for the same reason that Westerns are popular today: the sixteenth-century reader, like the twentieth-century viewer, admired the straightforwardness, the strength, the individualism, and the independence of the loner. Both pastoral romances and Westerns have served as vehicles of momentary escape. For a brief, fleeting moment, we readers and viewers can share the shepherd's and the cowboy's freedom; we too can thumb our noses at the foolish dictates of society; we too can decide for ourselves, without social pressures or constraints, what is essential and what is not; and, most important of all, we too can shape our destinies and retain control over our lives.

ENDNOTES

[1] Francisco Santos, *Periquillo el de las gallineras*, Ch. i, in *La novela picaresca española*, ed. A. Valbuena Prat, 6th ed. (Madrid: Aguilar, 1968), pp. 1853–1854.

[2] Ibid., Ch. viii, p. 1881. Not all *pícaros*, however, praise solitude; indeed, Marcos de Obregón, the pseudo*pícaro* of Vicente Espinel's *Vida de Marcos de Obregón*, attacks solitude for being the source of evil, fear, and temptation: "Fui . . . maldiciendo la soledad y a quien quiere andar sin compañía, considerando qué bien puede traer, si no es estas cosas y otras peores. ¿Qué temores no trae? ¿Qué imaginaciones no engendra? ¿Qué males no causa? ¿Qué desesperaciones no ofrece? Los que tienen aborrecida la vida buscan la soledad para acabarla de presto; quien huye la compañía no quiere ser aconsejado en su mal." (*Nov. pic. esp.*, pp. 961–962.)

[3] Fray Antonio de Guevara, *Menosprecio de corte y alabanza de aldea*, Ch. vii, 2nd ed. (Buenos Aires: Espasa-Calpe; Austral, 1947), p. 72.

[4] Ibid., Ch. iv, pp. 50–51.

[5] Cristóbal de Villalón (attributed to), *Viaje de Turquía*, ed. A.G. Solalinde, 4th ed. (Madrid: Espasa-Calpe; Austral, 1965), p. 24.

[6] Garcilaso de la Vega, second *Égloga*, in *Obras*, ed. T. Navarro Tomás (Madrid: Espasa-Calpe; CC, 1963), p. 29.

[7] Lope de Vega, "A mis soledades voy," from his *La Dorotea*, Act I, in *Obras escogidas*, ed. F.C. Sainz de Robles, 4th ed. (Madrid: Aguilar, 1964), II, 1400.

[8] Ibid., "Oh libertad preciosa," from his *Arcadia*, ed. E.S. Morby (Madrid: Castalia, 1975), pp. 130–132.

[9] Luis de Góngora y Argote, first *Soledad*, in *Obras completas*, ed. J. and I. Mille y Giménez, 5th ed. (Madrid: Aguilar, 1961), p. 637.

[10] Ibid., "Ándeme yo caliente y ríase la gente," pp. 289–290.

[11] Fray Luis de León, "Vida retirada," in his *Poesía*, ed. J.M. Alda Tesán (Zaragoza: Ebro, 1967), p. 24.

[12] Ibid., p. 25.

[13] Ibid., p. 27.

[14] Ibid., p. 28.

[15] Ibid., "Al salir de la cárcel," p. 85.

[16] Whether or not Fray Luis reached the state of mystic union with God, he shared much in common (including imprisonment) with the great sixteenth-century mystic poet San Juan de la Cruz (Saint John of the Cross). Solitude is a predominant theme in the poetry of both men: Fray Luis sought solitude to free himself of an imprisoning world, and San Juan sought solitude so that his soul could flee his imprisoning body.

[17] Count of Villamediana, "Silva que hizo el autor estando fuera de la corte," in his *Obras*, ed. J.M. Rozas (Madrid: Castalia, 1969), p. 331.

[18] The famed medical doctor and literary critic Gregorio Marañón offered a particularly provocative theory concerning the Count's untimely demise. According to Marañón, the Count led a double sexual life: on the one hand, he was a womanizer (and might have served as the model for Tirso de Molina's Don Juan, *El burlador de Sevilla*); on the other, he was the leader of a group of homosexuals, for which he was assassinated. See Marañón's "Gloria y miseria del conde de Villamediana."

[19] Francisco de Quevedo, "A un amigo que retirado de la corte pasó su edad," in *Obras completas*, ed. F. Buendía, 6th ed. (Madrid: Aguilar, 1967), II, 32.

[20] Antonio Enríquez Gómez, "A la quietud y vida de la aldea," in BAE, XLII, 369.

[21] Not all poets, however, sought solitude or followed the literary trends of the *Beatus ille* theme and the pastoral. Indeed, several wrote poems in which they condemn the craving for solitude as unhealthy, antisocial, and indicative of evil motives or of mental instability!

[22] Francisco de Aldana, "Octavas . . . sobre el bien de la vida retirada," in his *Poesías*, ed. E.L. Rivers (Madrid: Espasa-Calpe; CC, 1966), pp. 99–100.

[23] Miguel de Cervantes, *El ingenioso hidalgo don Quijote de la Mancha*, Pt. I, Ch. xiv, in *Obras completas*, ed. A. Valbuena Prat, 12th ed. (Madrid: Aguilar, 1962), p. 1078.

[24] Ibid., pp. 1078–1079.

[25] According to C.B. Johnson, the kindredness between Don Quijote and Marcela lies in the fact that their desire for freedom is symptomatic of the terror they both feel at the thought of sexual intimacy. Don Quijote and Marcela try to deny their sexual impulses and, as a result, search for life-styles in which they can live devoid of sexuality; see Johnson's *Madness and Lust: A Psychoanalytical Approach to Don Quixote*, Ch. 4: "Dulcinea and the Real Women: Part I."

8

The Quest for Self-Realization and Freedom in Cervantes' Characters

Of all Golden Age writers, Miguel de Cervantes ranks foremost in creating stories about individuals like Marcela who determine to lead their lives as they choose. Cervantes' characters exert their will to a remarkable degree, given the social strictures of sixteenth- and seventeenth-century Spain, a world most of them inhabit.

Whether or not one of these characters succeeds fully in realizing his individuality depends on the nature of his aspirations. If society judges that his goals conform to its moral and religious precepts, and if he does not overly disrupt the orderliness of established society, then Cervantes, reflecting that society, allows him to triumph. But if the individual's goals are irrational, or if they pose a risk to himself and to society, then Cervantes cannot let him prevail.

Regardless of the outcome of their personal quests, what we admire in Cervantes' individualistic characters is their courage. They have elected to follow the courses they themselves have charted, and they struggle in the midst of seemingly insurmountable odds, personal danger, and the derision and rejection of society.

Self-realization and freedom do not come easily to these men and women. To achieve these goals, they must sever the bonds of family and friendship that link them to their pasts and to their worlds. They must disassociate themselves from the familiar, the routine, and the comfortable.

In their courageous pursuits of individuality, Cervantes' characters point out the frailties and defects of the societies that attempt to frustrate their every move. Conflict between these individuals and their cultures or subcultures is as inevitable as it was between the *pícaro* and established society. On the one hand, the character's conscience impels him to seek the freedom to live as he wishes, even if his dream of a new life conflicts with the way of life into which he was born. His world, on the other hand, finds it difficult to tolerate an individual who disregards its traditions.

The quest for self-realization and freedom is a fundamental theme in Cervantes' works. The interpretations of these pursuits vary from character to character and range from the lofty to the mundane. Don Quijote, for example, associates individuality and liberty with living according to his conscience in order to revive the ancient order of chivalry. Sancho Panza, however, equates them with becoming a governor and with doing and saying whatever he pleases whenever he so desires.

Cervantes' characters, even those whose individualistic notions smack of self-interest, are not usually antisocial. Rarely do they impinge on the social institutions of marriage, family, and friendship. They do, however, ignore many of the irrelevant, nonessential customs and usages that their world deems essential.

Before exploring Don Quijote's and Sancho Panza's quests for self-realization and freedom, let us consider how some of the characters in Cervantes' short stories aspire to these same goals.

One reason for the continued popularity of Cervantes' short "exemplary" novels is the diversity of life-styles he recreates, ways of life that are marginal as well as mainstream. Two subcultures he presents, the picaresque and the gypsy, not only offered security and a sense of identity to their members but also appealed to youthful members of established society who were searching for adventure and for freedom from the restrictions of their world. Just as young American men and women have flocked in recent times to the bohemian meccas of Greenwich Village and San Francisco to become antiestablishmentarian beatniks and hippies, so too did the picaresque and gypsy modes of life prove fascinating to many a "well-bred" Spaniard. Given the closeness of the family unit and the strongly regulated environment in which sixteenth- and seventeenth-century youths—especially girls—grew up, it is not likely that a significant proportion of them left home to adopt these marginal cultures. Nevertheless, the fact that Cervantes wrote two tales about young men who did leave home indicates that his readership might have identified in some way with them.

The plots of both tales, "La ilustre fregona" and "La gitanilla", center around two young women who, the reader may recall, discover that they are not a washerwoman and a gypsy maiden, respectively, but noblewomen.

The illustrious washerwoman serves at an inn, a haven for men and women of often dubious reputations. One guest is the noble Don Diego de Carriazo. Impelled by a strong desire to become a *pícaro*, not by parental abuse, Carriazo took off one day from his home. Relishing his new-found freedom, Cervantes relates, he never looked back:

> Carriazo, . . . llevado de una inclinación picaresca, sin forzarla a ello algún mal tratamiento que sus padres le hiciesen, sólo por su gusto y antojo, se desgarró, como dicen los muchachos, de casa de sus padres, y se fue por ese mundo adelante, tan contento de la vida libre.[1]

Eventually he stops at the inn. His parents, meanwhile, are frantic, but all ends happily. His mother and father recover their long-lost son and wind up with a daughter as well, since it turns out that the washerwoman is none other than Carriazo's half sister.

Gypsy life, like the picaresque, also captured the imagination of those who tired of mainstream society. Spanish gypsies, whose forefathers had migrated from India during the first millennium A.D. and settled in Spain by the fifteenth century, have never formed part of established society. Bonds of kinship have traditionally joined them together, and their tightly knit social system has fostered self-sufficiency and a sense of belonging.

146

As a result, they have not felt the need to assimilate into the dominant culture, a point that distinguishes them from *Conversos* and *pícaros*.

Cervantes admired many aspects of their world, particularly their simple, spontaneous, nomadic life-style. Like *pícaros*, gypsies roam from place to place, but they differ from *pícaros* in that they serve no masters. Nobody and nothing enslave them. As Cervantes was an orthodox Catholic, however, many of the gypsies' customs regarding sex and marriage struck him as immoral and anarchistic. One old gypsy in "La gitanilla", for instance, says that incestuous relations are common (although adultery is harshly punished). Divorce is a frequent occurrence, since husbands tend to prefer young wives. What is more, gypsies do not proscribe premarital sex. Cervantes suggests that sexual love alone provides the basis for marriage between gypsies.

Preciosa, the independent-minded heroine of the story, has been raised among gypsies. But her noble birth, which she subsequently discovers, has exerted an unconscious influence on her. Her principles reflect her establishmentarian, Catholic origin rather than her gypsy milieu, and they affect her relationship to the noble Juan, who has fallen in love with her. She refuses to marry him until he consents to abide by a series of terms that she, not her gypsy clan, imposes on him:

Juan must first live as a gypsy for two years in order to test the strength of their love. He readily agrees, and the gypsies induct him into their membership and "baptize" him with the name "Andrés".

Second, Juan/Andrés must curb his possessive nature. Fearful that another man might win her heart, he has asked Preciosa not to venture into Madrid. She is a free spirit, she replies, and she will not allow jealousy to smother her independence: "Conmigo ha de andar siempre la libertad desenfadada, sin que la ahogue ni turbe la pesadumbre de los celos."[2]

It is Preciosa's third stipulation that attests to her innate morality (in the Christian sense of the word). When the old gypsy gives Juan/Andrés permission to take her as his bride *or con-*

cubine, she rebels. Although gypsy legislators have decreed that she belongs to Juan/Andrés, her conscience, which is stronger than any gypsy law, decrees that she will never be his mistress; nor will she marry him until he has met her conditions:

> Puesto que estos señores legisladores han hallado por sus leyes que soy tuya, y que por tuya te me han entregado, yo he hallado por la ley de mi voluntad, que es la más fuerte de todas, que no quiero serlo si no es con las condiciones que antes que aquí vinieses entre los dos concertamos.[3]

Her soul, she declares, is free, was born free, and must remain free as long as she wishes: "[Mi alma] es libre, y nació libre, y ha de ser libre en tanto que yo quisiere."[4]

Preciosa shares with Marcela a defiance of a world that goes against the dictates of her conscience. When Preciosa's real ancestry is revealed, however, she willingly leaves the gypsy world behind to marry Juan and to claim her heritage of nobility and Catholicism. She will live in a society that is guided by the same moral code that guided her conscience during her nomadic, gypsy years.

Another example of a non-Catholic girl who severs her ties with her culture, family, and friends in order to become a Catholic Spaniard is Zoraida, the heroine of Cervantes' "Captive's Tale". Zoraida is a Moslem of whom the Captive has become enamored while languishing in an Algerian dungeon. They flee Islam, and he takes her to Spain,[5] where she wholeheartedly embraces Catholicism and receives the sacrament of baptism. Discarding the name "Zoraida", she assumes the name "María", an act symbolic of her new religious, social, and political membership.[6]

Don Quijote, undoubtedly the most famous of Cervantes' characters, is known to his family and friends as Alonso Quijano. A seventeenth-century *hidalgo* of modest means, he has spent some fifty uneventful years in rural La Mancha. His is a household dominated by two women: his Niece and his Housekeeper. The combination of this female omnipresence and his noble lineage, which bars him from working or doing anything truly productive, has made his existence comfortably stable and terribly sterile. To relieve his monotony, he has taken to reading romances of chivalry. He knows them all by heart, and his mind has become so full of knights and their feats that he has lost his sense of judgment. No longer able to discern between reality and fantasy, he believes that he too is a knight-errant. The age of chivalry has become his reality, and he has forgotten that his cherished romances bear little resemblance to life in the Middle Ages. These tales offer their readers a vision of a mythical world that never was nor ever could have been. For Alonso Quijano, however, the medieval chivalry depicted in literature did exist, and he intends to reinstate it singlehandedly. He will experience for himself what he has hitherto experienced vicariously.

Alonso Quijano's gradual metamorphosis is a classic case of life imitating art. Indeed, Cervantes emphasized in the early seventeenth century the power that fiction could wield over a susceptible individual. Such a warning seems eerily familiar to the twentieth-century reader, who has heard of numerous incidents in which a person has committed an act in imitation of one he viewed on television or in a movie.

While blinding Alonso Quijano's eyes to historical reality, literature has opened them up to a fantastic world, one in which he can find personal fulfillment. It has embedded in him a dream, which he will convert into a reality of his own making. He will become his dream incarnate. Society gave him an identity, that of the *hidalgo* Alonso Quijano, and prescribed the roles he would play. Casting aside the old, he gives himself the new identity of Don Quijote de la Mancha. As he has created his new self, he has no past that might distract him from his knightly mission. His former existence will not deter him from being what he wants to be. Each man, he reiterates, is the son of his deeds: "Cada uno es hijo de sus obras." A man's works, not his heritage, give meaning to his life. He should not rest passively on his forefathers' laurels but should forge his own future.[7]

In the first of the two parts comprising *El ingenioso hidalgo don Quijote de la Mancha*, Don Quijote is quite sure of his new identity. Notwithstanding the protests of the Niece and the Housekeeper, who fail to understand why his inherited roles do not satisfy him, he repeatedly affirms that he *knows* who he is ("yo sé quien soy") and that he *is* who he is ("yo soy quien soy"). *Conversos* and *pícaros*, as we have seen, encountered difficulties in shaping new destinies for themselves, since society interpreted their aspirations as pretentious and threatening. Don Quijote, however, does succeed in breaking free of the restrictions his heritage placed on him, but only because society considers him mad and therefore not responsible for his actions.[8] Were it not for his madness, Alonso Quijano would never have ventured forth into the world as Don Quijote. A madman dares to rush in where a sane man fears to tread.

Literary critics have long debated the nature and the extent of Don Quijote's madness. An idealist, he dreams of reviving the age of chivalry. Visions of a better world are hardly symptomatic of an imbalanced mind. But Don Quijote's visions reveal his inability to distinguish fantasy from reality, a traditionally held symptom of insanity. He believes that his visions are based on truth; that is, he believes in the veracity of the romances he has so avidly read without realizing that chivalry is but an idealized memory of a fictionalized past enshrined and immortalized in literature. His self-imposed mission is truly noble, but his methods are irrational. Literature has misguided him into thinking that knights-errant personified justice and mercy in an age when all wrongs could be righted.

Don Quijote's madness, nonetheless, is limited only to his chivalric calling; otherwise, he is perfectly reasonable and is able to discourse rationally on almost any subject.

Not only does Don Quijote transform fantasy into his deranged view of the real world; he transforms reality into fantasy as well. He has chosen a new identity, which is his for as long as he can mold objective reality to it. Since he finds fulfillment solely as a knight-errant, he must remain madly out of touch with objective reality *insofar as it affects his new persona*. In one sense, he has chosen to become mad, and he must also choose to remain mad.

At the beginning of his first series of adventures as Don Quijote, he is deeply troubled. A true knight, he knows, should be dubbed, and he must abide by the formalities of chivalry if he is to be an exemplary knight. He spots an edifice. Objectively, it is an inn, but his mind cannot perceive it as an inn since innkeepers do not have the authority to dub knights. So his mind changes the inn into a castle and the Innkeeper into its lord. These transformations serve Don Quijote's knightly purpose. As Alonso Quijano, he would have seen an inn and an innkeeper; as Don Quijote, however, he must see a castle and its lord because they are crucial to his self-realization. Such transformations ensure that he will be able to live in the world of his own making. Only when his resolve weakens and he ceases to transform external, objective reality into internal, subjective reality does he begin to see the former as it truly is. It is then that he begins to doubt the validity of his life; doubts sow the seed of sanity, whereupon he reverts to his original identity and shortly thereafter dies.

Don Quijote's peers think that his madness stems solely from his inordinate fondness for romances of chivalry. They fail to comprehend why he began to read those books in the first place. A bored, frustrated man, he thirsted for excitement and freedom, which he never would have found within the confines of his static, fruitless, and unfulfilling existence. His horizons extended beyond his ancestral property and the uninteresting roles society expected him to play. As Alonso Quijano, he would have stagnated in an existence that presented him with very few options. He would not have dared to challenge the reality of his life—that his future would be merely a humdrum continuation of his past. Madness, to the contrary, gives him the strength to break from his past and the freedom to forge a future of his own creation. He will stop playing the role of an insignificant cog in society's wheel and will struggle to be a driving force. Despite tremendous hurdles, he will persevere in his efforts to count as an individual. For the first time, he will live, not merely exist.

Don Quijote's mission is both social and personal. He explains that the order of knights-errant, which he intends to revive, was instituted for the purpose of defending damsels, aiding widows, and succoring the needy: "Se instituyó la orden de los caballeros andantes para defender las doncellas, amparar las viudas y socorrer a los huérfanos y a los menesterosos."[9] Becoming a knight-errant is a suitable and necessary course of action if he is to serve others and thus increase his honor. With his arms and his horse, Cervantes tells us, Don Quijote will seek out adventures and will engage in all the chivalric feats about which he has read. Placing himself in dangerous situations, he will right all manner of wrongs, and he will earn renown and fame:

[A Don Quijote] le pareció convenible y necesario, así para el aumento de su honra como para el servicio de su república, hacerse caballero andante, e irse por todo el mundo con sus armas y caballo a buscar las aventuras y a ejercitarse en todo aquello que él había leído que los caballeros andantes se ejercitaban, deshaciendo todo género de agravios, y poniéndose en ocasiones y peligros donde, acabándolos, cobrase eterno nombre y fama.[10]

Romances of chivalry have taught Don Quijote that every knight must have a trusted squire to accompany him into the perilous unknown. And so he chooses for his squire Sancho Panza, his neighbor. Sancho is a poor farmer, but he is quite proud of his Old Christian stock. Why, the reader might ask, would Sancho agree to accompany a madman? Because Sancho, like Don Quijote, dreams of a life that has hitherto lain beyond his reach. Don Quijote has promised him wealth and the governorship of an isle, prospects that appeal to Sancho's ambitious streak. Caught up in Don Quijote's optimism and determination, Sancho soon comes to believe that anything is possible. Each person is the child of his deeds, he proclaims in imitation of Don Quijote's credo. What is more, Sancho believes that he can become pope or even governor of one of the many isles that Don Quijote will surely win: "Y cada uno es hijo de sus obras; y debajo de ser hombre puedo venir a ser papa, cuánto más gobernador de una Ínsula, y más pudiendo ganar tantas mi señor."[11]

Just as Don Quijote has created himself, so has he transformed Sancho into a squire. He will even make him a count, provided that he finds a kingdom to rule. The naive Sancho feels that he already meets the most important qualification of nobility, Old Christian blood: "Yo cristiano viejo soy, y para ser conde esto me basta."[12] Even if Sancho were not an Old Christian, Don Quijote responds, it would not matter. By virtue of the office he expects to hold, Don Quijote will confer noble status on him without Sancho's having to buy it or serve him in any way: "Y aun te sobra, y cuando no lo [cristiano viejo] fueras, no hacía nada al caso; porque, siendo yo el rey, bien te puedo dar nobleza, sin que la compres ni me sirvas con nada."[13]

Don Quijote's pronouncement is quite radical, considering the theoretically closed nature of the seventeenth-century society in which he and Sancho live. A realist when it suits his purpose, Don Quijote alludes to the "tainted" origin of many noblemen. At the same time, he challenges the hypocrisy of a world that would snub a poor, Old Christian commoner while welcoming into its fold a rich New Christian. A man's religious heritage, like his social level, is irrelevant in Don Quijote's estimation. The only factor that should determine whether or not a person merits a title of nobility is his worthiness as an individual. Don Quijote knows full well that his beliefs regarding noble status run counter to those held by most noblemen. Despite what people may think or say, however, they will one day have to call Sancho "lordship": "Porque en haciéndote conde, cátate ahí caballero, y digan lo que dijeren; que a buena fe que te han de llamar señoría mal que les pese."[14]

Sancho is aware that the world laughs at Don Quijote's escapades, but he is ambivalent regarding the degree of his beloved knight's madness. Loyally defending his master, he frequently states that Don Quijote is saner than many of the people whom they encounter in their travels. Sancho must be willing to believe in the sanity underlying Don Quijote's apparent madness, because his destiny depends on Don Quijote's success. If he acknowledges that Don Quijote is an outright madman whose dream cannot possibly come true, then he dooms himself to failure. Since his hopes rest with Don Quijote, he must begin to view external reality as Don Quijote does. He must see giants instead of windmills and wine gourds. Although the realist in Sancho at times struggles to prevail, he forces himself to reject what his reason tells him is imaginary and to accept Don Quijote's chivalric world as well as all the characters, visible and invisible, who inhabit it.

In spite of the many hardships and occasional doubts that plague him, Sancho would gladly serve Don Quijote to the end of his days, for the two men share much in common. Each cares for the other, and their lives and fortunes are intertwined. Both are happy men since at last they have found that most precious of states, freedom.

For Sancho, as well as for Don Quijote, freedom represents potential. He can and will become governor, an office that he never would have held, had he remained in his village. Freedom for Sancho is also the absence of social constraints. He can eat and drink what and when he pleases and can belch when he feels so disposed. No longer must he follow the monotonous routine that farming and domesticity brought to his life. Although he still loves his wife Teresa, he is relieved not to hear her nagging voice. To a certain extent, however, Don Quijote has taken Teresa's place, and Sancho's life is not entirely devoid of reminders and scoldings. Don Quijote, for example, constantly corrects his colloquial speech and admonishes him not to interject so many proverbs. He also tries to teach him the etiquette befitting the squire of a soon-to-be illustrious knight.

There comes a time when Sancho tires of Don Quijote's lessons. His bread and onions taste much better than turkey, Sancho claims, especially if he can eat them by himself in a quiet corner where he does not have to pretend to be finicky or overly respectful. He prefers not to sit at a banquet table because he wants to enjoy his meal without worrying about chewing slowly, drinking moderately, wiping his mouth excessively, and not sneezing, coughing, and doing the other socially unacceptable things one does when one is alone and free:

> Mucho mejor me sabe lo que como en mi rincón sin melindres ni respetos, aunque sean pan y cebolla, que los gallipavos de otras mesas donde me sea forzoso mascar despacio, beber poco, limpiarme a menudo, no estornudar ni toser si me viene gana, ni hacer otras cosas que la soledad y la libertad traen consigo.[15]

Eventually Sancho Panza is named governor of an isle. The great paradox of his new station in life is that the governorship, of which he has long dreamed, deprives him of the freedom he has craved every bit as much. He thought that the office of governor would enable him to gorge himself with the richest and most succulent dishes money could buy. To his immense disappointment, however, the resident physician hovers about him at every meal and places stringent limitations on the quality and quantity of his intake. Sancho governs wisely and justly and is greatly loved, but he yearns for his former freedom. He begs his subjects, the Islanders, to let him return to the life he shared with Don Quijote (who at the moment is a guest of the Duke and Duchess). Sancho wants to rise from the dead, a metaphor he uses to describe the imprisoning governorship, and to live as a free man again, even if "resurrection" and freedom mean renouncing earthly power: "Abrid camino, señores míos, y dejadme volver a mi antigua libertad; dejadme que vaya a buscar la vida pasada, para que me resucite de esta muerte presente. Yo no nací para ser gobernador."[16]

For Don Quijote, freedom signifies unshackling himself from his past in order to become a knight-errant, a role that will enable him to restore justice and mercy to a static, callous world. He eagerly escapes the rigid conventions that bound Alonso Quijano, but he is not antisocial; indeed, his calling is eminently social. In order to attain the fame of an exemplary knight, he forsakes one social order for another and wills to adhere to the rules that governed knights of yore.

Don Quijote is a knight-errant; that is, he must travel ("errant") the highways and byways in search of dangerous adventures, for the key to his success lies in seeking out adventures in which to display his prowess. Although his wanderings are a means to a heroic end, they represent, nevertheless, the freedom of movement that he has long associated with knighthood. Madness has given him the ability to flee the narrow horizons of his former sedentary, passive existence and has transformed him into a knight whose fulfillment depends on his actively participating in as many adventures as he can happen upon.

In his travels, Don Quijote meets up with several passive, idle noblemen in search of the amusement with which he unwittingly provides them. Delighted to have made Don Quijote's acquaintance, they invite him to be their guest. Two such aristocrats are the Duke and the Duchess, who make their appearance in Pt. II. Anxious to brighten their boring existence, they welcome Don Quijote and Sancho to their palatial estate and contrive to simulate Don Quijote's imaginary world of chivalry. The adventures they concoct give Don Quijote the opportunity to play his knightly role to the fullest.

During this sojourn, the longest in the book (and the one in which Sancho is given an isle to govern), Don Quijote feels hemmed in and no longer willing to submit to a lengthy confinement, no matter how luxurious it is. Furthermore, he is coming to the subconscious awareness that these so-called "adventures" are false and that he is being manipulated by others. Although he is grateful to the Duke and Duchess for their hospitality, he yearns to be the master of his own destiny. Besides, he needs a break from the onslaught of stressful, strenuous adventures, which come in such rapid succession that he barely has time to enjoy a little peace and quiet.

When Don Quijote finally does bid the Duke and Duchess farewell, his relief is as great as was Sancho's at renouncing the governorship. Likening his stay at the ducal palace to captivity, Don Quijote tells Sancho that freedom is one of the most precious gifts that Heaven gave mankind, more precious than all the treasures contained in the earth and hidden beneath the sea. One can and should risk his life, Don Quijote states, for freedom, as for honor. Captivity, to the contrary, is the greatest evil that has ever beset mankind:

> La libertad, Sancho, es uno de los más preciosos dones que a los hombres dieron los Cielos; con ella no pueden igualarse los tesoros que encierra la tierra ni el mar encubre; por la libertad, así como por la honra, se puede y debe aventurar la vida, y, por el contrario, el cautiverio es el mayor mal que puede venir a los hombres.[17]

Referring specifically to his sojourn with the Duke and Duchess, Don Quijote complains that his indebtedness to them left him bereft of the freedom he otherwise would have enjoyed. Obligations stemming from benefactions and favors received are chains that confine a man's free will, he declares. Lucky is he, Don Quijote continues, to whom Heaven, not his fellow man, gave a piece of bread! Such a person can take pleasure in what he eats with the knowledge that his indebtedness extends no further than to Heaven:

> Las obligaciones de las recompensas de los beneficios y mercedes recibidas son ataduras que no dejan campear el ánimo libre. ¡Venturoso aquél a quien el Cielo dio un pedazo de pan, sin que le quede obligación de agradecerlo a otro que al mismo Cielo![18]

What Don Quijote does not realize is that he needs not feel indebted to his hosts, because his knightly antics have given them the entertainment they sorely require to fill their vacuous existence.

Apart from representing freedom, Don Quijote's travels are therapeutic. They afford him a momentary escape from the world, during which time he can recover from the physical and psychological blows that form an inevitable part of his life. Alone or with Sancho during these moments of recuperation and introspection, he reflects on his knightly role and searches within himself for keys to unlock the many mysteries of the fantasy world he has created. He does not overly indulge himself in solitude, however, since isolation is counterproductive to his mission. He needs society as much as he believes that society needs him. He must, nonetheless, withdraw periodically from the world to regain his strength. Following these brief respites of solitude, he emerges renewed and revitalized to sally forth once again.[19]

Part of Don Quijote's mission is to restore justice to a world that has lost sight of what justice is. In his opinion, a just society is one that respects the rights and the individuality of its members and in which all men and women can live free of fear and coercion. Many of his ideas concerning justice and freedom are found in his discourse to the goatherds (at which time the shepherdess Marcela defends herself in the face of their accusations). Don Quijote recalls the mythical Golden Age of mankind, an idealized and blessed age that existed only in the hearts of men and women, an age in which individuals lived in harmony with each other and with their world. Then, Don Quijote maintains, people did not know the words "yours" and "mine", for all things were held in common. Peace, friendship, and harmony prevailed; fraud, deceit, and malice did not mingle with truth and simplicity. Justice stood its own ground without being tarnished by favor and self-interest, which so harm and persecute it nowadays, Don Quijote continues. A chaste maiden could go unaccompanied wherever she wished without fearing that a man's lewdness and lustful intentions would discredit her; and if she gave herself to a man, it was because she wanted to, not because she felt pressured:

Dichosa edad y siglos dichosos aquellos a quien los antiguos pusieron nombre de dorados, . . . porque entonces los que en ella vivían ignoraban estas dos palabras de *tuyo* y *mío*. Eran en aquella santa edad todas las cosas comunes: . . . Todo era paz entonces, todo amistad, todo concordia: . . . No había la fraude, el engaño ni la malicia mezclándose con la verdad y llaneza. La justicia se estaba en sus propios términos, sin que la osasen turbar ni ofender los del favor y los del interés, que tanto ahora la menoscaban, turban, y persiguen. . . . Las doncellas y la honestidad andaban . . . por dondequiera, solas y señeras, sin temor que la ajena desenvoltura y lascivo intento las menoscabasen, y su perdición nacía de su gusto y propia voluntad.[20]

Don Quijote's travels lead him to several adventures in which he tries to alleviate victims of what he interprets as injustice and to revive the ideal of true justice.

In one episode, he meets up with young Andrés, who is tied up to a tree while his master, a farmer, flogs him. Enraged that the boy is powerless to defend himself, Don Quijote demands that the farmer untie him. The fact that the lad has neglected his duties to his master matters not to Don Quijote, who believes that neither man nor society should hold a person against his will. Alas, Don Quijote's intervention backfires: the moment Don Quijote is out of sight, the farmer beats the boy much more severely than before.

In another adventure, one that incurred the wrath of the Holy Brotherhood (*Santa Hermandad*, or rural police force), Don Quijote and Sancho happen upon a group of galley slaves who are being led shackled to a port. Don Quijote cannot fathom how his King would force anyone against his will. Sancho explains that the slaves are criminals, and they themselves confess their crimes to Don Quijote. He regards as immaterial the reasons behind their present condition and sees only that they are victims of oppression and that they suffer in misery. Obeying his knightly calling, he resolves to go to their aid. From everything they have said, he tells them, it is clear that they are not pleased with their sentences and that they will row the galleys with the utmost reluctance. It could be, Don Quijote continues, that one tortured prisoner's lack of spirit, another's lack of money, yet another's lack of influence, and the twisted judgment of the judge are to blame for their predicament. Justice has surely miscarried in their cases, Don Quijote concludes.

Furthermore, Don Quijote states, it is cruel to make slaves of men whom God and Nature have made free. Each man must answer to God alone for his sins. Since God does not hesitate to punish the evil and reward the good, mortals should not usurp His power. Therefore, no man, no matter how honorable or upright he is, has the right to judge or execute other men, especially if their crimes have nothing to do with him:

> Me parece duro caso hacer esclavos a los que Dios y Naturaleza hizo libres. . . . Allá se lo haya cada uno con su pecado; Dios hay en el Cielo, que no se descuida de castigar al malo, ni de premiar al bueno, y no es bien que los hombres honrados sean verdugos de los otros hombres, no yéndoles nada en ello.[21]

As mankind cannot expect to find justice on earth, Don Quijote naively asks the guards to set the slaves free. When the guards refuse, he charges their officer. Meanwhile, the slaves take advantage of the pandemonium and break loose from their chains. Don Quijote entreats them to present themselves to Dulcinea, the lady of his dreams, and to tell her of his heroic undertaking. One of them replies that they cannot all go together for fear of the Holy Brotherhood, and he suggests that they all say some prayers instead. Furious at his ingratitude, Don Quijote calls him a whoreson, whereupon he and his comrades shower Don Quijote and the hapless Sancho with stones and strip them of their outer garments. The galley slaves' ungratefulness has made a mockery of Don Quijote's sense of freedom and justice. Once again, his good intentions backfire because madness has caused him to lose touch with reality.

Although Don Quijote has unwittingly done more harm than good in freeing Andrés and the galley slaves, the ideals shaping his actions reflect his belief that God did not create man to live defenseless and oppressed. How sad, therefore, that Don Quijote should be taken home in a cage at the end of Pt. I. He fought to free others, and he winds up deprived of his own freedom. He ventures forth again with Sancho, however, at the beginning of Pt. II, and when he returns home the final time, he does so voluntarily and with dignity.

Don Quijote never realizes his impossible dream. He never establishes a utopian, chivalric society, nor does he reform the justice system of seventeenth-century Spain. He does, nevertheless, exert a strong and even lasting effect on many of the

160

individuals who become caught up in his madly anachronistic life. They too proceed to act out their fantasies, to live as they would like to live, not as society expects them to live.

These characters don the disguise of chivalry for a variety of reasons: to flee their limited existences, to improve their lot in life, to amuse themselves, and to rescue Don Quijote from his madness. Most of them recognize that they are playing a game. A few, however, are so swept up in their new roles that, for a time, their chivalric disguises and adventures seem to them true to real life.

Whether their intentions in joining Don Quijote's world are altruistic, egotistic, or a combination of both, these characters in effect deceive him. Their pretending to be what they are not only confirms in Don Quijote's mind the validity and the sanity of his knightly role. What is more, in deceiving him, some of his more credulous friends and acquaintances ultimately deceive themselves (a theme, we have noted, that permeates Golden Age literature).

Of all the characters in the book, it is Sancho Panza who most approximates Don Quijote in his desire to believe in his new identity. Don Quijote's spirit of adventure and his promise of an isle to govern have whetted Sancho's appetite for freedom and wealth and have prompted him to sally forth with his knightly friend. Many adventures later, when well-intentioned friends bring Don Quijote home in a cage at the end of Pt. I, Sancho is no richer than when he left, nor has he yet found any isle. He is, nonetheless, delighted that his name figures prominently in a romance of chivalry about Don Quijote's exploits, which a mysterious author has penned. In spite of the hardships that knight and squire have undergone, Sancho's awareness of his fame inspires him to journey with Don Quijote another time. After all, he cannot give up his quest now that he has a reputation to live up to. This is one of the reasons why Sancho readily agrees to accompany him at the beginning of Pt. II (although his practical wife Teresa goads him into asking his master for a salary).

Shortly after they set out together this second time, Sancho tells Don Quijote a lie, one that, unbeknownst to him, will change the nature of Don Quijote's mission. As they are traveling along a road, they spot an exceedingly ugly peasant girl, and Sancho assures Don Quijote that she is none other than Dulcinea. Aghast that the girl does not fit his image of her, Don Quijote blames her metamorphosis on the cruel Enchanter, his nemesis. No longer will his primary goal be to reinstate chivalry; rather, he will have to seek a way to disenchant Dulcinea.

Don Quijote does not question the validity of his squire's words because he presumes that Sancho has already met Dulcinea. In Pt. I, he had entrusted Sancho with a letter to deliver to her. As Dulcinea exists only in Don Quijote's mind, Sancho clearly could not carry out his assignment. To placate his master, however, he told him that he had indeed visited her, and now he must cover up one lie with another.

Sancho knows that the peasant girl is not Dulcinea and that he, not the Enchanter, "transformed" her. He feels cocky that he alone holds the key to Dulcinea's "enchantment"—and to her "disenchantment"—, but he never consciously confronts reality; to do so would mean losing faith in Don Quijote. He refuses to consider that Don Quijote's world may be as unreal as the Dulcinea whom he has just "enchanted". Sancho's self-confidence, nevertheless, suffers a severe blow when the Duchess, whom he reveres, informs him that the peasant girl really *was* Dulcinea. Don Quijote is right, she informs him, to believe that the wicked Enchanter had practiced his magic arts on the radiant Dulcinea. Sancho, the deceiver, is deceived; his ego, deflated; and he resumes believing in the Enchanter.

The Duke and Duchess, who have already read the book about Don Quijote and Sancho, treat them with the pomp befitting a famous knight and his loyal squire. They provide the environment in which their guests make some of their dreams come true: Don Quijote is given the key to Dulcinea's "disenchantment" (although he never succeeds in restoring her to her pristine state), and Sancho is given an isle to govern. What prompts their hosts to reconstruct a fantastic, chivalrous world, however, is not a genuine appreciation of Don Quijote's knightly mission but boredom and selfishness. So eager are they for a little fun that they go to great lengths to recreate the trappings of chivalry: the ceremonies, the pageantry, the costumes, and even the speech. At the same time, they make laughingstocks of their guests, whose escapades never cease to amuse the ducal household. The Duke and Duchess deceive Don Quijote and Sancho into accepting as real a world that is as artificial as a theater. They write the script and set the stage on which knight and squire perform. But Don Quijote and Sancho are not professional actors. They are simply puppets manipulated by their callous, pleasure-seeking hosts.

The Duke and Duchess, as well as the Innkeeper who dubbed Don Quijote a knight, pretend to enter Don Quijote's world of chivalry in order to humor him; besides, his eccentric behavior has injected a touch of mirth into the tedium of their daily routines. Recent acquaintances, they consider him harmless enough and do not comprehend that his madness could prove threatening to his life and to the lives and property of other people. From society's standpoint, however, Don Quijote is a disruptive individual who wreaks havoc wherever he goes. He has tilted at windmills and wine gourds that do not belong to him; he has challenged two Benedictine monks whom he accused of holding a princess against her will; and he has freed the galley slaves, although he had no authority to do so. Had he been sane, the Holy Brotherhood would have arrested him.

Society clearly cannot permit a destructive, mad individual to wander about unrestrained, which is why several of Don Quijote's friends take it upon themselves to bring him back to safety. They know that they cannot persuade him to return to the reality of the seventeenth century, since he has sworn to obey the dictates of a mythical age. They also know that they cannot necessarily count on Sancho for assistance, for Sancho has tasted freedom and reknown and is generally content with his squirely role.

Two of Don Quijote's friends, the Priest and the Barber, have already failed once in their attempt to prevent him from embarking on his first journey with Sancho. At the beginning of

Pt. I, they ordered the Housekeeper to burn his treasured romances, which only added fuel to his fire. Saddened but undaunted, he is convinced that the relentless Enchanter spirited away his books and that Heaven ordained him to vanquish the evil knight whose cause the Enchanter champions.

No sooner do Don Quijote and Sancho leave home together the first time than the Priest and the Barber begin to draw up their plan of action. The only way they will have any positive effect on Don Quijote is to assume temporary identities in keeping with the world he has created. They then disguise themselves as a damsel in distress and her squire. Dressing as a young maiden, however, thrills neither the Priest nor the Barber. Fortunately for them, they happen upon Dorotea, a real damsel in distress. Dorotea, the reader may remember, is pursuing her erstwhile lover Don Fernando, and her appearance allows them to remove their ludicrous disguises. When they and Dorotea finally catch up with Don Quijote, she makes believe that she is Princess Micomicona of Guinea, and she implores him to avenge the wrong done her by an evil giant. Don Quijote is delighted to come to her rescue, but the plan miscarries when Dorotea meets up with her real-life seducer, who agrees to marry her.

Left without a princess for Don Quijote to succor, the Priest and the Barber hatch another plot. Concealing their identities once again, they tie Don Quijote up and place him in a cage, which they then load onto a wagon. In an effort to salvage his wounded pride, they convince him that the pathetic state in which he finds himself is the Enchanter's work. Sancho, however, knows that the robbers of Don Quijote's freedom are really his "friends". Insinuating to his master that their motives are not as altruistic as they appear, Sancho wonders aloud whether they might be jealous of Don Quijote. A keen observer of human nature, Sancho implies that sane people, who must conform to the limitations of time, place, and social circumstance, might feel envious of a madman who manages to live free of those constraints.

The Priest and the Barber deliver Don Quijote safely home,

where he stays long enough to regain his strength—though not his sanity—before venturing forth with Sancho for the second and last time. During this series of adventures, another friend, Sansón Carrasco, replaces the Priest and the Barber in an effort to lead Don Quijote home for good. Like his predecessors, Sansón meets with success only because he adopts Don Quijote's chivalric ways.

Disguising himself as the Knight of the Wood, Sansón challenges Don Quijote to a duel. Since he is considerably younger than his opponent, he expects to win, in which case he will exercise his right as vanquisher and will demand that the exemplary knight return home. They duel, and—surprise of surprises—Don Quijote defeats Sansón! The latter cannot now discard his new identity any more than Don Quijote can, but for different reasons. Sansón must continue to play the game of chivalry not only to restore Don Quijote to his loved ones and to his senses but also to win back his own honor. His motives are much baser than the Priest's and the Barber's. Humiliation makes him vindictive and compels him to avenge his defeat. He has assumed his knightly guise so completely that he forgets what his purpose is: to save Don Quijote, not to cause him needless harm.

Sansón again encounters Don Quijote in an episode that marks the turning point of Don Quijote's career. Disguised this time as the Knight of the White Moon, Sansón once more challenges him; this time, however, he wins, and he demands that Don Quijote return to his Niece and friends, in whose company he is to remain for a year. Don Quijote has no choice but to comply with Sansón's stipulation, whereupon he regains his sanity and dies.

As far as the plot of *Don Quijote* is concerned, only a lapse of a month separates the end of Pt. I from the beginning of Pt. II. The Don Quijote who emerges in the second, however, has changed from the Don Quijote of the first.

Madness enabled Alonso Quijano to transform himself into Don Quijote. Reborn, he was free to plot the course of his

165

knightly career and to interpret reality in accordance with his new identity. The first part of the book reflects the desire for self-realization and freedom and the idealism commonly associated with youth. In the second part, Don Quijote tends to view external reality as it is, not as he imagines it to be. An inn is an inn, not a castle. He is, in short, maturing into the adult phase of his new life. His gradual coming to terms with external reality forces him to come to terms, at least subconsciously, with himself. Perhaps he realizes that his mission is impossible, but he cannot now cast it aside. On the one hand, he basks in the fame he has acquired; on the other, his identity and reputation entrap him and require that his actions unflaggingly reflect the chivalric principles he has vowed to uphold. His acquaintances expect him to carry out his knightly activities with youthful vigor. But Don Quijote is a worn-down, middle-aged man, and he wearies of continually playing his self-appointed role.[22]

Don Quijote's stamina reaches a low ebb when Sansón, alias the Knight of the White Moon, deals him the crushing blow. That Don Quijote does not blame his humiliation on the Enchanter indicates an increasing acceptance of reality. He resorted to the Enchanter in order to rationalize why he saw reality in one way while the rest of the world saw it in another. Now, however, his perception of reality is becoming more objective, and he will soon have no further need of his nemesis. He is also coming to an awareness of his poor physical condition. When Sansón extracts from him the promise to return home, he might even secretly feel a degree of relief at the prospect of spending a year in passive tranquility.

Don Quijote remains, nonetheless, a knight of exceptional dignity to the end. Although he is dejected that another knight has routed him, he courageously accepts defeat and holds his head high as he and Sancho ride into their town.

Shortly thereafter, the melancholia from which Don Quijote suffers takes its toll, and he falls gravely ill. Fever wracks his body for six days, and when it subsides, he is cured of his madness. He awakens from his feverish sleep as Alonso

Quijano and repudiates Don Quijote. He then emphatically denounces romances of chivalry, which poisoned his mind to the point that he confused fantasy with reality. His mind is now free and clear of the misty clouds of ignorance that enveloped it, he proclaims, and he now sees the light of reason. Now he realizes how foolish and fraudulent romances are, and he regrets that he came to this awareness so late:

> Yo tengo juicio ya, libre y claro, sin las sombras caliginosas de la ignorancia, que sobre él me pusieron mi amarga y continua leyenda de los detestables libros de las caballerías. Ya conozco sus disparates y sus embelecos y no me pesa sino que este desengaño ha llegado tan tarde.[23]

Don Quijote never rejects the chivalric ideals of valor, justice, and compassion. He does, nonetheless, censure romances of chivalry because they made him believe that he could don the arms of yesteryear to right the wrongs of contemporary society. In the end, prudence triumphs over folly; and conformity to spacial, temporal, and social limitations prevails over the will to disregard them.

Alonso Quijano's loved ones have gone to great lengths in their attempts to cure him. And yet they do not rejoice that their once-errant friend and uncle will never again stray from the course charted for him by reality and society. To the contrary, they are filled with sadness, for they know that he will soon die. Only now do they realize that defeat, while it has brought him to his senses, has also brought him to his deathbed. It has rid him of his delusions—and of his illusions. Bereft of all earthly hopes, he has nothing to live for.

The Priest, the Barber, and Sansón, in particular, feel somewhat remorseful for having set in motion the chain of events that has led Don Quijote to sanity, disillusionment, and imminent death. Consequently, they try to rekindle his madness and insist on calling him "Don Quijote". Since he is in no condition to resume his chivalric way of life, they encourage him to assume the pacific role of a shepherd. They hope that he will transform pastoral literature into life just as he once transformed romances of chivalry. How ironic! His friends burned those romances because of the deleterious effect they had on him; now, they turn to similarly fictional and escapist pastoral literature in the desperate hope that it prove salutary.

The exhortations of Don Quijote's friends are of little avail, however, for Alonso Quijano is no longer Don Quijote. He begs them to stop their foolishness since he has more serious things on his mind: the material and spiritual affairs he must put in order if he is to die in peace.

Don Quijote's loved ones weep at the death of their friend and uncle. We, his readers, may also shed a tear or two, for Don Quijote has become almost as real to us as knights of chivalry were to him. He has bequeathed to all who have grown to love him the indelible memory of his indomitable will and of his courage. Although reality and society beset him with insurmountable obstacles and doomed his mission to failure, he persevered in his struggle to restore freedom and justice to the world. His life exemplifies the potential within each person to exert his or her individuality in order to transform society for the better.[24]

ENDNOTES

[1] Miguel de Cervantes, "La ilustre fregona," in *Obras completas*, ed. A. Valbuena Prat, 12th ed. (Madrid: Aguilar, 1962), pp. 921–922.

[2] Ibid., "La gitanilla," p. 783.

[3] Ibid., p. 790.

[4] Ibid.

[5] The plot of "The Captive's Tale" (included in Pt. I, Chs. xxxix-xli of *Don Quijote*) is similar to Cervantes' play *Los baños de Argel*. Yet another young lady who flees her non-Catholic culture is Transila, a character in Cervantes' last novel *Los trabajos de Persiles y Sigismunda*. Like Preciosa, she deplores her society's customs regarding premarital sexual relations, specifically the custom whereby the male relatives of a maiden's fiancé may deflower her on the eve of her wedding.

[6] Another Moorish character who appears in *Don Quijote*, the reader may recall, is Ricote. But his and Zoraida's aspirations and destinies are diametrically opposed. Together with his fellow Moriscos, he has been expelled

from Spain and is planning to settle in Germany, where he hopes to find an environment of religious tolerance. Zoraida, on the other hand, is a true Christian and seeks refuge in Spain, where she can practice her faith without fear of discovery. Nevertheless, both characters are similar in that they desire to live according to their consciences.

[7] Many literary critics see in Don Quijote's insistence that a man's deeds give meaning to his life a reflection of Cervantes' own life. For some critics, Don Quijote's words reflect Cervantes' desire to be recognized for his heroic deeds during the Battle of Lepanto and the years he spent in an Algerian dungeon. For others, these words are indicative of Cervantes' *Converso* heritage, which has been neither proved nor disproved; according to this theory, both he and Don Quijote were thwarted by a world that would not see in them what they saw in themselves. Whether or not Cervantes was a *Converso*, however, he knew firsthand the frustration an individual experiences when he is judged not on the basis of his merits but on the basis of factors entirely extraneous to his worth as a person.

[8] Cervantes' short "exemplary" novel "El licenciado Vidriera" also concerns a madman and bears certain similarities to *Don Quijote*. Agustín Moreto borrowed from this tale to write his own *El licenciado Vidriera*, which differs from Cervantes' story in that Moreto's character feigns madness in order for the world to shower him with riches so that he can win the hand of his ladylove.

[9] Miguel de Cervantes, *Don Quijote*, Pt. I, Ch. xi, in *Obras completas*, p. 1067.

[10] Ibid., Ch. i, pp. 1038–1039. As mentioned before, Cervantes too sought recognition for his noble feats; unlike Don Quijote, however, recognition would always elude him.

[11] Ibid., Ch. xlvii, p. 1250.

[12] Ibid., Ch. xxi, p. 1111.

[13] Ibid.

[14] Ibid. This is another of several passages that have led certain literary critics to conclude that Cervantes was a *Converso*.

[15] Ibid., Ch. xi, p. 1066.

[16] Ibid., Pt. II, Ch. liii, p. 1456.

[17] Ibid., Ch. lviii, pp. 1468–1469.

[18] Ibid., p. 1469.

[19] J. Ortega y Gasset writes about the necessity of therapeutic solitude in his *El hombre y la gente*, Ch. 1: "Ensimismamiento y alteración."

[20] *Don Quijote*, Pt. I, Ch. xi, pp. 1066–1067.

[21] Ibid., Ch. xxii, p. 1116.

[22] Ten years elapsed between the publication of Pt. I (1605) and Pt. II (1615). It is likely that Don Quijote's disillusionment and acceptance of objective reality reflect the change that Cervantes underwent in those ten years of frustration, disappointment, and growing *desengaño*.

[23] *Don Quijote*, Pt. II, Ch. lxxiv, p. 1521.

[24] In 1614 an unknown author, writing under the pseudonym "Alonso Fernández de Avellaneda", published an apocryphal *Don Quijote*. This book so incensed Cervantes (as Mateo Luján de Sayavedra's spurious second part of *Guzmán de Alfarache* had infuriated Mateo Alemán) that, in *his* second part, he has Don Quijote disavow the deeds Avellaneda "erroneously" recounted about him. Avellaneda's Don Quijote and Sancho Panza are hollow caricatures of their originals; what is more, Avellaneda treats Don Quijote unsympathetically and shows no understanding of his real mission.

9

The Undeceived Individual

However saddened we may feel that Alonso Quijano renounced Don Quijote and illusion, Alonso only felt saddened
that his disillusionment came so long overdue. His awakening
to reality, he believed, was a priceless gift that God in His in-
finite mercy gave him. *Desengañado*, or undeceived, he then saw
reality as it was, not as he had imagined or willed it to be.

This theme of *desengaño* pervades seventeenth-century Spanish literature. Its origins can be traced to the ideals of stoicism
and asceticism, which have traditionally exerted a strong influence on the Spanish character, and of the Counter-Reformation,
whereby art should move men and women to a heightened
awareness of the apparential and deceitful nature of the world.

When a person reaches the state of *desengaño*, he comes to
the realization that the things he craved—beauty, wealth,
power, and even glory—are transitory and meaningless in the
face of death. Life, in the words of many a poet, is but a river
leading inexorably to the sea of death. As the only true reality
of life is death, the wise man prepares for eternity by repu-
diating all things and desires that might imperil his soul. This
explains why Alonso Quijano so forcefully recanted romances
of chivalry: had he read spiritual literature instead of romances,
he concluded, he would have been able to devote more time
readying himself for death.

The undeceived individual views the world in a new light.
He espoused godless values in order for society to accept him
and to deem him a person of importance. He now sees how
empty and insidious many of these values are, because his con-
forming to them has jeopardized his chance for salvation. On

the one hand, he belongs to the world; on the other, he must disassociate himself from the spiritual danger that certain worldly values pose.

It was not uncommon for Golden Age writers and literary characters, as we have observed, to retreat to the countryside in search of freedom and solitude. For the thoroughly undeceived individual, however, the freedom and solitude of rustic life take on a spiritual dimension. They offer him the opportunity to ponder the transitory nature of life and to put his aspirations in perspective.

One of the most eloquent expressions of *desengaño* is a poem in the form of a moral epistle, the "Epístola moral a Fabio", generally attributed to Andrés Fernández de Andrada. The court, declares Andrada, is a prison where the ambitious man dies. Andrada needs no distant climes or seas to discover nor gold and silver to pursue. He is content in the countryside with his unpretentious home, a book, a friend, and a brief nap, which no debt or burden can perturb:

> Fabio, las esperanzas cortesanas
> Prisiones son do el ambicioso muere,
> . . .
> ¡Mísero aquél que corre y se dilata
> Por cuantos son los climas y los mares,
> Perseguidor del oro y de la plata!
> Un ángulo me basta entre mis lares,
> Un libro y un amigo, un sueño breve,
> Que no perturben deudas ni pesares.[1]

Unlike the courtier, Andrada desires nothing more, for truth has taught him that position and possessions are short-lived. Life, he realizes, is but a brief day in which the sun rises and quickly becomes lost in the darkness of the cold night: "¿Qué es nuestra vida más que un breve día, / Do apenas sale el sol, cuando se pierde / En las tinieblas de la noche fría?"[2] Truth has revealed to him its essence, and he has made up his mind to arrange his priorities accordingly: "Así, Fabio, me enseña descubierta / Su esencia la verdad, y mi albedrío / Con ella se compone y se concierta."[3] Therefore, he flees what he once loved in his foolish simplicity, and he has broken the chains that bound him to falsehood: "Ya, dulce amigo, huyo y me retiro; / De cuanto simple amé rompí los lazos."[4]

In his poem, Fernández de Andrada makes use of three closely related motifs that permeate seventeenth-century literature, particularly poetry: the brevity of life, the fugacity of time, and the vanity of things. These motifs convey the fundamental truth that *desengaño* teaches: the futility of placing one's hopes and trust in temporal life. When the undeceived, God-fearing individual like Andrada contemplates human existence, he understands that its sole purpose is to test him. He realizes that the way he has led his earthly life will determine the nature of his afterlife. He now grasps the true significance of his role in society, and the conflicts in which he has lived with his conscience, with other individuals, and with the world take on new meaning. He now sees that he will be worthy of salvation only if he has the strength to resist worldly temptations and if he plays his social roles virtuously.

One most famous literary character who ultimately learns the true meaning of life is Segismundo, the lead protagonist in Pedro Calderón de la Barca's *La vida es sueño*. The enduring popularity of this play lies, to a great extent, in the two principal themes it incorporates: honor and *desengaño*. Both themes treat the individual's relationship to the world around him. Honor, which we will explore in Pt. V, pertains to his earthly existence and enables him to safeguard his dignity and his membership in society. *Desengaño* pertains to his life after death and enables him to understand the transcendental nature of his earthly existence and to interact with society accordingly.

The Polish Prince Segismundo has been the victim of misfortune since birth. At the very moment he was born, his mother died, and the moon eclipsed the sun. King Basilio, Segismundo's father and an avid student of astrology, concluded that these catastrophic events portended a life of violence for his son. Should Segismundo succeed him on the throne, Basilio feared, he would rule tyrannically. To spare Poland needless suffering, Basilio proclaimed that his infant son had died; he then secretly banished Segismundo to an isolated castle where, as the play opens, Segismundo is already a young man. He has spent his youthful years in abject misery and is unaware of his royal blood. The only human being whom he has ever known is Clotaldo, his warden.

Basilio, in the meantime, has begun to wonder whether he acted too harshly with Segismundo. Perhaps he read too much meaning into the ominous circumstances surrounding his son's birth. Perhaps he was wrong to have deprived him of his rightful place in the court. As a result of his misgivings, Basilio resolves to give Segismundo a chance to disprove the dire forebodings. He will arrange for his son to be brought drugged to the palace. If, after he arouses, Segismundo should prove the stars right, Basilio will have him drugged once more and removed to his secluded castle; upon reawakening, Segismundo will think that his experiences at the court were all a dream, and he will not plunge into despair.

Basilio sets his plan in motion, and soon his son is brought to him. When Segismundo regains consciousness, Clotaldo reveals to him who and where he is. Enraged, Segismundo turns on Clotaldo and calls him a traitor for having withheld his birthright from him. Segismundo's anger is clearly justifiable; it is, nonetheless, misdirected, for he does not realize that Clotaldo has sworn loyalty and obedience to the King, not to him. Then Segismundo rightly denounces Basilio for having robbed him of his humanness, for having condemned him to spend his youth in chains as if he were a wild beast.

From the moment he awakens, Segismundo behaves like an instinctive animal, and his violence does not subside. First, he throws a defiant servant off a balcony; the servant dies. Next, he attempts to rape Rosaura, a young lady who has aroused his affection as well as his sexuality. Last, he tries to kill Clotaldo, Rosaura's father, who has rushed to her aid.

It comes as no surprise that Segismundo fulfills his father's worst expectations of him. Raised in virtual solitude, he has never known parental love and guidance. Barred from society, he has never had the opportunity to become socialized. Treated like a wild beast, he acts like one. And yet Basilio, for all his reputed wisdom, overlooks the truth—that he, not the stars, created this willful, unbridled monster. The stars did not compel Segismundo. Even if they had impelled him toward the course of brutality, paternal love might have overridden their power. Basilio, however, still has not comprehended the magnitude of his folly, and he sends his son back to his isolated existence.[5]

When Segismundo awakens to find himself once again in the dungeon, he wonders whether he dreamed his sojourn in the palace. If what seemed so real, especially his love for Rosaura, was only an illusion, then perhaps he is also dreaming the reality of his imprisonment. Life (*vida*) is a dream (*sueño*), he concludes. Still, it is far more preferable to dream a life of freedom and dignity than one of shackles and degradation.

Clotaldo has counseled Segismundo to practice self-mastery and virtue, and Segismundo now begins to see the wisdom— and the practicality—of his jailer's words. *Desengañado*, he begins to realize why he failed to redeem his rightful place in society. Having followed his instincts, he countered the evils of abandonment and negative solitude with evil, not with virtue, and he is now more wretched than before. In order to win vindication, he reasons, he must discard egotism and adhere to a higher ethos. Consequently, he resolves to abide by the dictates of God and society, a resolution he voices in what is perhaps the most famous soliloquy of Spanish Golden Age theater.

At the beginning of his soliloquy, Segismundo expresses his determination to repress his fierceness, his fury, and his ambition, in case he dreams again. And he will dream again, he declares, for his world is so singular that living is only dreaming. Experience has taught him that a man dreams what he is until he awakens. Segismundo dreams that he is weighed down with chains, and he dreamed that he saw himself in another

175

more pleasing state. What is life, he asks himself? A frenzy. What is life? An illusion, a shadow, fiction. The greatest good is but a trifle. All of life is a dream, he concludes, and even dreams are dreams:

> Es verdad; pues reprimamos
> Esta fiera condición,
> Esta furia, esta ambición,
> Por si alguna vez soñamos.
> Y sí haremos, pues estamos
> En mundo tan singular,
> Que el vivir sólo es soñar;
> Y la experiencia me enseña
> Que el hombre que vive, sueña
> Lo que es, hasta despertar.
> . . .
> Todos sueñan lo que son,
> Aunque ninguno lo entiende.
> Yo sueño que estoy aquí
> De estas prisiones cargado,
> Y soñé que en otro estado
> Más lisonjero me vi.
> ¿Qué es la vida? Un frenesí.
> ¿Qué es la vida? Una ilusión,
> Una sombra, una ficción,
> Y el mayor bien es pequeño;
> Que toda la vida es sueño,
> Y los sueños, sueños son.[6]

Like all dreams, the dream of life must come to an end. In preparation for that day when he will emerge from illusory life to true life, Segismundo vows to play his earthly, God-lent role with virtue. It is not the nature of a man's role, he realizes, that ultimately matters but how he enacts it and how he interacts with others.[7] Life is an illusion, but it lies within his power to live his dream without illusions and in such a way that he will one day awaken to the joyous reality of everlasting life.

Toward the conclusion of the play, circumstances allow Segismundo to prove to his father and to Poland that he has

176

mended his ways, that the stars were wrong. The discovery that Basilio deprived Poland of its rightful crown prince throws the kingdom into civil war, and rebellious soldiers free Segismundo. When he confronts his father a second time, all traces of his former rage (justifiable as it was) have disappeared. Segismundo forgives Basilio, who at long last understands the enormity of his error. And when he meets his beloved Rosaura again, he sublimates his love for her. Curbing the sexual desire she still arouses in him, he generously resolves to marry her to Astolfo, his cousin and the prince who had seduced her.

The emergence of the newly transformed Segismundo signals an end to the social and personal upheavals that had commenced on the day of his birth. Poland rejoices that Segismundo has risen forth from the obscurity of cruelly enforced solitude, and Segismundo is at last vindicated. Disillusioned, he sees life as it really is. Accordingly, he determines to play his social roles properly. He will live the rest of his dream with compassion, self-sacrifice, and courage, the attributes that comprise an individual worthy of society's esteem and, most importantly, of God's blessing.[8]

The dying Alonso Quijano and the spiritually reborn Segismundo ultimately came to an awareness that temporal life is but a preparation for afterlife. Having renounced the things of transitory, human existence that might endanger their souls, they set their sights on eternity.

For many an individual, however, the immortality of the soul is not the only goal that gives meaning to earthly life. While it is undoubtedly the most important, it does not satisfy the very human yearning for immortality in this world, for something of a person's individuality to survive long after his soul departs his body.

Numerous medieval and Golden Age writers treat the subject of fame, whereby a person lives in the memory of posterity; indeed, what prompted Don Quijote to sally forth was not only his desire to right the wrongs of society but also his desire for eternal reknown.

A famous fifteenth-century poet who discusses the significance of fame is Jorge Manrique, who composed one of the most moving Spanish poems ever written, a tribute to his late father Rodrigo Manrique. In this poem "Coplas por la muerte de su padre", Jorge sets forth his ideas concerning the three lives of such exemplary men as his father: earthly life, the life of fame, and eternal life.

Death approaches the knight Rodrigo and tells him to leave the first life of deceit and flattery and to let his heart of steel manifest its famed courage in this most difficult hour. The dread battle he expects should not make him bitter, Death consoles him, for he is leaving behind an honorable life of fame. While this second life is neither eternal nor true, it is longer lasting and much better than perishable, temporal life:

> . . . 'Buen caballero,
> Dejad el mundo engañoso
> Y su halago;
> Vuestro corazón de acero
> Muestre su esfuerzo famoso
> En este trago;
> . . .
> No se vos haga tan amarga
> La batalla temerosa
> Que esperáis,
> Pues otra vida más larga
> De la fama glorïosa
> Acá dejáis,
> (Aunque esta vida de honor
> Tampoco no es eternal
> Ni verdadera):
> Mas, con todo, es muy mejor
> Que la otra temporal,
> Perecedera.'[9]

Death assures Rodrigo that his military feats are not in vain. The "pagan" (Moslem!) blood he caused to be shed in God's name, Death promises him, has won him fame on earth and the reward of the third and everlasting life:

'Y pues vos, claro varón,
Tanta sangre derramasteis
De paganos,
Esperad el galardón
Que en este mundo ganasteis
Por las manos;

. . .

Que esta otra vida tercera
Ganaréis.'[10]

Father and son can rest peacefully in the knowledge that Jorge's poem immortalized them both.

The hope of being remembered consoled Don Rodrigo in the hour of his death. To the contrary, the possibility of being forgotten makes other individuals disconsolate, for it signifies that their endeavors may meet the same earthly fate as their bodies—nothingness. A poem written by the Golden Age poet Lupercio Leonardo de Argensola poignantly exemplifies this fear of oblivion. To be forgotten, he says, is like not being, and there is nothing worse than not having been: "La sombra sola del olvido temo, / Porque es como no ser un olvidado, / Y no hay mal que se iguale al no haber sido."[11]

While most authors agree that it is better to die with fame than without it, several of them, nonetheless, caution their readers against an inordinate thirst for reknown. Writing in the spirit of *desengaño*, they stress the mortality of fame and admonish their readers to shape their lives in accordance with the criteria that God, not necessarily society, will use to judge them (which explains why Alonso Quijano rejected the fame he had acquired as Don Quijote and why Tirso de Molina, as we shall see, condemned Don Juan to the fires of Hell). The fear of oblivion, these authors warn, drives a man to pursue fame, which in turn enslaves him fully as much as the pursuits of wealth and power. He who craves glory is never free. Depending on others for an enviable reputation during his earthly life and for enduring fame after he dies, he must always heed the criteria for reknown that society has established irrespective of whether or not such criteria are divinely inspired.

Fame and disillusionment are the two predominant themes in the literary works of Baltasar Gracián, one of the foremost seventeenth-century prose writers. Four of his treatises concern the dilemma of the individual, who is destined to live in a world Gracián considers essentially negative. The exceptional man whom Gracián idealizes, however, has partially solved his quandary by learning to cultivate his individuality and to prepare himself for the conflicts with society and the vicissitudes of Fortune, which he will inevitably encounter. At the same time, he has endeavored to achieve eminence, on which hinges his dream of reknown.[12]

The heroic, discreet, and prudent individuals whom Gracián discusses in three of his works, *El héroe, El discreto*, and *Oráculo manual y arte de prudencia*, are well aware of the deceptiveness and treachery that surround them. Nevertheless, they elect to remain in society. Whereas numerous sixteenth- and seventeenth-century authors, as we have noted, advocated solitude as a means of recovering or retaining one's equilibrium, Gracián does not, for his ideal individual cannot live without society. Only in the world can he realize his potential for greatness, and only in the world can his excellence be acknowledged. Without acclaim, eminence means nothing.

Gracián analyzes in detail the ways in which a man should strive for excellence in order to attain recognition. His profession, for example, often determines whether or not society will heap praise on him. Therefore, he should choose a "reputable" and visible career (the military, for example) instead of a highly ostentatious profession that lacks credibility: "Empleo plausible llamo aquél que se ejecuta a vista de todos y a gusto de todos, con el fundamento siempre de la reputación, por excluir aquéllos tan faltos de crédito cuan sobrados de ostentación."[13]

Fame was and is the sister of giants, Gracián declares. Assuming extreme proportions, it is either monstrously abominable or prodigiously applaudable: "Fue y es hermana de gigantes la fama; anda siempre por extremos: o monstruos o prodigios, de abominación, de aplauso."[14] A man whose reputation arises from evil deeds will be deemed an abomination;

180

virtuous deeds, to the contrary, will be considered prodigious. To be regarded with benevolence, Gracián reiterates, requires acting with beneficence; to be loved requires loving: "Requiérese, pues, para la benevolencia, la beneficencia: . . . amar para ser amado."[15] Good deeds, in effect, are not an end but rather a means to an end, and Gracián makes no effort to dissimulate the egotism behind them. Since society will ultimately benefit from virtue, however, Gracián believes that the end fully justifies the means.[16]

In these three books, Gracián rarely alludes to a person's spiritual goal of salvation. What concerns Gracián more than the individual's relationship to God is his relationship to society. Gracián instructs the reader to cultivate his individuality without letting society dominate or suffocate him. He can gain the upper hand in his struggle with the world if he shrewdly balances the expectations he has of himself with those society has of him, and if he manipulates men and events to his advantage.

The first of Gracián's works, El héroe, treats the making of a heroic man. Gracián defines a hero as an intrinsically self-confident and superior young man whose seed of greatness has reached fruition. The percentage of heroic men is extremely small, as most potentially superior men fail to develop their latent attributes and consequently personify mediocrity, a trait Gracián greatly disdains.

The hero is not a solitary figure, for only in the arena of society can he prove his mettle. He must demonstrate his ability to resist, not to escape, the social pressures that might detract from his heroic individuality.

In El discreto, Gracián advises the reader how to acquire the discretion needed in order to make the best use of his mature years. The discreet man, though not necessarily heroic, has lost the cockiness of youth, and he tempers his words and deeds at all times. Discretion and prudence, the subject of Gracián's Oráculo manual y arte de prudencia, are noninherent characteristics an individual must learn. They enable him to overcome many of the difficulties that living in the world presupposes.

Whether he is a hero or simply a man of discretion, prudence makes it possible for him to avail himself of the best that society has to offer him. It is the tool an individual employs in his attempts to thrive undefeated in a hostile world. Strongly linked to self-interest, it dictates how he should deal with society.

The prudent man exercises critical judgment in all aspects of his life. Reason, not whim, determines the choices he makes, and he should never act against his better judgment. He associates with those who can teach him something, and he shuns the company of fools: "Tratar con quien se pueda aprender."[17] He is very careful to pick friends who will be useful as well as pleasant company: "No sólo se ha de procurar en ellos [los amigos] conseguir el gusto, sino la utilidad."[18] This same utilitarian criterion also holds true for a man's choice of a wife.

The prudent man readily discerns between reality and appearances. Things, warns the undeceived Gracián, pass for what they appear to be, not for what they truly are. Rare is the man who examines the inside of things, for most men are satisfied with the outside: "Las cosas no pasan por lo que son, sino por lo que parecen; son raros los que miran por dentro, y muchos los que se pagan de lo aparente."[19]

People, like things, also have a way of deceiving the unwary, Gracián cautions. But the prudent man unmasks their deception and deciphers their intentions in order to place himself in an advantageous situation. By the same token, he masks his own intentions and tells neither the whole truth nor outright lies: "Sin mentir, no decir todas las verdades."[20]

Another important attribute of the circumspect, sagacious individual is his independence. He relies solely on himself and depends on no other person, there being few people on whom he can count. However, he makes others dependent on him since he knows that he can extract more from people who need him than from those who are grateful or courteous to him: "El sagaz más quiere necesitados de sí que agradecidos. . . . Más se saca de la dependencia que de la cortesía; . . . Acabada la dependencia acaba la correspondencia, y con ella la estimación."[21]

Ten years elapsed between the publication of Gracián's *Oráculo manual* and the third part of his masterwork *El criticón*. This interval signaled a deepening of the author's pessimistic view of the world, which was already perceptible in *El discreto* and *Oráculo manual*. The cynicism and *desengaño* that fill *El criticón* reflect his own plight. To avoid censorship of his works by his Jesuit superiors, Gracián had penned *El héroe, El discreto*, and *Oráculo manual* under the pseudonym "Lorenzo Gracián". The publication of each of these books increased the tension between Gracián and his superiors, who knew that he was the author. Disregarding the Jesuit General's order to cease, Gracián continued to write under pen names. Following the appearance of the third part of *El criticón* in 1657, the Order ruled that he atone for his rebelliousness. It sentenced him to a diet of bread and water, curtailed his intellectual activities, and banished him from Zaragoza, where he held a professorship of Sacred Scripture. Like Fray Luis de León, Gracián paid dearly for having exercised intellectual freedom; he too blamed his misfortunes on the jealousy of his colleagues. Unlike Fray Luis, however, he never recovered from his punishment, and he died shortly thereafter.

El criticón is an allegorical, philosophical novel that chronicles the journeys of two characters—Critilo, the rational man, and his illegitimate son Andrenio, the natural man—along the path of human existence. Each of the three parts of the book corresponds to the three stages of a man's life: youth, maturity, and old age.

Whereas *El héroe, El discreto*, and *Oráculo manual* treat the individual and the steps he must take to realize his unique potential, *El criticón* emphasizes the wretchedness of the human condition and the malice of society. Critilo, Gracián's alter ego, personifies *desengaño*. Imprisoned, robbed, shipwrecked, and compelled to forsake his truelove, Andrenio's mother, he becomes thoroughly disenchanted with life, with nature, and with man, who is the least trustworthy of all creatures. Accursed is he, says Critilo, who places his confidence in another person. He should not trust his friends, his brothers and sisters, or his children. He cannot even be sure of his own parents, because fathers have been known to roll their sons loaded dice, and many mothers have sold their daughers:

> Maldito el hombre que confía en otro, y sea quien fuere. ¿Qué digo amigos y hermanos? De los mismos hijos no hay que asegurarse, . . . Ni aun en los mismos padres hay que confiar, que algunos han echado dado falso a los hijos y ¡cuántas madres hoy venden las hijas![22]

Although Critilo does not specifically include wives in his litany of people unworthy of men's trust, he does bemoan the fact that a man can live neither with a woman nor without her: "No hay vivir con ellas ni sin ellas."[23]

Gracián portrays the human condition as essentially solitary. In his first three books he opposed solitude, for only in his relations with the world could an individual prove his worth. Nor does he advocate total withdrawal from society in *El criticón*. Virtuous living is the key to immortality, he stresses, and a man cannot practice virtue in a social vacuum. However, Gracián does recommend a sort of psychological withdrawal from the world. He urges the reader to shield himself from harm wherever and whenever possible, particularly in his relationships with his fellow men and women. Critilo admonishes Andrenio to proceed with caution in everything he sees, hears, and says. He should listen to everybody without placing his confidence in anybody. Bitter experience has taught Critilo/Gracián that wariness is the key to survival and that trust opens the doors to disappointment, conflict, and defeat.

Critilo's pessimism concerning human existence reaches its peak during the autumn of his years. His only consolations are the knowledge that death will soon claim him and the hope that he will live forever on the Isle of Immortality.

Gracián's depiction of afterlife does not specifically allude to the joys of the Beatific Vision but rather to the joy of everlasting fame; indeed, Gracián equates immortality with fame. What is death for most men is life for the few who have attained reknown: "Lo que para otros es muerte, para los insignes hombres es vida."[24] The Supreme Maker advises man that it is in his hands to live eternally. He should strive for fame by performing courageous feats, irregardless of whether he is a man of arms or letters, or a government official. Above all, he should be eminent in virtue and heroism if he desires everlasting life. If he makes fame the focal point of his earthly life, he will be immortal, for reknowned men never die:

> Advierte que está en tu mano el vivir eternamente. Procura tú ser fa-
> moso, obrando hazañosamente, trabaja por ser insigne, ya en las armas,
> ya en las letras, en el gobierno; y lo que es sobre todo, sé eminente en
> la virtud, sé heroico y serás eterno, vive a la fama y serás inmortal. No
> hagas caso, no, de esa material vida, en que los brutos te exceden;
> estima, sí, la de la honra y de la fama. Y entiende esta verdad, que los
> insignes hombres nunca mueren.[25]

The reknown to which Gracián refers far transcends the re-membrance among the living of the deceased's accomplish-ments. Wickedness may win a man fame on earth, but only virtue earns him eternal fame—the applause of the Supreme Maker and a place on the Isle of Immortality: "Desengañaos, que aquí no entran sino los varones eminentes cuyos hechos se apoyan en la virtud, porque en el vicio no cabe cosa grande ni digna de eterno aplauso."[26]

Gracián's concept of fame has evolved considerably since his first three books. In all four of his works, he accepts the ob-vious—that man is destined to live in society; he also urges the reader to make the most of his often conflictive relationships with the world, relationships that are crucial to the reknown he seeks. What most distinguishes *El criticón*, however, from *El héroe*, *El discreto*, and *Oráculo manual* is Gracián's interpre-tation of fame. In his first three treatises, he stresses that the hope of societal recognition and prominence gives meaning to an individual's earthly endeavors. In *El criticón*, Gracián does not altogether censure the desire for earthly fame because he recognizes that such a desire can be a force for good if it mo-tivates a man to lead a life of courage and moral excellence.

Nevertheless, *desengaño* has opened Gracián's eyes to the hollowness of all things temporal, and now he turns his gaze toward eternity and the fullness of life that the Supreme Maker promises the virtuous individual.

ENDNOTES

[1] Andrés Fernández de Andrada (attributed to), "Epístola moral a Fabio," in *Floresta de lírica española*, ed. J.M. Blecua, 2nd ed. (Madrid: Gredos, 1963), I, 275, 278–279.

[2] Ibid., p. 277.

[3] Ibid., p. 280.

[4] Ibid.

[5] The motif of a child isolated from society appears in several of Calderón's plays, including *Eco y Narciso* and *La hija del aire* (about the Assyrian Queen Semíramis).

[6] Pedro Calderón de la Barca, *La vida es sueño*, Act II, in *Obras completas*, ed. A. Valbuena Briones, 5th ed. (Madrid: Aguilar, 1969), I, 522.

[7] Calderón's *auto sacramental, El gran teatro del mundo*, is similar in theme to *La vida es sueño*. He uses the motif of the world as a stage to impress on his audience the need for each man and woman (that is, the actors in the drama of life) to realize that their roles (the props in life's drama) are lent them by God (the director of the play) and must be returned to Him when life comes to an end.

[8] *La vida es sueño* bears a similarity to Lope de Vega's religious play *La fianza satisfecha* in that the births of both Segismundo and the protagonist of Lope's play portended violence and tragedy. Like Segismundo, the protagonist of *La fianza satisfecha* is a victim of paternal neglect, which causes him to fulfill his destiny. Eventually, however, he repents his wickedness, and his father belatedly realizes that he was at least partially to blame for his son's once-unbridled character.

[9] Jorge Manrique, "Coplas por la muerte de su padre," sts. xxxiv-xxxv, in his *Cancionero*, ed. A. Cortina, 5th ed. (Madrid: Espasa-Calpe; CC, 1966), p. 106.

[10] Ibid., st. xxxvii, p. 107.

[11] Lupercio Leonardo de Argensola, "No temo los peligros del mar fiero," in BAE, XLII, 262.

[12] Gracián is a misogynist. He treats only the making of a noteworthy man, not of a woman, since he considers women vastly inferior to men and devoid of any potential for heroism.

[13] Baltasar Gracián, *El héroe*, in *Obras completas*, ed. A. del Hoyo, 3rd ed. (Madrid: Aguilar, 1967), p. 19.

[14] Ibid., *Oráculo manual y arte de prudencia*, p. 156.

[15] Ibid., p. 164.

[16] These three works of Gracián clearly reveal the influence of Machiavelli's *Il Principe* and Castiglione's *Il Cortegiano*.

[17] Gracián, *Oráculo manual*, in *Obras*, p. 156.

[18] Ibid., p. 196.

[19] Ibid., p. 180.

[20] Ibid., p. 202

[21] Ibid., p. 154.

[22] Ibid., *El criticón*, Pt. II, p. 671.

[23] Ibid., Pt. I, p. 567.

[24] Ibid., Pt. III, p. 995.

[25] Ibid., p. 1000.

[26] Ibid., p. 1012.

V

The Individual
and the Societal
Code of Honor

10

Honor and Dishonor

The authors and characters who experienced *desengaño* came to a recognition of the true reality of human existence. They realized that the goal of salvation after death should guide their relationships with other individuals and with society at large. Literature, however, presents a multitude of characters who have not reached the state of *desengaño* and who never will. While the undeceived person sets his sights on the eternal, these men and women set theirs primarily on the temporal. What directs the course of their lives is not *desengaño* but worldly honor. All of these honor-bound characters are at least nominally Catholic. Those who are true Christians try to reconcile their spiritual and mundane concerns; those who are not disregard the transcendental nature of their lives in favor of the earthly.

Although readers tend to identify honor with sixteenth- and seventeenth-century literature, particularly with drama, this theme also occupies an important place in medieval literature. Indeed, most shades of meaning associated with the Golden Age honor code occur in medieval fiction and poetry and were codified during the Middle Ages.

Prince Juan Manuel is one of several medieval authors who stress that worldly honor signifies little if not accompanied by virtue. Goodness, he writes in his famous *El conde Lucanor*, increases a man's wealth and his *honra* 'honor',[1] and it adds luster to his lineage; a noble, rich man, to the contrary, will lose everything if he is evil: "Y vos, señor conde, . . . debéis saber que el hombre con bondad acrecienta la honra, y alza su linaje, y acrecienta las riquezas: y por ser muy hidalgo y muy rico, si bueno no fuere, todo será muy aína perdido. . . ."[2]

The honor-virtue to which Juan Manuel refers implies moral strength and emanates from the individual. It is an attribute that he can choose to attain and over which he can exercise control.

During the Middle Ages, *"honra"* also signified "manliness", a concept that suggests virility as well as physical courage and strength. Moreover, it is a key ingredient of a man's worth or value (*"valor"* and *"valer"* in Spanish, two words derived from the Latin *"valens"* 'strong').[3] Like goodness, manliness is a characteristic an individual can will to develop.

Medieval kings bestowed titles of nobility on their exceptionally courageous subjects, especially on those who had displayed great prowess on the battlefield. These titles would pass from generation to generation, from fathers to eldest sons. As a result, titleholders came to include not only meritorious individuals on whom monarchs had conferred noble status but their descendants as well.

Whether or not a person possessed this vertical aspect of honor[4] was contingent, more often than not, on circumstances entirely beyond his control. Only a small fraction of Spanish men actually was granted noble status. The rest fell into two categories: those who were born into noble families and those who were not. If they were noble-born, they inherited the degree of vertical honor corresponding to their rank, from grandees down to *hidalgos*. If they were not, they would have found it difficult to achieve noble status unless, as we have noted, they bought or falsified letters of nobility.

While original title holders might have deserved the acknowledgment their feats had earned them, their descendants did not necessarily live up to their forefathers' illustrious reputations. Spanish literature offers many examples of nobles, and even monarchs, who neglect the obligations of responsibility, altruism, and generosity—noblesse oblige—that are expected of them. They are remiss in enacting their social roles because their personal desires clash with the duties God and society

192

require of them. Should they not make amends for their immoral, antisocial behavior, they must pay the penalty in one way or another.

Virtue, manliness, and duty are those aspects of honor that arise from within the individual. They contribute not only to his sense of dignity and self-worth but also to his reputation, or horizontal honor, which is society's recognition of his merit.[5] The fact that the medieval Spanish word "honra" could connote "virtue", "manliness", "duty", and "reputation" is significant, for it reveals how interdependent the personal and social facets of honor were (and are): a character who fails to meet the societal standards of honor risks losing his or her reputation and, consequently, is subject to ostracism, a state tantamount to temporal nonlife and far worse for many an honor-driven individual than physical death.

Medieval authors used the word *"fama"* interchangeably with *"honra"* to signify "reputation". *"Fama"* also meant "fame", or the prolongation of one's reputation after death. Centuries before Gracián's time, writers were reminding their readers to conduct themselves in such a way that posterity would remember them long after they departed this world. Prince Juan Manuel's alter ego, the counselor Patronio, for example, warns Count Lucanor not to let vice or loose behavior stop him from doing good; knowing that he must die, he should see to it that the fame of his good deeds remains unblemished even after death: "Y vos, señor conde Lucanor, pues sabéis que habéis de morir, por el mi consejo, nunca por vicio ni por holgura dejaréis de hacer tales cosas [buenas] porque, aun desque vos muriereis, siempre hinque la fama de vuestros hechos."[6] And Jorge Manrique, as we saw in the last chapter, emphasizes that the life of fame is far superior to earthly life.

Just as *"fama"* signified "reputation" as well as "fame", its antonym *"infamia"* signified "infamy", or the lack of a good reputation in life and in death.

In the seventh of his *Partidas*, Alfonso X "the Learned" discusses at great length the factors that comprise an infamous individual. Infamy, he writes, may stem from circumstances surrounding a person's birth, over which he clearly exercised no control. Illegitimate children, for example, are born infamous. Furthermore, some people bring infamy on themselves. Pimps, go-betweens, and entertainers who perform for pay (Alfonso specifies jongleurs, bullfighters, and wrestlers) fall under the category of infamous. A variety of such sexual misdeeds as the homosexual act also causes an individual's infamy. An adulteress is considered infamous, as are a widow and her new husband if the couple should marry less than a year after her late husband's demise.[7] (Alfonso codified these strictures on a woman's sexual activities in the hope of ensuring legitimate paternity.)

Since, with the exception of illegitimacy, an individual wills to become infamous, he cannot seek legal redress or vengeance to clear his name; rather, he must bear his stigma for the rest of his life. In the words of Alfonso X, once a man is defamed, even though he might not be at fault, he is dead as far as any worldly good and honor are concerned. What is more, physical death would be better for him (or her) than life: "El hombre, después que es infamado, maguer no haya culpa, muerto es cuanto al bien, y a la honra de este mundo; y demás, tal podría ser el infamamiento, que mejor le sería la muerte, que la vida."[8] Alfonso's comments on the terrible nature of infamy underscore the individual's reliance on society's acceptance; without it, life is a state of conflict and isolation, to which even death is preferable.

Self-induced infamy, however, can be avoided if a person conducts himself with *vergüenza*, a Spanish word that has several interrelated meanings. In this particular context, *"vergüenza"* signifies a sense of shame, an acute awareness of the importance of a good reputation and of the steps a person must take to possess it. Society instills in the individual this sense of shame. If he acts accordingly, society will reward him with its approval and will not brand him infamous.

Learning a sense of shame plays an essential part in the process of socialization. Men and women who are sensitive to shame respect God, temporal authority, parents, and fellow men and women. Upholding the dignity and good name of their ancestors and family members, men conduct themselves with bravery and loyalty, and women, with morality, modesty, and decorum.

Medieval discoursers on the subject of honor also discuss shame, to which honor is closely linked. They recognize that a sense of shame serves as a restraint on an individual's behavior and that shamelessness leads to conflict and immorality in his relationships with other individuals and with his world.

Vergüenza, Alfonso X explains, does two things: first, it prevents men from boldly defying society's laws; second, it makes them obey the things they should: "[vergüenza] hace dos cosas, que conviene mucho al Pueblo, que haga a su Rey. La primera, que tuelle [quita] atrevimiento a los hombres. Y la segunda, que les hace obedecer las cosas que deben."[9]

Alfonso's son Sancho IV also stresses how powerful a deterrent of wickedness is *vergüenza*. In addition, he states that a sense of shame makes a man mindful of his lineage. He who has inherited an unsullied family name should desire the same good fortune for his descendants, Sancho declares: "La vergüenza hace conocer a hombre el linaje de donde viene y que tome vergüenza de su linaje y de sí mismo y de los que han de venir de él."[10]

For Prince Juan Manuel, Alfonso's nephew, *vergüenza* is an extraordinary attribute that impels a man to make great sacrifices. It is the best thing a man can possess, Juan Manuel claims, for it is the mother and the head of all good qualities. Because of their sense of shame, men suffer death, the most serious thing possible, and refrain from doing the unseemly things they otherwise might have done:

> Vos digo que la mejor cosa que hombre puede haber en sí, y es madre y cabeza de todas las bondades, dígovos que ésta es la vergüenza; ca por vergüenza sufre hombre la muerte, que es la más grave cosa que puede ser, y por vergüenza deja hombre de hacer todas las cosas que no parecen bien, por gran voluntad que haya de las hacer.[11]

"Vergüenza" also means "shame", the humiliation a person

feels when he is caught doing something he knows is wrong or when another person deliberately offends him in public. In the latter instance, the ashamed person feels dishonored and robbed of his dignity; what is more, he fears that his reputation will plummet.

In addition to shame, medieval writers treat the subject of dishonor, which is different from infamy. Although both may fill a person with shame, infamy is often self-motivated, whereas dishonor is other-motivated.

Alfonso X codified the many ways in which one individual could dishonor another: in word (by insulting or ridiculing him publicly) and in deed (by wounding him, holding him against his will, tearing at his clothes, spitting in his face, making offensive gestures at him or his home, or harassing a virtuous female member of his family).

A dishonored person, unlike an infamous one, could legally demand redress and could initiate the lawsuit up to one year after the offense occurred.[12] Should the offended party choose not to publicize his dishonor, he might seek vengeance, especially if the offense involved his wife, daughter, or sister. Both legal redress and vengeance served the same purpose as far as the victim was concerned: once his manliness and subsequently his reputation were restored, he regained his dignity and his sense of oneness with society.

The oldest Spanish literary masterpiece in which honor, in all its forms, is a prime theme is the twelfth-century, anonymous epic *Poema de mío Cid*. The hero of the poem, Rodrigo Díaz de Vivar, was a real-life Catholic warrior whom the Moors (at times his enemies; at others, his allies) honored with the title "Cid", the Arabic word for "lord".

The epic poem reveals that the numerous battles El Cid has won for his king, Alfonso VI of Castile and León, have aroused the envy of certain unscrupulous nobles. Believing the false, calumnous tales they have spread about the warrior, the King banishes him from his realms. Rodrigo is dishonored and shamed through no fault of his own. Not only has he lost the

King's esteem, but he must also abandon his loved ones and his home.

As dejected as he feels, El Cid nonetheless promises his loyal comrade Álvar Fáñez that they will one day return to Castile with great honor: "¡Albricia, Álvar Fáñez, ca echados somos de tierra! / Mas a gran honra tornaremos a Castiella."[13] This determination to right the dishonor that his enemies have done him offsets his feelings of alienation and loneliness.

Although the act of banishment has released him from all bonds of fealty to the King, El Cid still considers himself Alfonso's loyal vassal. During the course of his term of exile, he scores many victories and wrests Valencia from the Moors. On these occasions, he sends the King generous portions of the booty he has accumulated, even though he is not duty-bound to do so. He hopes that these demonstrations of loyalty will soften the King's heart, and his hopes come true when Alfonso, impressed with El Cid's exploits and the booty, consents to "forgive" him. El Cid beseeches Alfonso to pardon him in public so that all present may hear the King's words: "¡Merced vos pido a vos, mío natural señor, / Así estando, déisme vuestra amor, / Que lo oigan todos cuantos aquí son!"[14] The King readily agrees, thereby restoring El Cid's dignity and his reputation.

Meanwhile, the two archvillains of the poem, the Counts of Carrión, set their sights on El Cid's wealth. Despite the fact that El Cid, a member of the lower nobility, is their social inferior, they propose to marry his daughters Doña Elvira and Doña Sol. The King intercedes on the Counts' behalf, and El Cid consents to the double nuptials with great reluctance, even though his and his family's social status will greatly increase once Elvira and Sol become countesses.

El Cid's premonitions of doom become reality shortly after the weddings take place. The Counts, whose words and deeds bespeak the antithesis of true honor, prove cowards on the battlefield. Their ignoble behavior has made laughingstocks of them. Humiliated, they lose whatever sense of shame they might have had, and they vow to avenge themselves. Instead of confronting El Cid directly, they pusillanimously belittle their wives, mercilessly beat them, and leave them to die in the forest of Corpes. Luckily, Álvar Fáñez happens upon the hapless young women and leads them to safety.

Now it is El Cid who must avenge his dishonor. Since King Alfonso bore the responsibility for the marriages, El Cid reasons, he shares his dishonor and consequently should seek a way to right it.

The King agrees to convene the court and orders the Counts to attend. When the session opens, El Cid asks the Counts to return his two swords and the dowry he had given them. They do El Cid's bidding, whereupon he demands that they meet two of his trusted comrades in combat. The ignominious Counts are vanquished and will live out their lives in infamy. Their defeat vindicates El Cid and enables him to marry his daughters (once their first marriages are annulled) to the crown princes of Navarre and Aragon, a considerable step up the social ladder for El Cid and his family.

El Cid epitomizes honor in all its phases. He triumphed over envy and evil, avenged himself, and won the acclaim of his King and of posterity because he fought with the honorable arms of valor, loyalty, and generosity.

These same heroic qualities are also the guiding ideals of the fictional knights in romances of chivalry (the tales that inspired Don Quijote). The oldest known romance of Spanish origin is the anonymous *Historia del caballero Cifar*, written during the first years of the fourteenth century. To a certain extent, Cifar's personal attributes and his life parallel El Cid's. Cifar is a courageous, just knight whose feats spark the jealousy of his noble peers. They speak ill of him to the King, who unwisely heeds their slander and refuses to send Cifar into battle. Disappointed, Cifar then goes into self-imposed exile. In the course of his travels and adventures, he encounters the picaresque, proverb-spouting Ribaldo, who becomes his faithful page (and who bears a striking resemblance to Sancho Panza).

As a lad, Cifar had heard his grandfather mention that his family descended from kings of a distant land and that the last king had been an evil ruler whom a just, virtuous knight had deposed. When Cifar asked his grandfather whether he, Cifar, could one day reclaim the throne, the grandfather replied that Cifar could if he never stopped performing good deeds. Cifar then proceeds to fulfill his grandfather's hopes. His journeys take him to Mentón, the kingdom of his ancestors. The King of Mentón is so impressed with Cifar's valor that he marries him to his daughter, and eventually Cifar succeeds his father-in-law to the throne. Because of his virtue and bravery, Cifar redeems his dignity, his reputation, and his birthright. The moral of the story, concludes the author, is that the good man who strives to excel gains the things that are most important in this world and in the next, not the least of which is honor.

Honor, which is closely linked to the concepts of personal and social justice, constitutes the primary or secondary theme of the vast majority of Spanish Golden Age plays and is also a leitmotif of many novels and short stories written during that period.

While some poems and novels (especially the picaresque, as we have seen) suggest that the storm clouds of social change, avarice, and injustice were seriously threatening the structure of estate society, dramas in particular represent a world capable of maintaining its soundness in the face of those threats. Falsity, greed, lust, dishonor, and injustice may temporarily disrupt harmony among individuals and between one individual and society; in the end, however, harmony emerges victorious. These plays were clearly not intended to reproduce everyday social life but to recreate the ideals of honor (*honor* and *honra*, two words used interchangeably in Golden Age drama[15]) and of justice, ideals that were considered the bedrocks of a well-ordered world.

Unlike those novelists who hoped to open their readers' eyes to the hypocrisy and cruelty undermining true honor, dramatists were constrained to gear their plots, themes, and motifs to the requirements of producers, who in turn looked for plays that would appeal to the public. As a result, playwrights tended to pen their secular works more for the purpose of entertaining than of edifying or moralizing, and most of them would not have cared to jeopardize their popularity by explicitly probing the murky waters underlying the reality of the honor code.

Dramatists were not necessarily less aware than novelists of the gap separating the theory and the reality of honor; indeed, many plays implicitly criticize the primacy of reputation over virtue, as well as the excesses of the honor code. In general, however, playwrights presented the honor code (hypocritical and cruel as it might have struck them) as an instrument of temporal justice that society, including their public, demanded. Consequently, they conveniently overlooked the fact that sometimes the justice they portray runs counter to the Christian interpretation of true justice.

Virtually all protagonists and most minor characters of secular Golden Age plays belong to established society. They represent the monarchy, the nobility, and the commoners. (Hardly ever do clergymen and nuns appear.) Regardless of their social status, male and female characters alike are expected to carry out the responsibilities corresponding to their roles in life, roles they assumed the moment they were born.)

Monarchs form the pinnacle of society. As God's temporal regents, they ought to personify mercy, reason, justice, and wisdom. Should they or their family members fail to abide by *monarchie oblige*, they are rarely punished; in most instances, they see the light of *desengaño*, whereupon they repent their transgressions.

Noblemen possess vertical honor, which they either inherited or were granted by a king. Honorable status requires that a noble's conduct be always above reproach: he should manifest manliness, generosity, trustworthiness, moderation, decorum, and discretion in all aspects of his life; that is, he should be an honorable man as well as a man of honor. He must at all times demonstrate his loyalty to his monarch, the font of nobility and vertical honor; he should protect and respect women regardless of their social rank; and he ought to respect the dignity of his male social inferiors. Finally, he must conform to the rigid conditions set forth in the honor code, a system of rules governing the behavior of all noble protagonists (and of many peasants as well).

Noblemen, like Don Quijote, frequently proclaim: "Soy quien soy" 'I am who I am'. This statement is the nobleman's way of affirming that he is fully cognizant of the responsibilities his status entails and that, as a result, he *must* act accordingly. He has no choice in the matter. If he were to act otherwise, he would experience two grievous consequences: first, his dignity, or self-esteem, would suffer a severe blow; second, he would jeopardize his reputation and would run the risk of social ostracism. Since deviance from societal expectations would bring him into conflict with his world, he generally elects not to deviate, even in the rare instances when his conscience tells him that conformity might be sinful.

As honor implies discharging a series of simultaneous duties, it may happen that one imperative collides with another. How the confused nobleman solves this dilemma is the principal theme of several plays (and a secondary theme of a great many more).

The common denominator of some such plays is the friendship between two men, a bond that obligates one friend to protect the other and to be true to his word. As the typical plot unfolds, however, each friend discovers that the other has unwittingly wronged him. Both individuals vacillate between their obligation to avenge their dishonor and their obligation to keep their promise of friendship. Fortunately, circumstances reveal that the offenses were not intentionally committed (unlike in the more serious dramas involving the treachery of a false friend), thereby obviating vengeance altogether. Needless bloodshed is averted, and the comedies end happily for all concerned.

Juan Ruiz de Alarcón's *Ganar amigos* (*How to Win Friends*) is about two friends who embody generosity and self-sacrifice. Their friendship is so true that they overlook the offenses that might have driven less magnanimous noblemen to wreak vengeance. The two characters, the Marquess and Don Fernando, both love the ambitious Doña Flor. Then the Marquess discovers that Fernando has killed his brother. Although his sense of manliness dictates that he in turn murder Fernando, friendship prevails, and he intercedes on Fernando's behalf and arranges a royal pardon for him. Shortly afterward, an imposter claiming to be the Marquess seduces a woman. She rushes to the King and begs for justice. The King arrests the innocent Marquess and threatens to execute him unless he marries the woman, which he refuses to do. Now the indebted Fernando seizes the opportunity to repay the Marquess' generosity: he pleads with the King to spare his friend's life and even offers to die in his place. The King, however, learns the truth about the seduction and declares the Marquess innocent. So strong is the friendship between the Marquess and Fernando that not even Flor's choice of the Marquess over Fernando can estrange them, and Fernando graciously bows out of the amorous race.

Francisco de Rojas Zorrilla also treats this clash between friendship and vengeance in his *Obligados y ofendidos*. Whereas the Marquess and Fernando epitomize nobility in all senses of the word, Rojas Zorrilla's friend characters are merely slaves of the absurdly fine points of the honor code (*pundonor*). The hilarity of the comedy derives from the entangled web of obligations and offenses in which the friends find themselves. So excessively punctilious are they that neither can escape his duty as a friend for long enough to kill the other.

Rojas Zorrilla's *Sin honra no hay amistad* incorporates this theme in an equally uproarious way. The play concerns two friends, Don Antonio and Don Melchor, who love the same woman, Doña Juana. Both sneak into her boudoir at the same time, and each generously agrees to let her decide which of the two men she will have! At that very moment, her brother Don Bernardo appears, sees his sister in a most compromising situation, and demands vengeance of the two friends. Then Antonio and Melchor discover that Bernardo has offended *them*: he seduced Antonio's sister and killed Melchor's father. Now it is *their* turn to demand vengeance. The problem confronting them, however, is which one will kill Bernardo. Each is duty-bound to avenge his dishonor. Yet the one who kills Bernardo leaves the other's honor unsatisfied; he also destroys the bond of friendship joining them, for without honor there can be no friendship (*no hay amistad*). Finally, Bernardo *himself* attempts to mediate their friendly dispute by suggesting that they both duel him at the same time! However, the need for a duel disappears with a double marriage: Melchor consents to wed Juana, thus restoring Bernardo's honor, and Antonio's honor is restored when Bernardo agrees to wed his sister. Although Melchor's honor remains unsatisfied, he proclaims himself the happiest of the three men by far, for only he has been spared marriage!

Commoners also play leading roles in Spanish drama, but not nearly to the same degree as noblemen. They tend to fall into two categories: bourgeois and villeins.

Bourgeois are usually portrayed as rich, greedy, social-climbing merchants who are more than eager for the prestige of marrying off their daughters to noblemen.

An important innovation of Golden Age theater involves the role of the villein, who hitherto did not generally share equal billing with a nobleman. The typical Golden Age peasant is an upright and loyal subject of his king. Some peasants live under the protection of a great lord; others survive as poor journeymen; a few even own the land they farm. These villeins differ from their boorish, comic literary predecessors in a couple of ways: for one thing, their love for women transcends the merely carnal; for another, they are frequently as honor-driven as their noble brethren. In defending their family honor, they have effectively usurped the "noble" prerogatives of dignity, duty, manliness, and reputation.

Golden Age established society, like its medieval forerunner, expected a woman, irrespective of her social rank, to adhere to its norms and conventions regarding her conduct with men. She learned these rules as part of the socialization process and was fully aware of the dire consequences of disobedience. Literature, especially the theater, reflects these precepts and customs, and it bears witness to the importance society has traditionally attached to a woman's reputation—and to the appearance thereof. How a woman interacts with a man not immediately related to her affects her and her family's honor, to say nothing of her life expectancy.

An unmarried woman is expected to play her virginal role until her wedding night. The fact that peasant girls abide by this code of behavior comes as a great surprise, as we shall have occasion to see, to many arrogant noblemen characters who are hell-bent on bedding without wedding their female social inferiors. A good reputation is the key to a noblewoman's *and* a peasant woman's marriageability, which even the suspicion of extramarital relations might very well endanger. This explains why the fear of *¿qué dirán?*, or gossip, often—though not always—serves to curb her amorous inclinations.

Should a young maiden yield to a man's sexual advances, his social and marital status frequently decides her fate. If he is single and of her estate, she usually weds him in the end. If he is married and/or above her in rank, she may spend the rest of her days in a convent or even become an outlaw, for her chances of marriage to another man have all but vanished. And even if she could hide her past and wed another, she would always fear that her husband would one day discover that she had not taken adequate care of her reputation.

Several Golden Age plays involve the machinations of a young man who wishes to test his prospective fiancée's reputation. If she passes the test he imposes on her—that is, if she resists the temptations he sends her way—he rewards her by marrying her. That the young woman agrees to wed her beloved, after all he has made her endure, attests to the supreme importance of marriage, without which a young lady would not fulfill the mission that God and society have intended for her.

One of the most entertaining of these plays is Guillén de Castro's *Engañarse engañando*. In contrast to several of her counterparts, however, the heroine has her own sweet revenge when she pretends, much to her fiancé's consternation, to love the man whom he has sent to seduce her! But all ends well, and the fiancé realizes that he has only deceived himself (*engañarse*) in deceiving (*engañando*) her.[16]

As for a married woman, her one obligation is to remain faithful to her husband. Rarely do a loveless marriage and her spouse's extramarital adventures justify adultery on her part. Not only should she not have an affair with another man; she must also refrain from any occasion of temptation, real or apparent, that might give her neighbors grounds for gossip. Should she neglect to act decorously, she threatens her husband's honor, her life, and the life of her admirer; she also casts doubt on the legitimacy of her children.

In the patriarchal society that Spanish literature depicts, an unmarried girl falls under the tutelage of her father. In the event that he is deceased, her brother, uncle, or legal guardian supports her and does his best to safeguard her chastity and to arrange a suitable marriage for her. On her wedding night, she becomes the responsibility of her husband, who assumes the role of her watchdog.

Just as the king should maintain the order and integrity of society and defend it from outside assaults, so too must a man protect the female members of his household from men who would lead them astray. His sense of manliness, which might encourage him to seduce a nonrelated woman, compels him to protect his own women from seduction. When he fails, society considers him remiss in his duties. What is more, if the seduced woman is his wife, society ridicules him with the most degrading, demeaning name imaginable for a husband—*cornudo* 'cuckold'.

Try as he does to thwart his daughter, sister, or wife from succumbing to physical love, in the final analysis it is she who controls his honor. His reputation depends on her behavior and her reputation. If she is—and appears—virtuous, if she is willing to play her role properly, then his honor will remain unblemished. If not, both she and he will suffer the consequences.

This is the great irony of the honor code: a man strives to be the master of his family, his destiny, and his honor, but in reality he is not. Even when he epitomizes many of the facets of honor—exalted lineage, virtue, manliness, and duty—he cannot fully control his dignity and his reputation. This feeling of impotence leads male protagonists to bemoan the fragility of honor, to protest the fact that honor relies on the actions of other people.

The unfortunate man whose woman really or apparently dishonors him experiences hell on earth. He loses his self-esteem. Should his shame become publicized, he would certainly lose his good name and his social standing. Like other victims of wrongdoing, he feels terribly alone since he cannot confide his plight to anyone (except to us, his audience). How he rights his dishonor depends on his relationship to the woman involved. If his sister or his daughter submits either willingly or forcibly to a bachelor's sexual demands, he—and often she—attempts to coerce the man into marrying her. In the event that a wedding cannot take place, he usually kills the erstwhile lover. Although he might also contemplate slaying the young woman as well, he generally refrains and instead banishes her to a convent. If, however, his wife is guilty of adulterous intentions or deeds, he must kill not only her lover but her as well. Vengeance does not make the offense disappear or appear never to have happened. Rather, it enables the dishonored man to reclaim his most precious possessions—his dignity and his reputation. Unavenged, he would exist in a state of nonlife. Avenged, he feels able to live once again.

Vengeance has social and personal implications. As each man and woman belong to society, an affront to one member is an affront to his or her family and to society as a whole. Just as a man's honor reflects on the honor of the group, so too is his dishonor society's dishonor. Illicit passion destroys the harmony binding one individual to another and to his family, his community, his estate, and his world. Therefore, society urges the wronged individual to take the steps necessary to restore the harmony that had hitherto marked his social relationships.

The fact that vengeance reinstates him to his world is a tacit admission of society's approval of his measures. In addition, the monarch in many dramas ratifies the guardian's or husband's act(s) of vengeance. Since the sovereign in these plays personifies justice and honor, his endorsement signifies that the wronged man has acted justly, honorably, and in accordance with society's dictates.

Women characters infrequently assume the role of avenger, which society usually considers the exclusive domain of men. In the following chapters, we shall examine the comparatively few works involving single or married women who exact retribution for sexual offenses. As for nonsexual wrongdoings, writers seldom give the avenging role to a woman; they do, however, permit her to incite her menfolk to wreak vengeance. The rare female avenger who does appear in Golden Age literature contrasts markedly with the real-life women avengers of the Middle Ages, whom chroniclers generally portray as bloodthirsty and vindictive rather than as seekers of justice.

One female, fictional avenger of a nonsexual offense is Doña María, the heroine of Lope de Vega's aforementioned *La moza del cántaro*. A suitor of hers, Don Diego, has dishonored her elderly father. Her only brother, on whom it would have been incumbent to avenge the offense, is away in Flanders; consequently, María believes that it is her duty to act in her brother's place. She then mortally wounds Diego, who acknowledges just before dying that María was right to have sought redress. Moreover, all the world speaks respectfully of her deed, a sign that society would condone a woman's act of vengeance as a last resort.

All the interrelated phases of honor that appear in Golden Age literature also appear in medieval literature, with one exception: "purity" of blood. During the sixteenth and seventeenth centuries, as we have repeatedly observed, a person's Old Christian ancestry came to be a decisive factor in determining his social status. In theory, membership in established society implied «*limpieza*» 'purity'; in reality, however, many urban nobles descended from men and women of *Converso* heritage.

Following the pogroms of the late fourteenth century and the expulsion and forced conversion of Jews at the end of the fifteenth, the possibility of "contaminated" blood became a source of acute concern for noble men and women. Should their "tainted" ancestry be unmasked, they would suffer ostracism and even the stigma of infamy, of inherent vileness.

Few *Conversos* appear as protagonists in Golden Age plays, and the theater, unlike the novel, rarely treats overtly the plight of New Christians. Nevertheless, "purity" is a significant undercurrent in many plays because it determines a nobleman's good name. In several comedies, for example, the lead *galán* yearns for the honor of induction into a prestigious religious-military order. Whether or not the order admits him hinges on his "*limpieza*", which he must first prove. Until he is able to gather the requisite documents, the poor *galán* suffers great anguish. His fiancée postpones their wedding, for her good reputation would never allow her to undergo the humiliation of marrying a man whom an order rejected. Normally, however, these tales end happily: the order inducts the nobleman, who has proved to the world that his blood is "untainted", and his fiancée welcomes him back with open arms.

Unlike noblemen, the rural villeins of Golden Age theater never doubt the "purity" of their blood. Their unquestionable "*limpieza*" imbues them with honor and enables them to feel superior, in this one sense, to urban noblemen, whose "illustrious" backgrounds they often view with suspicion. Their innate sense of dignity, in turn, explains why they zealously defend their women and their reputations.

ENDNOTES

[1] See W. Poesse, "Utilización de las palabras 'honor' y 'honra' en la comedia española."

[2] Prince Juan Manuel, *Libro de Patronio* (a.k.a. *El conde Lucanor*), Ex. xxv, in BAE, LI, 394.

[3] See B. Dutton, "The Semantics of Honor."

[4] G. Correa introduced this term "vertical honor" in his "El doble aspecto de la honra en el teatro del Siglo XVII."

[5] Ibid., in which Prof. Correa uses the term "horizontal honor".

[6] Juan Manuel, *Libro de Patronio*, Ex. xvi, p. 384.

[7] King Alfonso X, *Las siete partidas*, Partida VII, Title VI, in *Los códigos españoles concordados y anotados* (Madrid: n.p., 1848), IV, 305–312.

[8] Ibid., Partida II, Title XIII, Law iv, in *Los códigos*, II, 390.

[9] Ibid., Law xvi, p. 397.

[10] King Sancho IV, *Castigos y documentos para bien vivir*, Ch. vi, ed. A. Rey (Bloomington, IN: Indiana Univ. Publications; Humanities Series No. 24, 1952), p. 60.

[11] Juan Manuel, *Libro de Patronio*, Ex. l, p. 422.

[12] Alfonso X, *Las siete partidas*, Partida VII, Title IX, in *Los códigos*, IV, 330–344.

[13] *Poema de Mío Cid*, Ll. 14–15, ed. R. Menéndez Pidal, 8th ed. (Madrid: Espasa-Calpe; CC, 1958), p. 105

[14] Ibid., Ll. 2031–2033, p. 215.

[15] W. Poesse, "Utilización de . . . 'honor' y 'honra'."

[16] Other plays involving a man who tests the reputation of the woman he loves are Lope de Vega's *El amante agradecido* and Juan Ruiz de Alarcón's *El semejante a sí mismo*.

11

Honor in Conflict with Love

One of the principal themes of Golden Age plays concerns honor in conflict with love. Male and female protagonists are occasionally torn between their obligations to act out their social roles, on the one hand, and the love they feel for their children, lovers, or spouses, on the other; in other words, they waver between doing what society expects them to do and what they, as individuals, would like to do. Sometimes, social roles and love mutually exclude each other, in which case honor must triumph at the expense of love. Other times, especially in the comedies of intrigue (also known as "cloak-and-dagger" comedies), honor and love are harmoniously reconciled; both prevail, and neither must be permanently sacrificed to the other.

Several plays treat as their primary theme a sovereign's conflict between honor and love for his willful son who has violated the laws his father has sworn to uphold impartially. What is the monarch-father to do? If he desists from punishing his child, he does not fulfill his duty as a just ruler. Yet the thought of meting out justice to his son strikes him with grief.

Rojas Zorrilla wrote a couple of so-called "Cain and Abel" dramas, *No hay ser padre siendo rey* and *El Caín de Cataluña*. In each of these plays, the rebellious brother is envious of the obedient one and kills him. The father is naturally enraged at his murderous son. Should he sentence him to die, however, he would be left childless. But Rojas Zorrilla does not force the fathers to avenge their virtuous sons' deaths; instead, circumstances solve their dilemma for them.

The King of *No hay ser padre* imprisons his son, but the country rises up (as it did in *La vida es sueño*) to protest the incarceration of its rightful heir to the throne. Realizing that he cannot play father (*no hay ser padre*) and king (*siendo rey*) at the same time, he abdicates, and his son succeeds him on the throne. The ex-King is now free to forgive him; since he is no longer the ruler, he cannot bring him to justice, for monarchs are traditionally immune from earthly retribution.[1]

Acting in his capacity as ruler, the Count in *El Caín de Cataluña* also jails his son, but when paternal instincts overpower his sense of duty, he has him secretly released. Nevertheless, justice emerges victorious: the guards spot the son fleeing and slay him.

Seleuco of Antioch, the King-father of Agustín Moreto's *La fuerza de la ley*, handles his predicament in a different way. His married son Demetrio is caught making love with Aurora, a married woman, and her husband cannot avenge his dishonor because of his rival's royal blood. The strict laws of Antioch regarding adultery prescribe blinding the male lover in both eyes. Even though Demetrio and Aurora were compelled to marry their respective wife and husband against their will, and even though they truly love each other, King Seleuco must bring the force of the law (*la fuerza de la ley*) to bear against his son. However, he blinds Demetrio only in one eye; in this way, once Demetrio ascends the throne, his sightless eye will remind him to rule justly, and his sighted eye, mercifully.

Another variation on the theme of honor versus love for a child involves the opposing loyalties of a nobleman who must choose between the king and his son. In Luis Vélez de Guevara's *Más pesa el rey que la sangre*, for example, Don Alonso has fallen out of favor with the King, but he demonstrates his loyalty, nonetheless, by refusing to assist the King's traitorous brother in overthrowing him. In an effort to coerce Alonso, the brother takes his son Pedro hostage and threatens to kill him unless Alonso betrays the King. In a moving soliloquy, Alonso balances loyalty to his king and love for Pedro to see which will prove the weightier:

> . . . ¡Bravo trance
> Entre el amor y el honor,
> Que ambos a dos se combaten!
> . . .
> Pongamos en dos balanzas,
> Aquí el Rey, aquí la sangre,
> Y llévese la victoria
> De las dos quien más pesare.[2]

He concludes, as he must, that the King outweighs his flesh and blood (*más pesa el rey que la sangre*). Despite the fact that the King's wicked brother slays Pedro, the play does not end on an entirely tragic note: having managed to avert insurrection, the King restores Alonso to his favor and bestows great honors on him, thereby rewarding the personal sacrifice that Alonso's sense of duty has entailed and restoring him to membership in society.

The most prevalent conflict in Golden Age theater concerns honor versus love between a man and a woman. In the following chapters, we will analyze some of the plays in which the attempted or real seduction of a woman provokes this conflict in her guardian or husband. In this chapter, however, we will examine only those works treating as their central theme the conflict that circumstances other than seduction have precipitated.

The theme of honor in opposition to love occurs in the so-called "sentimental" novels written in Spain during the fifteenth century. These immensely popular stories differ from some of their Italian models in that the love affairs they relate are not adulterous. Nevertheless, the tales end as unhappily as Shakespeare's *Romeo and Juliet*, to which they are often compared.

The women protagonists in many of these novels cannot wed their lovers because of the social differences separating them. Whether or not the young lady dies, her beloved must die, for his affection for her has weakened the bonds linking her to her family and to her world. In the end, the social considerations of rank, duty, and reputation defeat the individuals' natural inclination toward love.

In one type of "sentimental" novel, the lady rejects her lover's courtly overtures since they only serve to jeopardize her reputation and indeed her life. Her inconsolable lover laments her "cruelty" and eventually dies of a broken heart.

The most famous of all "sentimental" novels, Diego de San Pedro's *Cárcel de amor*, exemplifies this tragic chain of events. The noble Leriano adores Princess Laureola, but their difference in rank precludes any thought of marriage. The treacherous Persio, meanwhile, is also enamored of Laureola, but she does not reciprocate his love. Lying to the King, her father, Persio in revenge tells him that she and Leriano have made love. Deeply angered, the King imprisons her and sentences her to death. Leriano makes plans to free her, but she writes him a letter begging him to spare her already tainted reputation, which a rescue attempt would only further tarnish. If he does not help her, she explains, she will die. If, on the other hand, he carries her off to freedom, she will always be a condemned woman. Since her earthly fate is sealed regardless of what she does, she implores him to save her honor, not her life, for fame endures long after life has come to an end: "Si no me remedias, he de ser muerta; si me libras y llevas, seré condenada; y por esto te ruego mucho te trabajes en salvar mi fama y no mi vida, pues lo uno se acaba y lo otro dura."[3] Leriano, however, disobeys her and comes to her rescue. The King subsequently learns that he had given credence to lies, and he restores Laureola to his favor on the condition that she never meet Leriano again. Dejected, Leriano sees no way out of the prison in which love has kept him chained. He loses his will to live and induces death by eating the shredded remains of the letter she had sent him.[4]

Another kind of "sentimental" novel involves a young man and woman who consummate their love without benefit of a formal wedding ceremony. Society apprehends the defiant true lovers and condemns them to die for having violated its sacred norms. At least in death they will be together without fear of a cruel world that would part them. In one of these tales, Juan de Flores' *Historia de Grisel y Mirabella*, the pair commits suicide, the lovers' ultimate act of individuality, rebellion, and love.[5]

The tragic demise of true lovers is a motif that also appears in Golden Age theater. These plays, however, contrast with the earlier "sentimental" novels in that the young man, often a prince or a king, is enamored of a woman who is his social inferior, and not vice versa. Their love is sincere, albeit illicit. What is more, she is his mistress and has borne him children. He yearns to marry her, but his role of ruler requires him to put duty before personal happiness. When reasons of state compel him to wed a social equal, he must accede. As for the hapless mistress, she is killed in circumstances that vary from play to play.

Perhaps the most famous of these dramas is Vélez de Guevara's *Reinar después de morir*, based on the true story of the fourteenth-century Portuguese Prince Pedro (later King Pedro I) and Inés de Castro, the mother of his two children. When Pedro's father, the King, urges him to wed Princess Blanca, Pedro hopes that he can extricate himself from the marriage by telling her of his love for Inés. His plan, however, miscarries terribly: instead of understanding his plight and relinquishing him, Blanca feels dishonored and vindictive. The King sees no solution to the impasse that Inés' presence has created other than to have her murdered. Shortly after she is killed, the King dies, whereupon Pedro succeeds him on the throne and resolves that Inés should reign after death (*reinar después de morir*). Accordingly, he has her crowned posthumously, an honor that eluded her in life.[6]

A drama that closely resembles *Reinar después de morir* in plot is Guillén de Castro's *La tragedia por los celos*. The male protagonist is the King, whom duty has doomed to a loveless marriage. Guillén de Castro warns in many of his plays of the potentially tragic effects of forced wedlock, and this play is no exception: jealousy (*celos*) prompts the Queen to murder her husband's mistress, and the King spends the rest of his life brokenhearted.

As long as the romances depicted in Golden Age plays are not scandal-provoking or adulterous, the conflict between honor and love is usually resolved to the satisfaction of both. The individuals, who are portrayed as essentially positive, are allowed to achieve personal fulfillment and to retain their membership in society.

In one series of plays, honor and love collide when the young man or woman must first avenge a wrong done him or her by the other or by a member of the other's family. Only when the obligations of honor are carried out may the couple contemplate marriage. The path of their love is rocky, but each understands the other's need to restore honor lost, and the two are ultimately joined in matrimony.

One such play is Guillén de Castro's *Las mocedades del Cid*, which treats a fictitious episode in the life of the youthful (*mocedades*) Don Rodrigo, El Cid. He and Doña Jimena have fallen in love, but conflict ensues when her father slaps Rodrigo's father, thus dishonoring him. As Rodrigo's father is elderly, Rodrigo must challenge Jimena's father to a duel even though he risks forfeiting her love. Begging her forgiveness, he explains to her that he has balanced love against honor and that he must choose honor. He then kills her father, and now *she* is dishonored. She too balances love and honor. Although she is a woman, she tells Rodrigo, her honor compels her to do whatever she can to avenge her father's death; love, nevertheless, makes her want to be unsuccessful in carrying out her duty. In order to seek redress, she enlists the King's support, and he banishes Rodrigo from the court in an attempt to placate her. Rodrigo's victories soon earn him the King's gratitude. By now, the King has wearied of Jimena's melodramatic remonstrations and orders her to wed Rodrigo, a decree that secretly delights her in spite of her public protestations.[7]

Antonio Mira de Amescua's play *Obligar contra su sangre* follows a similar plot. Doña Sancha's brother, Don Nuño, has slain her beloved Don García's father, and García in turn wants to slay Nuño. Sancha also feels dishonored, for García will not keep his promise to marry her—a promise he gave in return for her sexual favors—unless he first avenges himself on Nuño. What is Sancha to do? Should she right her dishonor by marrying García, she would incur further dishonor by wedding the man who murdered her brother. But she is a plucky young lady, and García's precondition does not daunt her. Pistol in hand, she gives García her ultimatum: marriage or death. Since he truly loves her, García opts for the Golden Age variety of the shotgun wedding, and she regains her honor. Once she weds, her priorities change, and honor now obligates her to side with García against her flesh and blood. García, however, is so impressed with her courage that he magnanimously forgives Nuño, and the three live out their lives in peace.

Premarital sexual relations, which almost ruined Sancha's marriageability and her social standing, are a common motif in early Spanish literature. If the man and woman are single, social equals, and sincerely enamored of one another, authors generally reward their devotion with matrimony.

This motif of enduring love culminating in matrimony appears in medieval romances of chivalry. One of the most popular romances (and one that greatly influenced Don Quijote) was the anonymous *Amadís de Gaula*, which was known during the fourteenth century but not printed until 1508. Amadís, the hero of the tale, is the son of a princess who secretly wed the King of Gaul. To spare herself and her infant son shame, she placed him in a little boat and prayed that a kind soul would take pity on him. Her prayers were soon answered, and he was rescued and taken to Scotland. There he falls in love with Princess Oriana. Although their ostensible social inequality makes formal marriage impossible, they do marry clandestinely, as his parents had done years before, and Oriana gives birth to a son.[8] Meanwhile, Amadís' father formally weds his mother and recognizes him as his legitimate son. Then Oriana's father ratifies her marriage to Amadís, and their romance ends happily (in contrast to the ill-fated love affairs portrayed in the "sentimental" novels).

Golden Age comedies of intrigue also present numerous examples of the clash between honor-reputation and love. In these plays, the noble-born or bourgeois lovebirds outwit the *dama*'s guardian, who has placed obstacles in the path of their love. Often, the heroine has been forcibly betrothed to a rich, older man, and she has to exert her will if she is to wed whom she, not her guardian, chooses. Since she is kept under lock and key in order to safeguard her purity, she must resort to disguises and subterfuges. In doing so, she defies authority and imperils her reputation. She usually succeeds in her endeavors, however, because her aspiration, marriage, is an honorable institution that Church and society sanction. Her means are unconventional and sometimes immoral, but her goal is not.

When the guardian concludes that the *dama* has dishonored him, he swears to seek vengeance, but violence is averted in the nick of time. Because matrimony erases dishonor, he has no choice but to heed the couple's plea to wed, a decision that satisfies the demands of honor as well as of love. In the *dama*'s case, two wrongs—her greedy guardian's tyranny and her subsequent defiance—do indeed culminate in a right.

Several of Lope de Vega's *damas* risk their lives and sleep with their *galanes* in order to compel their menfolk to let them wed. One of Lope's best-known comedies, *La dama boba*, concerns a young lady who proves that she is not as stupid (*boba*) as people think, for her ingenuity ultimately gains her the husband of her choosing. She concocts a plan whereby she will hide her lover in her home with the knowledge that, when her father inevitably catches them together, he will demand that they marry. Her plot proceeds according to plan, and the father readily sees the urgency of a wedding. The lesson in another of Lope's comedies, *El mayor imposible*, is that the most impossible thing in the world is to lock up a woman against her will, something the heroine's brother learns the hard way. Despite his extreme measures to confine her, she sneaks her lover into her boudoir and manages to spend seven days and nights with him![9] And in a very daring comedy, Lope's *El acero de Madrid*, the young woman feigns illness so that she can rendezvous with her truelove. She summons her "doctor"—in reality, her beloved—to her bedside; in the course of the "cure", she becomes pregnant, which greatly expedites their wedding!

Tirso de Molina's heroines are also strong-willed *damas* who must outsmart their domineering, materialistic guardians. The central character of Tirso's *Marta la piadosa*, for instance, avoids marriage to a wealthy old man by telling her father that she has taken a vow of chastity. Assuming the role of a pious woman (*piadosa*), Marta visits the sick, and her new-found freedom gives her the opportunity to meet her sweetheart. Then she convinces her father that she must learn Latin if she is to become a nun. Her father agrees, and she hires her lover to teach her. So strong is her love for him that she even overlooks the fact that he killed her brother. Eventually they wed, and the father's anger at his daughter subsides considerably when he discovers that his son-in-law has just inherited a fortune.

Two of Calderón de la Barca's heroines boldly initiate their love affairs with the young men who have caught their fancy. To do so requires that the *damas* first establish contact with the *galanes* without endangering their own good names. Donning disguises solves the problem of their reputations and allows them freedom of movement, but it also creates unforeseen problems. When the heroine of *La dama duende* assumes the guise of a phantom (*duende*), her two brothers, unaware of her true identity, become attracted to her. The young lady in *Casa con dos puertas, mala es de guardar*, likewise changes her identity, and her beloved mistakenly believes that she and her brother are lovers. Like his counterpart in Lope's *El mayor imposible*, the brother learns too late that a house with two doors (*casa con dos puertas*) is impossible to guard. Once the heroines of both comedies reveal their identities and marry the men whom they have finally snared, however, their brothers' dishonor disappears.

Rojas Zorrilla and Moreto give a new twist to the comedy of intrigue in that the lead male characters in several of their plays are not *galanes* but pompous stuffed shirts (*figurones*) whom the young ladies are supposed to wed.

Don Lucas, the *figurón* in Rojas Zorrilla's *Entre bobos anda el juego*, is so stingy that the *dama*'s servant advises her to spend the rest of her days in a convent rather than marry him. She does neither; instead, she falls in love with Lucas' cousin, whom Lucas supports financially. But Lucas plots his revenge. Miserly to the end, he sweetly agrees to the marriage and then cuts the couple off without a cent. Deprived of money, he hopes, the newlyweds will not enjoy a moment's peace!

Moreto's *El lindo don Diego* involves a foppish (*lindo*), opportunistic fool, whose fiancée loves another man. Her *gracioso* saves her from a most unpleasant marriage to Don Diego when he introduces Diego to his girl friend, who appears disguised as a countess. Diego promptly falls in love with the "countess"—and with her "title"—and breaks his engagement. His pretentiousness, however, suffers a well-deserved blow when he discovers that the "countess" has tricked him. Wedding bells ring for his former fiancée and her truelove, as well as for the "countess" and the *gracioso*; Diego, to the contrary, winds up chagrined and mateless.

Impending forced marriage, defiance of societal convention, and the ultimate triumph of both honor and love through marriage are also motifs in several of Cervantes' plays and short "exemplary" novels. The heroines of his *El laberinto de amor* and *El gallardo español*, for example, leave home and assume new identities in order to pursue their lovers; one even follows her gallant Spaniard to Oran, in North Africa. For the protagonist of "La señora Cornelia", love poses the acute danger of imminent death. In spite of circumstances that have made it impossible for her fiancé to wed her, Cornelia becomes pregnant and gives birth. Fearing that her honor-bound brother will kill her, she flees, and her beloved has no idea where she has hidden. Buffeted for so long by the winds of Fortune, the lovers are at last reunited. Her brother forgives them and consents to their marriage, thus restoring these individuals to the society with which they had temporarily lived in conflict.

ENDNOTES

[1] A source of *No hay ser padre siendo rey* is Guillén de Castro's *La justicia en la piedad*, a play in which the Prince slays the husband of the woman whom

he attempted to seduce; the King imprisons his son, but the country rises up in arms and frees him, whereupon the Prince repents his crime and marries the woman.

[2] Luis Vélez de Guevara, *Más pesa el rey que la sangre*, Act III, in BAE, XLV, 107.

[3] Diego de San Pedro, *Cárcel de amor*, in his *Obras*, ed. S. Gili Gaya, 3rd ed. (Madrid: Espasa-Calpe; CC, 1967), p. 162.

[4] Diego de San Pedro's *Tratado de amores de Arnalte y Lucenda* is similar to his *Cárcel de amor* in that the heroine is concerned for her reputation, and the hero dies of a broken heart.

[5] Similar to *Grisel y Mirabella* is a short story by Juan Rodríguez del Padrón (a.k.a. Juan Rodríguez de la Cámara), "Estoria de dos amadores", which he included in his *Siervo libre de amor*.

[6] Pedro and Inés are buried in the monastery church of Alcobaça, Portugal. Their magnificent tombs lie feet to feet so that, as they rise from the dead on Judgment Day, they will face each other.

[7] *Las mocedades del Cid* was the source of Pierre Corneille's famous play *Le Cid*.

[8] Garci Ordóñez de Montalvo not only published *Amadís de Gaula* but also wrote a sequel, *Las sergas de Esplandián*, concerning the adventures of Amadís' and Oriana's son Esplandián.

[9] *El mayor imposible* was the source of Agustín Moreto's hilarious *No puede ser*.

12

Honor, Illicit Passion, and the Unmarried Woman

Matrimony legitimizes and sacramentalizes passionate love. It ensures legitimate offspring and enables lovers to live in harmony, if not always with each other, at least with society and with God. When passionate love leads to marriage, as in the tales we have examined, it is considered a constructive force. To the contrary, the illicit, extramarital passion depicted in countless medieval and Golden Age literary works is viewed as a destructive force, for it disrupts the harmonious relationships that all of its victims had hitherto enjoyed with their families and with their world.

The unlawful passion that writers treat usually originates in the man, who is the antagonist in these stories. He differs substantially from the *galán* protagonist in many comedies of intrigue. The *galán* is generally portrayed as a fundamentally positive individual who may have even challenged materialism, appearances, and other false societal values; if he violated some of society's mores, he did so only to expedite his marriage to his truelove. The antagonist in these stories about illicit passion, on the other hand, is a negative individual who sows discord in a world viewed as essentially good. He thinks only of his own pleasure, never of matrimony or of the grave consequences of seduction on the lady whom he woos. He may delude himself into thinking that he is genuinely enamored, and he may use the word *"amor"* to describe his desires, but he is not really in love. True love is selfless and noble; the passion that grips him, however, is narcissistic, selfish, and ignoble.

Several writers employ the imagery of the hunter and his

prey to describe the impassioned man and the woman whom he resolves to snare. So determined is he to trap her that he resorts to all manner of devious, cruel wiles: the promise of marriage, if she is a maiden; the promise of requited love, if she is unhappily married; and even rape, if all else fails.

Should the woman succumb to seduction, she jeopardizes everything she and society value highly. The unmarried woman who hopes that an affair will culminate in matrimony risks abandonment, for the typical seducer in Spanish literature leaves his lady friend the moment he has won her favors. She may then pursue him in an attempt to convince him to honor his commitment; the greater their difference in social rank, however, the less likely it is that she will succeed. If she does not, she can hardly wed another man, especially if her family and neighbors suspect the truth. As for the married adulteress, her fate is usually more dire—death at the hands of her dishonored husband.

Not only do the man's passionate advances endanger his lady friend's welfare; they may also endanger his own. He may be forced to wed his unmarried victim, should she prove that he proposed marriage to her prior to their affair. If he or the woman is married, or if he is unwilling to wed the young lady whom he deflowered, society sentences him to death. It metes out this extreme penalty because his antisocial, immoral act has collided with the norms of honor, fidelity, and chastity that it expects its members to uphold. Furthermore, his infamous behavior has severed the bonds linking parent with child, brother with sister, husband with wife, and each of these individuals with society. Without these bonds, harmonious relationships would soon vanish.

Although the seducer type victimizes his prey, he too is a victim—of passion, which writers from time immemorial have described as a force so powerful that it blinds a person's mind to reason, truth, and duty; in effect, it enslaves him. It is no wonder that authors of the Middle and Golden Ages inveigh against illicit passion, for it places an individual in conflict not only with his world but also with himself.

MEDIEVAL LITERARY TREATMENTS OF ILLICIT PASSION

Illicit passion involving an unmarried woman is a motif that appears in medieval as well as Golden Age literature. Indeed, it sets the framework for Juan Ruiz's fourteenth-century masterpiece *Libro de buen amor*.

In keeping with the title of the book, Juan Ruiz, the Archpriest of Hita, extols *buen amor* 'good love', the love of God and the reasonable, moral, and socially acceptable love between man and woman. He warns women throughout the book to beware of worldly, "mad" love (*loco amor*) and of go-betweens, whose avarice and devious machinations can lead a virgin to ruination. While Ruiz, the priest, expresses the sentiments of the Church and society, Ruiz, the man, is a realist regarding carnal love. On the one hand, the priest reiterates what his readers ought to do; on the other, the man describes what sexual desire may compel them to do against their better judgment.

Moreover, Ruiz seems to delight in offering extremely salacious examples of "mad" love! The fables and tales he incorporates belong to the medieval tradition of Boccaccio's *Decameron* and Chaucer's *Canterbury Tales* and are supposed to teach moral lessons through examples of immorality. If we choose, says Ruiz, we can learn a great deal about worldly love from his stories; but if we are wise, he warns, we will learn only those lessons he claims that we should learn. Because of the ambiguous nature of the book, however, it is difficult to ascertain exactly what truths he wished to impart.

Ruiz penned the *Libro de buen amor* in autobiographical form, and what further contributes to the ambiguity of his book is the scarcity of information about his life. We do not know whether he was really as irreverent and individualistic as he would have us believe in some of his tales. Whether or not he was a worldly clergyman, it is unlikely that all the stories he relates are autobiographical, since several of them are not original but adaptations of earlier works.

A possible solution to the riddle of the *Libro de buen amor* is that Ruiz wrote it to satirize his amorously inclined colleagues. While his tales might have had some factual basis, they probably recreate the misadventures of a fictional, abstract priest rather than of a specific one. As for the "exemplary" nature of the book, the only lesson a reader might possibly derive, other than to stay clear of procuresses like Trotaconventos (who arranged the narrator's seduction of a beautiful young woman), is to beware of hot-blooded priests.

Illicit love also provides the framework of Fernando de Rojas' *La Celestina*. This book was immensely popular during the sixteenth century and left its mark on several Spanish works of fiction, including two we have already seen, Francisco Delicado's *La Lozana andaluza* and Alonso Jerónimo de Salas Barbadillo's *La hija de Celestina*.

La Celestina is the story of the passionate, ill-fated love affair between Calisto and Melibea. At first, Melibea turns a deaf ear to Calisto's amorous pleas, and with good reason. Since he makes no proposal of marriage, she recognizes that the love he offers her is dangerous. She knows that a meeting between them would imperil her good name and her social standing. Desperate to possess her, Calisto then goes to the go-between Celestina (portrayed in far greater depth than her literary predecessor Trotaconventos) and begs her to intercede on his behalf. The fact that he resorts to such a woman reflects his egotism: as her fame proceeds from arranging sexual liaisons and repairing broken hymens, society might deem Melibea guilty of "mad" love if she were merely *seen* speaking to Celestina.

Lured by Calisto's offer of gold, Celestina agrees to take him as her client, but she frets that she may be unable to break down Melibea's resistance. She *must* succeed, she tells herself, for the sake of her professional reputation, on which rests her "honorable" place in society. In an effort to attain her desired end, she conjures up the Devil (whom she addresses as "Pluto") and demands that he come to her aid. The extent of Celestina's diabolism, in the literal sense of the word, is a matter of speculation; at any event, the Devil's presence, real or imagined, encourages Celestina to embark on her mission.

Under the pretext of selling household goods, Celestina gains admittance into Melibea's home and speaks to her of Calisto's "illness", which only she, Melibea, can "cure" by sending him her sash (a very personal love token).

Melibea reacts to Celestina's words even more harshly than she had to Calisto's. Calling Celestina an evildoer, she replies that, were it not for her modesty and her wish to keep Calisto's boldness a secret, she would kill her. Melibea then accuses Celestina of wanting to destroy her home, her virginity, and her father's honor in order to cure a madman and to further her own "honor": "¿Querrías condenar mi honestidad por dar vida a un loco? . . . ¿Perder y destruir la casa y la honra de mi padre por ganar la de una vieja maldita como tú?"[1]

Nevertheless, Celestina soon calms Melibea down, and Melibea's resolve begins to weaken. She sends Calisto her sash and finally consents to meet him at night. She is still, however, concerned for her reputation and begs him not to dishonor her by telling anyone of their impending rendezvous.

Calisto and Melibea meet one another and make love, whereupon she berates him and herself for having sacrificed her most valuable possessions—her virginity and her good name—for a moment's pleasure. Notwithstanding her concern for her family name, however, her passionate love for Calisto impels her to continue their trysts for almost a month. Following their last night together, Calisto falls off a ladder leading to her balcony and dies. Brokenhearted, Melibea makes plans for her own death. First, she attempts to justify her actions before God, and she confesses that she has no choice but to take her life. She is powerless to do otherwise, she admits, for passionate love has consumed her and has made captives of her freedom and her senses. Next, she summons her father. After revealing to him the details of her love affair, she states that she simply cannot live without Calisto. Moments later, she plunges to her death.

La Celestina bears a certain resemblance to the fifteen-century "sentimental" novels in that the stories all involve star-crossed love affairs and the untimely demise of one or both lovers; in addition, the protagonists of some "sentimental" novels lost their will to live, as did Melibea, and committed suicide. *La Celestina*, nonetheless, departs from the tradition of the "sentimental" novel in the reasons underlying the lovers' tragic demises. Whereas the lovers in many of those novels could not wed because of parental objection to their social differences, Melibea and Calisto never mentioned marriage at all—in spite of the fact that her father probably would not have objected, had Calisto asked for her hand. Calisto and Melibea looked upon their passionate attraction to one another as an end in itself, not as a means to marriage (a reflection, according to some literary critics, of the medieval tradition of courtly love). Not only did Melibea never contemplate wedding Calisto; she also bristled at the thought of marrying anyone else. As she had no intention of discontinuing her trysts with Calisto, she would not have wanted to sully her conjugal bed.

Melibea did not deceive herself about the nature of her love affair. She knew from the beginning that it was immoral, antisocial, and destructive. She understood why Calisto died and why she would take her own life. Had passion not enslaved them, she realized, he would not have lost his footing, and she would not have rebelled against the laws of God and society. Passion blinded the lovers to reason and alienated Melibea from her family, the microcosm of society. As matrimony, which would have restored Melibea's good name, was never discussed, she had no alternative but to die. (Under the circumstances, entering a convent would have been utterly inappropriate and even sacrilegious.)

Inordinate passion motivated many of the characters in *La Celestina* and ultimately led them to their deaths. Illicit sexual love, which resulted in Calisto's and Melibea's deaths, also played an indirect role in the demises of Celestina and of Calisto's two servants, the treacherous Sempronio and the once-faithful Pármeno. What is more, another kind of passion—greed—was directly responsible for the deaths of these three.

Avarice drove Celestina to extract as much gold as she could from Calisto. To ensure that he would be amenable to her requests, she enlisted the support of her ally Sempronio; together, they began to corrupt Pármeno. In return for Pármeno's help, Celestina promised to arrange for him to visit Areusa, the independent-minded prostitute with whom Pármeno had become smitten. In the end, Pármeno so totally lost his innocence that he incited Sempronio to kill Celestina after she had selfishly refused to share with them the gold chain Calisto had given her. Avarice and violence, however, got the servants nowhere, for they died fleeing the scene of the murder.

The central theme of *La Celestina* is the disastrous effects of uncontrolled lust, whether for sex, money, or power. Passion places an individual on a collision course with reason, with other people, with society, and with God. Struggling to fulfill his own desires and ambitions, the inordinately impassioned individual inevitably clashes with the world around him. Melibea's and Calisto's illicit affair threw into turmoil the apparent orderliness of their lives; avarice turned the two servants against their master (self-centered as he was) and their greedy ally Celestina. Ultimately, all five perished.

THE IMPASSIONED HUNTER AND HIS PREY

Spanish Golden Age theater is the great repository of the theme of the unmarried woman involved in the conflict between honor and illicit passion. The catalyst of this conflict is a willful man, generally a nobleman or a monarch, who makes sexual demands on a young maiden. His negatively individualistic impulses collide with the positive social roles he ought to be enacting properly and with the principle of chastity, which society expects him to respect. Havoc ensues, and order is restored in a variety of ways that have to do with the man's marital status, the woman's social rank, the degree of force he used in an endeavor to possess her, and the outcome of his entreaties.

Besides the male antagonist and the female protagonist, these dramas usually involve a third lead character, the young woman's guardian or fiancé, who seeks to avenge the dishonor into which he and the young lady have fallen as a result of the antagonist's actions.

One group of plays concerns a lustful overlord who tries to take a peasant girl against her will. He wickedly neglects his obligations toward his social inferiors and disrespects their rights; instead, he insists on the privileges to which, in his misguided opinion, he is entitled by virtue of his seigneurial rank. Many of these plays are set in medieval Castile, a kingdom that frowned on the droit du seigneur (a customary practice in other European kingdoms). However, the noble-born antagonist in these dramas behaves as if he were a feudal lord and earnestly believes that he has the right to take the peasant girl to his bed whenever he pleases, even on her wedding night. Needless to say, it never crosses his mind to marry her. He has inherited vertical honor but fails to abide by noblesse oblige; in effect, he embodies false honor.

The nobleman has ruptured the tranquility and the dignity of the villeins' lives. He expects them to accept his intrusion with resignation and to play the role of subservient feudal vassals. To the contrary, they react strongly. Although they tolerate other manifestations of his abusive personality, they refuse to condone his sexual abuse of their women, for they are as protective of their family honor as he would be, should a man assault a woman of his household. The nobleman and the peasants live worlds apart in all respects except honor, an attribute that the peasants ardently defend and that the nobleman considers exclusively his. His incomprehension of their inherent sense of dignity explains why he is genuinely perplexed and greatly angered when the peasants seek to avenge their dishonor. In his mind, they are usurping his prerogative, and he sees only that the old feudal order (which was never as strong in Castile as elsewhere in Europe) is crumbling to pieces beneath his very eyes. Wondering what the world has come to, he dies unrepentant, for he cannot understand the magnitude of his folly.

Despite the fact that the wronged villein often kills or instigates the slaying of the nobleman, these plays were not intended to foment social revolution. The masses are not rebelling against the nobility, nor do they aspire to social equality. While they are proud of their Old Christian stock and suspect the urban nobility of "tainted" ancestry, they accept the hierarchical structure of society and respect the vertical honor that a true noble possesses. What they do not accept is a nobleman who neglects the obligations incumbent on him, who fails to play his God-given roles as he should.

The nobleman has placed his own desires before the well-being of other individuals and of society as a whole. The punishment the peasants often exact serves to remove all traces of the negative individualism that has upset their lives and that threatens to throw into turmoil the harmony governing their relations with each other and with all other members of society.

A fourth protagonist in these dramas is the just king, who usually appears on the scene in the last act. If he did not personally order the nobleman's execution, he sanctions the act of justice that the villein has committed; without the king's stamp of approval, the villein might be accused of having overstepped his bounds. Once the king formally ratifies this unusual deed, the peasant and his family can resume their peaceful lives. Furthermore, the monarch then honors them in some way: he may give the wronged girl a dowry or bestow a title on a member of her family. His sense of justice and his magnanimity serve the important function of strengthening the bonds between himself and the peasants, bonds that were crucial in maintaining the idealized society that playwrights strove to present.

Two of Lope de Vega's most popular dramas, *Fuenteovejuna* and *El mejor alcalde, el rey*, are loosely based on historical fact and treat tyrannical noblemen who abduct peasant girls on their wedding days. The disruption of the marriage festivities symbolizes harmony thrown into chaos; order and justice will prevail only with the deaths of these two evildoers.

Fuenteovejuna takes place in Castile during the reign of Fernando and Isabel. The antagonist, the Commander of the religious-military Order of Calatrava, is a tragic travesty of a Christian knight. A libertine, he has already enjoyed the favors of many girls in the village of Fuenteovejuna. He believes that he honors them, and he cannot understand why the villagers think otherwise. Therein lie his tragic flaws: unrestrained lust and the failure to comprehend the peasants' sense of dignity, which lead him inexorably to his demise.

As the story opens, the Commander has set his sights on Laurencia. The animal imagery he employs underscores the nature of his intentions: he is the wolf (*lobo*); she, the lamb (*oveja*, a word that is doubly significant since she lives in the village of "Fuenteovejuna"); and her father Esteban, the shepherd (*pastor*). The Commander's arts of persuasion have not ensnared Laurencia, so he has her forcibly seized at her wedding feast. He also orders her bridegroom Frondoso arrested for having challenged him. When Esteban, who is the mayor of Fuenteovejuna, defends Frondoso's action, the Commander strips him of his staff and beats him with it. Esteban bears his humiliation and pain with resignation. He will submit to the Commander's seigneurial authority in all matters except the honor of his family.

When the Commander leaves to join Laurencia, Esteban summons the town council and points out that the Commander has wronged every member present. Inspired to do something about their plight, they swear to deliver a complaint to the King. At that very moment, the disheveled Laurencia enters the room. She has escaped after a fierce struggle and vehemently urges them to do more than simply talk. She insultingly calls them sheep and tells them that their docility makes them truly worthy of living in Fuenteovejuna. As her marriage was not consummated, she reminds her father Esteban, it is incumbent on him, as her custodian, to avenge her dishonor. If he delays, she intends to act alone and will lead the other dishonored women of the village against the Commander.

Laurencia's words have their desired effect. Ashamed that she has accused them of cowardice, the villagers revolt against the Commander and slay him, in spite of the fact that he released Frondoso in an effort to pacify them.[2]

Apprised of the situation, the King sends a judge to interrogate the villagers. The judge proceeds to torture some three hundred of them, but none will reveal (if indeed they know) which one killed the Commander. Instead, each and every villager replies that Fuenteovejuan slew him. The King does not approve of the Commander's execution, which he calls a grave crime. The collective nature of the villeins' act of justice, however, rules out punishing any or all of the villagers, and he has no choice but to pardon them all.

Because Laurencia successfully defended herself against the Commander's sexual attack, she is able to return to Frondoso; presumably, they will live happily and peacefully under the benevolent authority of the new commander whom the King will soon appoint.

El mejor alcalde, el rey, set in twelfth-century Galicia, incorporates two interrelated plots: the abduction of the peasant girl Elvira and the struggle for power between Don Tello, her feudal abductor, and Alfonso VII of Castile and León, the titular sovereign of Galicia. Sancho, Elvira's fiancé, complains to the King about the haughty and tyrannical Tello, a nobleman who makes and breaks laws at will and who has no reason to fear the King. In an attempt to impose his authority on his disobedient subject, the King writes him to free Elvira. Tello disregards the letter, and the King decides to take harsher measures. Since a just king (*rey*) is the best possible mayor (*mejor alcalde*), he vows to act as an exemplary upholder of the law and to bring Tello to justice. In a personal confrontation with him, the King forces him to marry Elvira (an indication that Tello had raped her). The King then executes him for insubordination and bequeaths half of his estate to Elvira. Now a wealthy widow, she is free to marry her beloved Sancho.

Pedro Calderón de la Barca also wrote of the impassioned nobleman versus the honorable villein in his famous play *El alcalde de Zalamea*. What makes this drama particularly special is the depth of character with which Calderón portrays Pedro Crespo, the peasant protagonist.

Pedro Crespo, the reader may recall, is a dignified, virtuous, and wealthy villein who enjoys an enviable reputation in his town of Zalamea. He is proud of his Old Christian heritage and is content, unlike his son, to reside in the countryside. Crespo's antagonist is the noble Captain Álvaro, who is billeted in Crespo's house. Álvaro has heard of the beauty of Isabel, Crespo's daughter. Hoping to seduce her, he gains entry into the room where Crespo has tried to keep her hidden from his lecherous gaze. Crespo angrily challenges him, at which point Álvaro's commanding officer, the crusty but kindhearted Don Lope, makes his entrance. Lope prevents Crespo from harming Álvaro and asks the latter to find lodging in another house.

As Lope and Crespo come from different worlds, each is initially distrustful of the other. Had Lope not intervened, Crespo complains to him, he would have killed Álvaro for jeopardizing his reputation. Lope replies that abuses such as Álvaro's are the burdens that peasants must bear. Crespo then explains to Lope exactly what honor means to him. In this oft-quoted passage, Crespo declares that he will bear financial burdens if need be, but he will not give up his reputation for any man. He will give his worldly possessions and his life to the King if he must, but his honor is the patrimony of his soul, which belongs only to God:

> Al Rey la hacienda y la vida
> Se ha de dar; pero el honor
> Es patrimonio del alma,
> Y el alma sólo es de Dios.[3]

God has endowed him with honor-dignity, which his virtuous conduct has enhanced. Moreover, he has rightly earned his peers' esteem. If another man unjustly tarnishes his reputation,

Crespo will seek to restore it to its pristine state, for duty obliges him to protect what God has given him and what he has long striven to attain.

Astonished at Crespo's wisdom and sense of honor, Lope concedes that he is right. Lope is beginning to respect Crespo for personifying the very attributes he himself prizes so highly. Unfortunately for Crespo, however, Lope soon departs, and Álvaro then sends his soldiers to abduct Isabel. Crespo pursues them, but the soldiers overpower him, tie him to a tree, and rape Isabel, whom they later abandon.

Poor Isabel is caught in the horns of a dilemma. If she returns home, her presence will compound her father's dishonor; besides, she fears that he will kill her. Should she not go home, on the other hand, her family will likewise incur further dishonor, for people will conclude that she willingly yielded to Álvaro. As she is wandering dazed and confused through the woods, she finds her father and unties him. He quickly assures her that he has no intention of murdering her, and the two head for Zalamea.

Knowing that public vengeance would broadcast his dishonor, Crespo plans to kill Álvaro in secret. When he and Isabel arrive home, however, he learns that the townsfolk have elected him mayor. This honor, ironically, threatens to increase his dishonor, for his new mayoral role must take precedence over his paternal role of avenger. Rather than resort to secret vengeance, he must now arrest Álvaro and bring him to trial, even if proceeding legally means disclosing his shame.

Before carrying out his plan, however, Crespo pleads with Álvaro to marry Isabel. He stresses his good reputation and offers him his riches if only he will wed the girl whom he wronged. Many readers express disappointment that Crespo humbles himself before the wicked Captain. Yet so strong is his concern for his good name that he will go to any length to avoid publicizing the rape. Álvaro, nonetheless, is as disdainful of villeins as was the Commander in *Fuenteovejuna*, and he refuses to consider Crespo's offer.

Unable to settle the matter amicably, Crespo orders Álvaro

seized and convinces Isabel to sign a formal complaint against him. Lope is indignant that Crespo has detained the Captain. After all, he asks, what jurisdiction do the civil authorities have over a military man? The King now appears and orders Crespo to hand over the prisoner, but when they enter the cell, they find Álvaro garroted.

Don Lope is less appalled at Álvaro's death than at the manner in which he was killed. Álvaro, he claims, should have been beheaded, a method of execution befitting his military rank. Crespo responds that the local hangman never did master the technique of beheading. The King sides with Crespo in this dispute: justice is justice, no matter how it was carried out. Crespo has adhered to the spirit of the law; that he did not conform to its letter should not be held against him. The King then names him mayor for life, an honor that partially compensates for the publicity surrounding his dishonor.

With Álvaro's death, order is restored to Zalamea and its inhabitants. Crespo has fared better than he had expected, and Isabel will enter a convent as the bride of a Husband Who will not look disdainfully on her humble origins and her dishonor.[4]

A variant of the honor-versus-illicit passion theme concerns a sovereign who attempts to seduce a noble-born, unmarried young lady. (Rarely does a monarch seek to wrong a peasant girl.) In the dramas we have just seen, the king protagonist plays his social role as he should: he is wise and just, and he honors his subjects. In these plays, however, passion so deters him from his sense of duty that he momentarily loses sight of his role and dishonors his loyal, noble subjects.

In several of these dramas, the king or prince is unhappily married. This circumstance somewhat mitigates his consuming passion and makes the reader feel slightly more sympathetic to him than to the wicked, arrogant overlord whose sole reason for wronging the peasant girl was lust. Notwithstanding the reasons behind the royal-born antagonist's interest in the young woman, nevertheless, his sexual aggressiveness dishonors her and her male guardian, who is often his confidant. Torn between the opposing duties to his ruler and to his daughter or sister, the guardian decides, as he must, that loyalty to his monarch supercedes every consideration *but honor*. He cannot give his tacit approval to an illicit relationship, however exalted the would-be seducer's rank.

How can the guardian resolve his predicament? If the seducer were unmarried and noble-born, he could try to coerce him into marrying the young lady; should the nobleman refuse, he might kill him in vengeance. But this seducer type is royal-born and usually married; even if he were single, the guardian could not place demands on him. Besides, a king or prince is traditionally immune from vengeance. The murder of a sexually abusive monarch would have severely ruptured the structure of society, for his authority was considered divine in origin; therefore, vengeance would be considered an affront to God and to society. Moreover, the sovereign, on whom the nobility depended for its social status and its privileges, symbolized honor, and one could not kill the font of honor in the name of honor. As a result, few wronged noblemen characters resort to regicide, a controversial solution appearing only in plays that are not set in Spain and in which the monarch's tyranny extends to matters other than the merely sexual.

The antagonist's royal blood, then, normally bars a nobleman from actively righting his dishonor. Impotent in the face of circumstances beyond his control, he must try to forestall the lustful king or prince. Sometimes he hides the young lady in the country. He may hastily wed her to her beloved. As a last resort, he may even try to slay her in order to save their family's reputation and to spare her the ignominy of surrendering to the antagonist against her will.

Fortunately, most monarchs come to their senses and realize in the nick of time that passion has prevented them from behaving dutifully. Repentant, they discard their negative individualism and resume the social role they had temporarily abandoned; once again, they rule justly and wisely.

As in the case of those dramas involving lustful noblemen, playwrights criticize neither the monarchy in general nor the social system responsible for the sovereign's exalted position. Rather, they portray a particular king or prince who has violated the very ideals he has sworn to uphold. His individualistic and aberrant behavior has provoked conflict and has threatened to weaken the bonds linking him with his subjects. His remorse signals an end to the chaos he has created and a restoration of order and harmony.

Vélez de Guevara's *El diablo está en Cantillana* is one of the few humorous renditions of this potentially tragic motif. This comedy is about the amorous adventures of the fourteenth-century King Pedro I of Castile. (Pedro frequently makes his appearance as a lead character in Golden Age theater; depending on the role he plays, he is dubbed either "the Cruel" or "the Just".) The King becomes smitten with the fiancée of his trusted friend Don Lope, and he sneaks off toward her house with the idea of seducing her. Suddenly he hears a phantom wailing in the night. Terrified, he thinks that the phantom is the Devil (*diablo*). Then he learns that Lope has donned the ghostly disguise in order to deter him! Lope's strategy works, and the King promptly desists.

Vélez de Guevara also wrote another, more serious variation on this motif, *A lo que obliga el ser rey*, which involves King Alfonso X "the Learned". According to his play, Alfonso has taken enough time away from stargazing (and law codifying) to set his sights on a young woman. After unsuccessfully pursuing her, he eventually reverts to his more successful intellectual pursuits.

Lope de Vega penned several dramas about the impassioned monarch and the innocent noble maiden, the most tragic of which is *La Estrella de Sevilla* (a play that certain critics feel is not Lope's). This drama concerns the thirteenth-century King Sancho IV and the ignominy to which he descends (despite his treatise on the virtues of a sense of shame) in an attempt to seduce Doña Estrella of Seville. He bribes a slave to gain entry into her house, whereupon her brother Don Busto spots him and tells him how difficult it is for him to believe that the King, who bestows honor, should seek to take his honor away. Nonetheless, Busto has no alternative but to let the King go, although he does slay the treacherous slave. The King feels belittled by Busto's words and plans a horrible revenge: he summons Don Sancho, Estrella's beloved, and orders him to kill a man whom he refuses to identify; this man, he claims, has done him wrong. Sancho reluctantly accedes to the King's order, but when he learns that the man is his truelove's brother, he is filled with anguish. Unaware that Busto was in fact defending his honor, Sancho carries out the King's bidding. In doing so, he sacrifices the woman he loves because Estrella, unlike several of her counterparts, cannot bring herself to marry the man who has murdered her brother.

Sancho ponders the tragic events that have enveloped him. In a revealing and introspective dialogue with Honor, he declares that he is an honorable fool who has become Honor's servant: "Honor, un necio y honrado / Viene a ser criado vuestro."[5] Honor cynically replies that he, Honor, has been dead for a thousand years, and he agrees with Sancho's assessment of himself: indeed, he was a fool for having kept his word of honor in an age when not keeping one's word is a sign of gallantry:

> ¡A mí me buscáis allá,
> Y ha mil años que estoy muerto!
> . . .
> . . . Riendo
> Me estoy: ¿palabras cumplís?
> Parecéisme majadero;
> Que es ya el no cumplir palabras
> Bizarría en este tiempo.[6]

How sad! Sancho sacrificed his individuality in order to abide by the societal code of honor, as a true *caballero* should, and he is now left with the lingering thought that perhaps he was a fool after all. The King, meanwhile, repents. In an effort to make amends for having deprived Estrella of a fiancé, he arranges for her to wed another nobleman of his court. His remorse, however, comes too late to stem the tide of suffering and tragedy that has engulfed his innocent victims: Busto died unnecessarily; Estrella must marry without love; and Sancho, grief-stricken and plagued with self-doubts, rides off alone into exile.

Guillén de Castro also wrote dramas about lustful sovereigns; what makes them particularly noteworthy are the ways in which they contrast with the plays that we have just examined.

For one thing, the Princess and the Queen in two of his plays, *Cuánto se estima el honor* and *El amor constante*, take an active role in attempting to "cure" the Prince and the King, respectively, of the "sickness" that blinds them to all else. These remarkably understanding and astute women recognize that reasons of state, not love, compelled the monarchs to unite with them, and they entreat their rivals to yield to the monarchs' amorous overtures. Once the men's passion is spent, they hope, the Prince and the King will forget the young ladies and will return to them. These young women, however, refuse to submit to their sovereigns.

The Prince of *Cuánto se estima el honor* comes to his senses after his sexual advances prompted the young lady's father, who holds his honor in the highest of esteem, to stab his daughter. Luckily, she survives and marries her beloved, and the Prince and Princess are reconciled.

The King of *El amor constante* is crueler than his princely counterpart and kills his own brother, the young woman's beloved, in an effort to possess her. So constant is her love for her dead lover that she drinks poison rather than become the King's mistress. The son whom she and her beloved had conceived out of wedlock then slays the King in revenge, accepts the crown, and gives it to the King's daughter, whom he marries. This radical solution of tyrannicide, the other novelty in several of Guillén's plays, terminates once and for all the turmoil that the sovereign's evil, passionate, and antisocial nature has engendered in his subjects' lives.

The right to resist a ruler who abused his authority was a subject of considerable debate during the Spanish Middle and Golden Ages. Several notable political theorists defended tyr-

238

annicide. Others, including the conservative Francisco de Quevedo, viewed the murder of a tyrannical king, for whatever the reason, as a disruptive, defiant act against the divinely inspired order of society; in other words, a monarch's was the only form of unprincipled and violent individualism that society must condone.

The reader will recall that Calderón de la Barca alluded to the potential for regicide in his *La vida es sueño*. King Basilio shares with Guillén's monarchs one crucial feature in common: they all rule non-Spanish kingdoms; therefore, the question of tyrannicide could be posed without unduly upsetting the social order, which the Spanish monarchy symbolized and on which it depended for its very existence.

Calderón spared Basilio's life because he was misguidedly rather than intentionally cruel; what is more, he repented his folly. Guillén de Castro's king characters, on the other hand, felt no remorse. Inordinate passion made them unjust, unreasonable, inhumane, and vindictive. Only the deaths of these individuals would restore a semblance of harmony to the lives and the society they had thrown into disorder. As for the tyrant killers, Guillén not only spares their lives but allows them to live happily ever after, an indication that he endorsed their extreme measures.

THE DISHONORED WOMAN'S QUEST FOR JUSTICE

Of all the female protagonists whom we have seen in the aforementioned plays, only one took an active role in bringing the antagonist to justice: Laurencia, who incited the villagers of Fuenteovejuna to kill the Commander. Many other unmarried heroines of Golden Age plays and short stories also seek out the men who have wronged them; these girls, however, differ from Laurencia in that they are victims of real rape or seduction. They pursue the antagonists in order to wed them, for only marriage restores the honor that the rapists or seducers have stolen from them, and only marriage restores them to their rightful place in society. These heroines temporarily defy social convention in assuming the role normally corresponding to their male guardians, but their unconventionality is forgiven when the antagonists finally agree to wed them.

A number of Golden Age tales involves rape, a particularly heinous crime that robs a woman not only of her virginity and her reputation but of her free will as well.

One play attributed to both Tirso de Molina and Lope de Vega, *El rey don Pedro en Madrid y el infanzón de Illescas*, treats the noble (*infanzón*) Don Tello's rape of the peasant girl Elvira. The girl complains to King Pedro (who in this play is portrayed as just) and beseeches him to dispense justice. The plot closely resembles Lope's *El mejor alcalde, el rey* except for the fact that the King spares Tello's life once he has won the rebellious noble's respect and has compelled him to wed Elvira. As a consequence of the King's magnanimity toward Tello, Elvira gains in honor but loses in love, for she will never be able to marry her sweetheart.[7]

Cervantes' short "exemplary" novel "La fuerza de la sangre" and Calderón's drama *No hay cosa como callar* are strikingly similar in that the young ladies are violated in the rapists' houses. After performing their evil deeds, the men hurriedly leave. Even though both women are bruised, dazed, and frightened as they prepare to head for home, they have sufficient presence of mind to take with them little mementos, which they will use in order to identify their assailants.

Doña Leocadia, the heroine of "La fuerza de la sangre", becomes pregnant as a result of the rape, and she bears a son, whom her wonderfully compassionate and unconventional parents welcome with great affection. One day, a horse kicks the little boy. A kindly old man takes him into his house to recover, and Leocadia recognizes the room where she was violated. The old man and his wife acknowledge the crucifix she offers them as proof of her misfortune, and they ask her and the child to await their son's return. When the rapist arrives home, no one reveals to him the guests' identities. Nevertheless, a mysterious force draws him to Leocadia and to his flesh and blood. Only after he falls genuinely in love with Leocardia does he learn who she and the child are, whereupon he wholeheartedly agrees to wed her and to transform his dissolute life.[8]

Unlike Leocadia, the heroine of Calderón's *No hay cosa como callar* has good reason to fear for her reputation, and she believes that there is nothing (*no hay cosa*) more crucial than to keep quiet (*callar*) about the rape she was forced to endure. That vicious crime has spelled not only dishonor and potential ostracism for her but heartbreak as well, because it has compelled her to break her engagement to her beloved. When she at last confronts her attacker, he at first refuses to marry her. She then threatens to inform his father of his ignominious deed. Concerned more for his reputation than for hers, he reluctantly weds her. Like Elvira in *El rey don Pedro*, she has redeemed her honor, but at the expense of love.

Another group of tales involves young ladies who are seduced under the promise of matrimony by ambitious bachelors who promptly discard them in order to be free or to marry wealthier, more socially prominent women. These victims of seduction may seem gullible, but they consider themselves married. They base their belief on a tradition of the Church, according to which a promise of wedlock followed by sexual intercourse constituted a valid union. The Church discouraged these informal marriages for obvious reasons: the lack of witnesses and the possibility that the man might disavow his promise (a situation that forms the basis of numerous Golden Age stories). These factors could endanger the woman's reputation, cast doubt on the legitimacy of any offspring that might have issued from the clandestine marriage, and bring into question her and/or her children's right to inherit the man's worldly possessions. Not until the Council of Trent did the Church decree that a man and woman must observe the formalities of banns and witnesses for their union to be valid. Playwrights and novelists, nonetheless, conveniently overlooked that fact and incorporated the motif of secret matrimony into their works for its dramatic potential.

One case of seduction that we have already noted appears in *Don Quijote* and involves Dorotea, alias Princess Micomicona of Guinea. This astute, ambitious peasant girl planned for the noble-born Don Fernando to bed her in order to force him into wedlock. Her scheme backfired when he abandoned her, but she chased him, cornered him, and convinced him that she was indeed his lawful wife.

Seduction tests the ingenuity of young ladies like Dorotea, a point that Lope de Vega makes in his *La prueba de los ingenios.* The social-climbing seducer in this play is about to enter a marriage of convenience with a duchess. Donning a disguise, the wronged heroine boldly follows him and becomes her rival's maid. Her cleverness pays off when her erstwhile lover recognizes her as his wife, and the Duchess is left to find herself another husband.

Tirso de Molina also penned plays of this type, many of which involve a variety of disguises and mistaken identities. His hilarious *Don Gil de las calzas verdes,* for example, concerns the travails of Doña Juana, who takes on the identity of the ficticious "Don Gil" in order to woo Doña Inés, the wealthy woman whom her lover Don Martín aspires to marry! Juana hopes to distract Inés and to snag Martín for herself, and her ruse works to perfection. As it turns out, Inés has no intention of wedding Martín, and she falls in love with Juana/Gil! Much to Inés' astonishment, Juana then discards her masculine disguise, including her green breeches (*calzas verdes*). She has outwitted Martín, who rightly blames greed for having made him abandon Juana. The fact that Martín, however, still professes to adore Inés does not trouble Juana, for a loveless marriage in her condition is better than none at all. As for the frivolous Inés, she marries a man whom she had loved before Juana/Gil entered the picture.

Calderón de la Barca uses the seduction motif in several more serious dramas, including his masterpiece *La vida es sueño.* Rosaura, the noblewoman with whom Segismundo falls in love,

242

has come to Poland in search of Segismundo's cousin, Prince Astolfo, who seduced her just as Clotaldo, her father and Segismundo's warden, had seduced her mother. Astolfo may still love her, but ambition dictates that he marry Princess Estrella, his coclaimant to the throne. Rosaura thirsts for revenge and demands that Clotaldo kill Astolfo. Clotaldo, however, faces a dilemma: not only is Astolfo royal-born, but he has also saved Clotaldo's life. Attempting to reconcile these conflicting obligations, Clotaldo weakly suggests that Rosaura enter a convent. She rejects his solution and resolves to seek vengeance herself. Once the rebellious soldiers liberate Segismundo, she enlists his support. Segismundo is torn between his word of honor to help Rosaura and his love for her. If he assists her, he loses her. If he does not, he imperils his chances for a felicitous ending to the dream of his life. Nevertheless, his sense of duty prevails, and he orders the arrogant Astolfo to marry her. Poor Estrella suddenly finds herself with neither a throne nor a fiancé, but Segismundo gallantly comes to her rescue and offers to make her his queen, an offer she accepts with delight.[9]

Perhaps the most famous Golden Age treatment of seduction is Tirso de Molina's *El burlador de Sevilla y convidado de piedra*. This play, which has spawned numerous imitations and adaptations, involves the ignoble Don Juan Tenorio and the four women whom he wronged. Strongly religious in tone, Tirso's work graphically depicts the punishment God metes out to this negative individual for having violated most of His commandments and many of society's mores.

Women are objects that Don Juan must possess and then discard. As if he were a military strategist planning the conquest of a fortress, Don Juan studies the object of his desire and notes her weaknesses. He needs not use brute strength to force her into submission since his powers of impersonation and persuasion more than suffice. He risks death each time he proceeds to take a woman to bed; yet the dangers he courts whet his appetite for more of the same. He also revels in the fame these escapades have won him, for the more he dishonors a woman, the more his reputation increases. Don Juan epitomizes the double standard of sexual behavior in that his promiscuity contributes to his sense of manliness, which in turn heightens his reputation. Don Juan himself boasts that Seville calls him *the Seducer* (*el Burlador*) and that his greatest pleasure is to seduce a woman and leave her without honor:

> Sevilla a voces me llama
> *El Burlador*, y el mayor
> Gusto que en mí puede haber
> Es burlar una mujer
> Y dejarla sin honor.[10]

Of the four young ladies whom Don Juan seduces, two are noblewomen who at different times in his life have become betrothed to him against their wishes. They have secretly invited their sweethearts to late-night rendezvous in their boudoirs. When Don Juan learns of their less-than-honorable intentions, he impersonates the men whom they were expecting. Although we may sympathize with the young ladies' quandary, they have, nonetheless, defied parental and royal authority as well as the sanctity of betrothal in agreeing to meet their true-loves. They will pay for their waywardness, for their reputations are now at stake, and they may forfeit the opportunity to wed. Nor are their beloveds entirely blameless, since only Don Juan's treachery has prevented them from illicitly making love with the ladies.

When the first of these women, the Neapolitan Doña Isabela, realizes that her beloved Don Octavio is not the man who enjoyed her favors, she rashly announces that an intruder sneaked into her bedroom. Meanwhile, Don Juan escapes to Spain, and Isabela sees that her imprudence has compounded her dishonor. She then tells the King of Naples, in whose palace she resides, that her seducer was none other than Octavio. The news angers the King because the seduction has violated the strict laws of decorum governing royal palaces. When his anger subsides, Isabela hopes, he will force Octavio to marry her. The

King orders Octavio seized, but Octavio escapes and sets sail for Spain, as will Isabela.

The second noblewoman is Doña Ana, whom the King of Castile has betrothed to Don Juan. But when the King hears of Don Juan's infamous impersonation of Octavio, he breaks Don Juan's engagement to Ana, betroths him to Isabela, and promises to give Ana's hand in marriage to Octavio. Unhappy at the prospect of marrying Octavio, Ana writes a letter inviting the Marquess of Mota, her sweetheart and Don Juan's best friend, to a tryst. Don Juan intercepts the letter and cannot resist the challenge of seducing the woman who is at once his former fiancée and his friend's secret love. Pretending to be Mota, he enters her room, but Ana realizes his deception before it is too late. Like Isabela, she cries for help. Her father Don Gonzalo rushes in, and Don Juan mortally wounds him. Unbeknownst to Don Juan, Don Gonzalo's final words have sealed his fate: Gonzalo calls him a traitor and a coward, and he vows that his furor will always follow him. After Don Juan flees, Gonzalo dies, and the King orders Mota apprehended for his murder; fortunately, Mota is eventually exonerated.

The other two wronged women, Tisbea and Aminta, are peasants whom Don Juan deceives with words of love and promises of marriage. Tisbea is extremely proud that love has hitherto not enslaved her. She most willingly yields to his embrace, whereupon he deserts her. She has always laughed at passion; now, passion has the last laugh. As for Aminta, her ambitious streak proves her undoing. She has just wed Patricio when Don Juan appears at their wedding feast. He assures her that he can arrange for her unconsummated marriage to be annulled, and he offers to wed her himself. Captivated at the prospect of marrying a nobleman, she quickly surrenders to his amorous entreaties. When she wakes up the next morning, he is gone.

The first part of the play deals with Don Juan, the seducer. The second treats the dire punishment that his defiance of God and of society has earned him. As he is wandering through the cemetary where Don Gonzalo lies buried, Don Juan reads the inscription on his tomb: "Here a most loyal cavalier awaits God's vengeance on a traitor." Knowing that the inscription refers to him, he boldly invites the stone (*piedra*) statue of Gonzalo to be his guest (*convidado*) for dinner. The statue comes to life, accepts the invitation, and reciprocates by inviting Don Juan to a ghoulish dinner at the grave site. Don Juan must accept the statue's invitation, for at stake is his dignity, to say nothing of his manliness and his reputation, which any public acknowledgment of fear would greatly diminish. Besides, Don Gonzalo has called him a coward, and he seizes the opportunity to disprove Gonzalo's defamatory (though justified) insult.

Don Juan duly joins the statue for a dinner of vipers, scorpions, and vinegar. When the meal is finished, Don Juan extends his hand to the statue as a final proof of his fearlessness. At that very moment, the statue seizes Don Juan's outstretched hand and drags him to his fiery death. Don Gonzalo has tricked the trickster who had tried to trick his daughter, and he has finally avenged his own death.

It is only fitting that God should have sent the spirit of Don Gonzalo to condemn Don Juan to the eternal flames of Hell, for Gonzalo represents all of Don Juan's victims. In treacherously deceiving them, Don Juan broke the laws God instituted to ensure social order; furthermore, he took the name of the Lord in vain for thoroughly dishonorable purposes, and he proudly challenged death itself. His end is a vivid reminder of the vengeance God wreaks on those individuals who have sinned without remorse against Him and society.

Tisbea and Aminta, in the meantime, complain to the King of Don Juan's deceptions, but an authority higher than the King has already exacted retribution. Each girl had threatened to invoke God's wrath, should Don Juan not honor his promise of marriage. God has heeded their invocations, though not in the manner they would have desired. Even if God had spared Don Juan's life, neither girl could have wed him, since marriage to one girl would have left the other dishonored. Both young women return home sadder and wiser than when Don Juan first entered their lives, and they console themselves with the knowledge that the wicked seducer has perished.

The noble-born Isabela and Ana, however, fare better than the peasant girls. Don Juan's death makes Isabela, his second fiancée, a semi-widow; she can thus marry Octavio despite the fact that Don Juan had seduced her. Having escaped his assault with her virginity intact, Ana weds Mota. Marriage restores honor to these two women, who were less responsible than the peasant girls for the dishonor that befell them.[11]

The age-old plight of the seduced girl whose lover recants his promise of marriage deeply troubled María de Zayas y Sotomayor, one of the very few female authors of the Spanish Golden Age. Zayas wrote a collection of ten short stories, *Desengaños amorosos*, in which she emphasizes how cruelly men act toward women. The unscrupulous man, she warns, lies to his victim and vows to wed her if she will give him the supreme gift of her love. Once he takes her to bed, he quickly tires of her; even worse, he gossips to his friends about her "loose" ways. Too late does she realize that she has lost her honor to a thoroughly dishonorable man.

The victims of seduction in Zayas' tales often meet with the same fate as Tisbea and Aminta, although they are far less deserving of their unfortunate lot. Belatedly undeceived about men, they have no option but to enter a convent. Zayas' lesson is plain: a woman should beware of amorous men and should never endanger her reputation for any reason whatsoever.

There is certainly nothing original about Zayas' advice. What is novel, however, is another recommendation she makes: should a woman behave unchastely and find herself abandoned, she should kill the man who made her go astray: "No seas liviana, y si lo fuiste, mata a quien te lo hizo serlo, y no mates tu honra."[12] In Zayas' mind, the man is the primary culprit of a woman's downfall;[13] therefore, he should pay for his crime with his life. Furthermore, she assures the reader, there would be fewer victims of seduction and of other offenses if all women avenged the wrongs done them: "Que yo aseguro que si todas vengaran las ofensas que reciben, . . .no hubiera tantas burladas y ofendidas."[14]

While numerous seduced female characters in Spanish Golden Age literature take an active role in righting their dishonor by convincing their seducers to marry them, wronged women seldom slay their seducers. The rare female avenger who does appear plays a most unconventional role in that she usurps the role society has given her male guardian. Disregarding a fundamental convention of the honor code, she takes the matter of vengeance into her own hands because she feels her dishonor as keenly as her guardian would, were he to discover it. Once this strong-minded individual redeems her honor, society normally forgives her two transgressions—losing her virginity and wreaking vengeance—and welcomes her back into its fold.

María de Zayas wrote several stories that treat the female avenger. One such tale, "La burlada Aminta y venganza del honor", is about Jacinto's seduction of Aminta. Unbeknownst to her at the time, Jacinto is separated from his lawful wife and lives with a woman who serves as his procuress. Poor Aminta despairs of ever finding a solution to her shame and to the social ostracism that threatens her. Then she meets Martín, an extraordinarily compassionate man who contrasts markedly with the cruelly selfish Jacinto. She and Martín fall in love, and he asks her to marry him (a most unusual proposal, considering her tainted past). However, Aminta cannot consent until she recovers her lost honor. Accordingly, she kills Jacinto and his perverse mistress, whereupon she happily marries her beloved Martín.

BANDOLERAS AND BANDOLEROS

A Golden Age variant of the woman avenger motif concerns the *bandolera*, or female bandit. She has been wronged by one or more men: her male guardian who forced her into an unwelcome betrothal, a suitor whom she rejected, or her lover.

The victim of oppression and deceit, she feels humiliated, ashamed, angered, and desperate, sentiments that impel her to forsake family and home and to become an outlaw.[15]

The *bandolera*'s initial impulse, like that of the avenging woman, is one of justice. But while the avenger solely challenged social conventions in assuming the masculine role of honor restorer, the *bandolera* defies the laws of God and society. Rage transforms her natural desire for justice into an unnatural thirst for needless revenge, for she not only wishes to avenge herself on the particular man or men who hurt her but on mankind in general. As a result, she waylays one man after another, plunders their money and jewels, and in some plays even murders them.

Because the *bandolera* carries godlessness and antisociality to an extreme, society must apprehend her. The lives of most *bandoleras* are spared, however, since they sincerely repent their heinous offenses. That these young women are pardoned might also reflect a tacit recognition on the part of their creators and of the society they portray that the ultimate blame for their criminality rests with the men who have done them wrong.[16]

Lope de Vega established the precedent of the *bandolera* as a lead character in theatrical works. One of his *bandolera* plays, *La serrana de la Vera*, concerns Doña Leonarda, an outlaw who differs from several of her literary successors in that a great deal of her dishonor is imagined, not real. The culprit of this rather contrived tale is Don Fulgencio, who hopes to win her love by telling her that her fiancé Don Carlos plans to break their engagement. Hurt and irate, she leaves home for the mountains (*serrana*), where she becomes a bandit. She encounters Carlos and refuses to believe that he still loves her and wants to wed her. She tries unsuccessfully to kill him but does succeed in murdering scores of other men. Nonetheless, she refrains from taking a distinguished nobleman's life, a compassionate act that merits her the King's pardon after the authorities finally seize her. Fulgencio confesses his treachery, and the remorseful Leonarda and her beloved Carlos then marry.

Lope's play inspired Vélez de Guevara to write his own version of the tale. Gila, the *bandolera* of his *La serrana de la Vera*, is a free-spirited, nonconformist peasant girl who shuns the thoughts of love and marriage. In an episode reminiscent of Calderón's *El alcalde de Zalamea*, the wicked Captain, vowing to seduce Gila, seeks lodging in her father's house. The father's initial suspicion and refusal to billet him, however, quickly turn to joy when the Captain shrewdly asks for her hand in marriage. To see his daughter wed to a captain, the father declares, he would gladly lodge the entire company of soldiers! Gila reluctantly agrees to marry him and, since they are now betrothed, submits to his sexual demands, whereupon he abandons her. When Gila realizes that the man whom she never wanted to wed in the first place has duped her and her father, she becomes so enraged that she publicizes her shame and announces that she herself will murder the Captain. Eventually, she tracks him down. Frightened to death, he promises to marry her, but sweet words will not assuage her anger. She kills him in revenge—and then proceeds to kill 1,999 other men! She even ambushes the King, but his exalted rank saves his life. Her own father, the mayor, disavows her as his daughter and leads the Holy Brotherhood to her hiding place, where they take her prisoner. After the King (who is not as charitable as Lope's) sentences her to death, she begs forgiveness for her sins, but she never truly repents. In her mind, she had no choice but to wreak vengeance. She even accuses her father of setting in motion the tragic chain of events that culminated in so much bloodshed: had he treated her less indulgently, discouraged her spirit of independence, and been less gullible, she claims, he would have averted the tragedy that has enveloped her and all her victims. In society's mind, however, she is fully guilty of her crimes. She could have righted her dishonor by accepting the terrified Captain's second proposal of marriage; instead, she chose the path of unjustified lawlessness, for which she must pay.

Tirso de Molina also treats the *bandolera* in two of his religious dramas, *La condesa bandolera* (also known as *La Ninfa del Cielo*) and *La Dama del olivar*. In these plays, Tirso stresses the efficacy of grace, which ultimately reconciles the errant individuals with God as well as with society.

Tirso's *bandoleras* have fallen into seduction, but they are not totally innocent (Tirso's women characters seldom are). Having become enamored of their seducers, they willingly make love to them in the hope of snaring them into marriage. Little do these young ladies know, however, that their lovers are either married or betrothed to other women. Dishonored beyond remedy, they become *bandoleras*, but they are unable to kill the men who wronged them. Eventually, both *bandoleras* repent; shortly afterward, one is accidently killed by an arrow her lover's wife had aimed at a deer, and the other enters a convent. As for the two seducers, heavenly grace also descends on them, and they swear to amend their lascivious ways and to return to their wife and fiancée, respectively.

One of the best-known dramas involving a *bandolera* and her male counterpart, the *bandolero*, is Mira de Amescua's *El esclavo del demonio*. Mira based this play on a medieval Portuguese legend about a monk who became a slave of the Devil in order to win a woman's sexual favors.

The *bandolera* is Lisarda, whose father urges her to wed a man whom he has chosen for her. She adamantly refuses and insists, instead, on the right to wed her beloved Don Diego, despite the fact that he slew her brother in a duel and consequently is her father's sworn enemy. Lisarda places love before honor and obedience, the first of several steps leading to her eventual undoing. Enraged at her disobedience, her father hurls her a malediction in which he prays for the worst fate imaginable to befall her—social ostracism. Would to God, he curses, that she never marry, that she live a life of infamy, that she die poor, and that people abhor her. Would to God, he continues, that this wayward woman be destroyed, that people call her wicked, and that there be nothing as evil in all the world as her life:

Plega a Dios, inobediente,
Que casada no te veas,
Que vivas infamemente,
Que mueras pobre y que seas
Aborrecible a la gente.
Plega a Dios que, destruída
Como una mujer perdida,
Te llamen facinerosa,
Y en el mundo no haya cosa
Tan mala como tu vida.[17]

Smarting from these harsh words, Lisarda writes Diego to rescue her from her tyrannical father. At the duly appointed hour, Diego is about to climb the ladder to her bedroom when Fray Gil, the monk, appears and dissuades him from further dishonoring Lisarda's family. No sooner does Diego reluctantly depart than Gil, overcome by the temptation the ladder poses, climbs into her room. Lisarda thinks that he is Diego and lets him make love to her. She quickly sees her mistake and plunges into a state of despair. When Gil tells her that Diego sent him to dishonor her father even more, Lisarda gives credence to his lie. She feels betrayed by Diego, and she has nowhere to turn. No longer a virgin, she cannot remain home. Alienated from her world, she firmly believes that she is destined to fulfill her father's malediction. She interprets her plight as fitting punishment for having rebelled against her father (although modern readers may view her as the victim of paternal oppression and of clerical deceit).

As for the saintly-turned-wicked Gil, he too is filled with despair, for he believes that this one act of lust and treachery has irrevocably denied him any chance of eternal salvation. Since he sees himself estranged from God and condemned to Hell, he has nothing to lose, he feels, in proceeding to enjoy all the illicit pleasures the world has to offer him.

Alienation and despair drive Lisarda and Gil to a life of violent crime. Together, they become *bandoleros* and rob many an innocent passer-by. One day, they waylay Lisarda's father and sister. The father does not recognize his disguised daughter, nor does she reveal her identity. She initially intends to kill them but suddenly has a change of heart and takes only their jewels, not their lives. She then begs her father's forgiveness, which he grants her. It may seem ironic that he would forgive an "unknown" highwaywoman, on the one hand, and would damn his own daughter, on the other. His two opposite reactions, however, are indicative of his priorities: in his opinion, filial disobedience threatens the social order he represents far more than does banditry.

Gil, in the meantime, spots Lisarda's beautiful sister and lusts for her. He willingly sells his soul to Angelio, the Devil, in return for Angelio's help in seducing her. Angelio tricks him into assuming that he has slept with her, and when she appears to him in a vision, he realizes that the girl in bed with him was but a phantom. Gil now understands the folly of putting one's trust in the Devil, for Angelio deceived him, as he does all his disciples. Accordingly, Gil forswears him, wills to become God's slave, and resumes his saintly life.

In contrast to Gil, Lisarda never reaches the depths of evil. She has spared her family members and has given their jewels to a poor shepherdess whom Gil had seduced. Nevertheless, she still burns with the desire to avenge herself on Diego, the man who she falsely believes is responsible for her downfall. When she finally meets up with him, she resolves to slay him, but divine grace moves her to refrain from violence, at which point she too renounces wickedness and becomes the slave of God. She then takes on the guise of a real slave and offers her services to her father, who still does not recognize her. This act of submission to paternal authority signifies the obedience of a once-rebellious individual to the dictates of family and, by extension, of society.[18]

When Lisarda encounters Diego for a second time, all traces of her former rage have disappeared. He persuades her of his innocence, and shortly thereafter she dies in peace. Her reconciliation with the social order has prepared her soul for reconciliation with the divine. Only now that Lisarda is dead does her father realize that the highwaywoman and the slave were his daughter. He feels no remorse for having cursed her; to the contrary, he considers his malediction a blessing in disguise, for it ultimately paved the way for her salvation.

Fray Gil is one of many *bandoleros* who appear in Golden Age drama, especially in religious plays. The *bandolero*, like the *bandolera*, defies the laws of God and society and follows only his own instincts. He lives in the isolated woods or mountains, where he easily preys on travelers.

The *bandolero* should not be confused with the Robin Hood type, who fights social injustice by taking from the rich to give to the poor, for what the *bandolero* takes from the rich, he keeps for himself. He is devoid of the altruism that justifies a Robin Hood's seemingly antisocial methods. While a Robin Hood is viewed as a positive individual in a negative world, the *bandolero* is the reverse—a negative individual in conflict with a world seen as essentially positive.[19]

The *bandolero* shares with the seducer and the rapist an inordinately vindictive, proud, willful, and passionate nature. He lusts for women as much as for vengeance, and in the course of his violent life he violates the codes and institutions society holds dear: family, honor, and chastity. Unmarried women are not safe in his presence; some *bandolero* characters even attempt to take to their beds young ladies who are later revealed to be their sisters, and only because of a fortuitous turn of events is incest narrowly averted.

The *bandolero*, like his female counterpart, has committed crimes against society and has sinned against God. Society usually apprehends him in the end and sentences him to death, but God is more merciful. He will not condemn a sinner to eternal damnation without offering him His grace and, thereby, the chance for salvation. Most *bandoleros* accept God's gift and repent their rebelliousness. Society decrees that they must die in order to restore order to their victims' lives. God, however, is satisfied with the sincerity of their conversions and sentences their souls to spend eternity with Him.[20]

Calderón de la Barca wrote several dramas about violent, antisocial individuals, like Segismundo, who have been wronged by their tyrannical fathers. Deprived of paternal affection and guidance, factors that play such a crucial role in the socialization of children, these characters epitomize unbridled passion and lawlessness. Victimized, they become *bandoleros* and in turn victimize others. One such play, *Las tres justicias en una*, concerns the remorseless Don Lope, a *bandolero* who goes to his grave in the belief that the man and woman who raised him are his natural parents. In reality, however, his "mother" Blanca had concealed from his "father" Lope the Elder the news about their newborn son's death and had deceived him into thinking that Lope the Younger, her unmarried sister's son, was their own.

Lope's "parents" are partially to blame for his violent temperment. Blanca overindulges him, and Lope the Elder treats him coldly; indeed, young Lope is convinced that his "father" hates him.

One day, Lope tries to seduce a young woman. Don Mendo, her father, rushes in to kill him but then mysteriously loses his resolve. We know, although on a conscious level Mendo does not, that the young lady is Lope's half sister. Mendo, it is later revealed, had seduced, impregnated, and then abandoned Lope's natural mother, after which he married another woman, the young lady's mother.

No sooner does Lope desist from pursuing Mendo's daughter than he meets another girl. This time he succeeds in deflowering her and immediately afterward leaves her; what is more, he kills her brother. Both crimes force him to flee and become a *bandolero*. Lope the Elder persuades the King to pardon him, and he returns home. In a not unusual moment of anger, however, he strikes his "father" and leaves home a second time. Lope the Elder feels thoroughly dishonored and ashamed, and he implores the King to bring the young man to justice. The King orders Mendo to apprehend him, and when Mendo finally tracks him down, he again feels inexplicable compassion for the young miscreant and consequently helps him to evade the authorities.

Blanca, meanwhile, confesses to the King what she had hidden for so many years. The King concludes that three wrongs in all have been committed: Mendo had seduced Blanca's sister (Lope's natural mother), Blanca had deceived Lope the Elder, and young Lope has dishonored his "father". Once Lope is eventually captured, the King orders his execution, thus carrying out three acts of justice in one: grief is the punishment he metes out to Blanca and to Mendo, who belatedly learns that Lope was his son; death is the sentence he imposes on Lope for having rebelled against the laws of society.[21]

Unrestrained passion, which often takes the form of sexual assaults on young women, led *bandoleros* like Lope to throw into turmoil the peaceful lives of other people and the orderliness of society. With the exception of Fray Gil, all of them perished in order to satisfy the demands of earthly justice. In society's opinion, the fact that many of these *bandoleros*— and *bandoleras*—were victims of misguided or oppressive fathers did not mitigate their guilt. God offered them the chance of redemption, an offer that most *bandoleros* gratefully accepted, but temporal justice blinded itself to the circumstances that divine justice might have deemed extenuating.

The only form of victimization that society considers a justifiable cause for a man's descent into criminality is the sexual abuse of his wife, fiancée, daughter, or sister, a wicked deed that spurs him to seek revenge. Even though his methods exceed the limits that society imposes on an avenger, society spares his life. In doing so, it tacitly recognizes that his particular circumstances left him with no other alternative.

The second part of Juan Ruiz de Alarcón's *El tejedor de Segovia* exemplifies the extent to which society, as portrayed in Golden Age literature, tolerates the excesses of this kind of male victim-turned-*bandolero*. The play concerns Don Fernando, whose father was falsely accused of dealing with the Moors and was executed. Fearing that the same fate would befall him, Fernando climbed down the social ladder and assumed the identity of Pedro, the weaver (*tejedor*) of Segovia. Pedro has played his new role uneventfully until the appearance of the Count, who tries to force Pedro's wife Teodora against her will. Hearing the commotion, Pedro rushes in to protect her, strikes the Count, and slays his accomplice. The Count typifies the arrogant nobleman who cannot comprehend why a "commoner" would defend his honor. Pedro is jailed for his "temerity" but manages to escape. Eventually, he and Teodora join a group of *bandoleros*, and he becomes a notorious highwayman. Although he thirsts for vengeance against a world that, in his mind, has wronged him twice, he is not an unjust man. When his comrades seize a bailiff, for example, he refuses to let them kill him because he identifies with him: both men, in his opinion, embody justice; what differentiates them is that the bailiff administers justice within the law, whereas Pedro operates outside the law.

Pedro's hatred of the Count doubles when he learns that the Count had seduced his sister, whom Pedro had long given up for dead. The Count has lived with her for seven years but refuses to wed her. Now Pedro has another reason to avenge himself on his enemy. When Pedro finally apprehends him, he compels him to marry his sister, and then he mortally wounds him for having attempted to dishonor Teodora. In his dying breath, the Count confesses that he and his father had been responsible for the death of Fernando/Pedro's father, an admission that makes Pedro's act all the more justifiable. Like the King in *Las tres justicias en una*, Pedro has effectively administered three acts of justice with one fatal blow.

The King pardons Pedro for having engaged in a life of banditry, and he ratifies the Count's death. Moreover, he publicly acknowledges that Fernando/Pedro's father was not a traitor after all. The King's intervention vindicates Pedro, puts an end to the conflict in which he has lived with society, and enables him to resume his rightful role as the noble Don Fernando.

ENDNOTES

[1] Fernando de Rojas, *La Celestina*, Act IV, ed. J. Cejador y Frauca, 9th ed. (Madrid: Espasa-Calpe; CC, 1968), I, 178–179.

[2] Lope de Vega's *Las famosas asturianas* also concerns a woman who incites the villagers to wreak vengeance on the men who have wronged her; the story is based on an historical episode in which one hundred Leonese damsels were sent against their will as tribute to the Moors. This particular young lady, however, rebels and demands that her beloved and his soldiers confront the Moors in battle. He and his men then rout their enemies, and the couple is able to marry.

[3] Pedro Calderón de la Barca, *El alcalde de Zalamea*, Act I, in *Obras completas*, ed. A. Valbuena Briones, 5th ed. (Madrid: Aguilar, 1969), I, 549.

[4] Lope de Vega also wrote a version of *El alcalde de Zalamea*; his play, however, involves two daughters and two captains. The two young ladies, who are flirtatious social climbers, allow the captains to seduce them in the hope of marrying them. When Crespo realizes that he has been dishonored, he forces the captains to wed his daughters and then executes the young men; as for the daughters, they repair to a convent to atone for their waywardness.

[5] Lope de Vega (attributed to), *La Estrella de Sevilla*, Act III, in *Obras escogidas*, ed. F.C. Sainz de Robles, 5th ed. (Madrid: Aguilar, 1966), I, 563.

[6] Ibid.

[7] Agustín Moreto used *El rey don Pedro en Madrid* as the source for his *El valiente justiciero*.

[8] Guillén de Castro recast Cervantes' "La fuerza de la sangre" in a play bearing the same title; Guillén's play is similar in plot to Cervantes' tale except for the fact that two women are raped, not one.

[9] In Calderón's *La niña de Gómez Arias*, which also involves the seduction motif, the Queen forces the seducer to marry his victim and then has him executed for treason. Calderón's model for this play was an identically entitled play by Vélez de Guevara; in Vélez' play, however, the traitor's life is spared.

[10] Tirso de Molina, *El burlador de Sevilla y convidado de piedra*, Act II, in *Obras dramáticas completas*, ed. B. de los Ríos, 2nd ed. (Madrid: Aguilar, 1962), II, 656.

[11] Tirso de Molina's third part of his *Santa Juana* series is similar in plot to *El burlador* except for the fact that the seducer marries the one noblewoman whom he seduced. *El burlador*, in turn, was the source of numerous literary works, including Antonio de Zamora's *No hay plazo que no se cumpla ni deuda que no se pague, y convidado de piedra* (in which Don Juan begs for mercy and is saved), Molière's *Dom Juan ou le Festin de Pierre*, Goldoni's *Don Giovanni Tenorio*, the libretto that Lorenzo da Ponte wrote for Mozart's *Don Giovanni*, Lord Byron's *Don Juan*, José Zorrilla's *Don Juan Tenorio*, and George Bernard Shaw's *Man and Superman*.

[12] María de Zayas y Sotomayor, "La inocencia castigada," in *Novelas completas*, ed. M. Martínez del Portal (Barcelona: Bruguera, 1973), p. 407.

[13] The views that María de Zayas presents in *Desengaños amorosos* are strik-

ingly similar to those expressed in a poem by the prominent seventeenth-century Mexican nun and writer Sor Juana Inés de la Cruz: men are foolish, declares Sor Juana, to accuse women without reason, for they fail to see that they themselves are the cause of what they censure: "Hombres necios que acusáis / A la mujer sin razón, / Sin ver que sois la ocasión / De lo mismo que culpáis." This poem is entitled "Arguye de inconsecuentes el gusto y la censura de los hombres que en las mujeres acusan lo que causan" [in Sor Juana's *Obras completas*, ed. F. Monterde, 4th ed. (Mexico City: Porrúa, 1977), p. 109].

[14] María de Zayas, "La más infame venganza," in *Novelas completas*, p. 392.

[15] A most detailed study on the *bandolera* is M. McKendrick's *Woman and Society in the Spanish Drama of the Golden Age: A Study of the Mujer Varonil*, espec. Ch. 4: "The *bandolera*."

[16] See A.A. Parker's "Santos y bandoleros en el teatro español del Siglo de Oro" for a study on the chain of causality linking the *bandolera*'s childhood to her descent into criminality.

[17] Mira de Amescua, *El esclavo del demonio*, Act I, in his *Teatro*, ed. A. Valbuena Prat (Madrid: Espasa-Calpe; CC, 1960), I, 12.

[18] See A.A. Parker's "Santos y bandoleros."

Attributed to Tirso de Molina is another famous play about a holy man-turned-*bandolero*, *El condenado por desconfiado*. Unlike Fray Gil, however, the antagonist of this play despairs of salvation and is condemned, like Don Juan, to the fires of Hell.

[19] One *bandolero* who bridges the gap between a Robin Hood type and the typical *bandoleros* of Golden Age theater is Roque Guinart, the outlaw who appears in Pt. II of *Don Quijote*. He is just and compassionate in his own way, he declares to Don Quijote, but the desire to avenge a wrong done him years before made him become a public, professional avenger.

[20] See A.A. Parker's "Santos y bandoleros" for a detailed study about *bandolero* characters in Golden Age literature.

[21] Another of Calderón's plays about individuals whose fathers have wronged them is *La devoción de la Cruz*, a religious drama involving a brother and sister who become *bandoleros* and who subsequently repent. A.A. Parker explores this theme of conflict between parents and children in his "The Father-Son Conflict in the Drama of Calderón."

13

Women, Wedlock, and the Threat of Adultery

Established society gave its young women, nobles and commoners alike, the choice between two reputable ways of life: they could marry, or they could enter a convent.

Medieval and Golden Age literature rarely treats the devout girl who heeds the calling of religious life; by its very nature, her story would lack the conflict and drama so essential to fiction. Literary works do, however, make frequent references to the fact that young ladies often became nuns for reasons other than religious vocation. As we noted in the last chapter, the convent offered refuge to a victim of rape or seduction. There, she could at least live in peace with a Husband Who, unlike a secular husband, would forgive her unfortunate past.

The plight of the young, unwilling novice appears in traditional, anonymous Spanish poems, which were sometimes written in the first person as if by the girl herself. These poems give us no concrete motive for her dilemma, but a few insinuate that her parents have objected to her sweetheart. She bemoans her fate and berates her mother and father for condemning her to live without love. One girl, for example, laments the irony of her predicament: now that she knows that a cavalier loves her, her parents have placed her in a convent. My God, she cries, what a grave thing!:

> ¿Ahora que sé de amor me metéis monja?
> ¡Ay, Dios, qué grave cosa!
> Ahora que sé de amor de caballero,
> Ahora me metéis monja en el monasterio.
> ¡Ay, Dios, qué grave cosa![1]

The repetition of the word *"ahora"* 'now' underscores the despair she feels at the thought that she will never experience the *caballero*'s love. Another young lady tells her parents that she does not want to be a nun, for she is prone to falling in love. She begs them to let her enjoy pleasure and happiness:

> No quiero ser monja, no,
> Que niña enamoradica só.
> Dejadme con mi placer,
> Con mi placer y alegría.[2]

Young women who refused to enter a convent and who found it impossible to wed their trueloves would have had to adopt such disreputable life-styles as prostitution and banditry. Prostitutes occupied a marginal place vis à vis the mainstream society in which they performed their services. *Bandoleras,* as we have seen, operated outside the law and preyed on established society.

THE UNCONVENTIONAL MAIDEN'S DISDAIN OF MARRIAGE

Literature also portrays the chaste, unmarried woman who shuns all the aforementioned ways of life. She has no desire to become a nun, a prostitute, or a *bandolera*. What is more, she avidly rejects any thought of love and all proposals of marriage. She insists on her right to remain single because she views matrimony as a form of tyranny. She cherishes her independence and vows never to surrender it to any man.

This type of woman appears frequently, though not exclusively, in Golden Age theater.[3] Reflecting the attitudes of their times, playwrights did not sympathize with her liberated, nonconformist ideas about love and marriage. In their opinion, her refusal to wed (or to enter religious life) constituted an act of rebellion against the divine, the natural, and the social orders. Unlike nuns, who sublimate their sexuality as a sacrifice to God,

261

this aloof (*esquiva*) young lady has opted to suppress her sexuality for the wrong reasons. She is not sincerely devout and altruistic but selfish, haughty, disdainful, and vain—negative traits that cannot go unpunished. Since she has not defied the laws of morality, dramatists do not let her perish; they do, nonetheless, make her fall in love in spite of herself, a cruel form of punishment, indeed! She struggles against love, but to no avail, for love gradually wears down her resistance. She now sees the light of conventional wisdom and finally comprehends that she only deceived herself into assuming that she could disregard her reputation and live without a man. Eventually, she resigns herself to domesticity and even to the fate of subservience she had so zealously avoided. More often than not, she weds, though not always to the man who has stolen her heart.

Lope de Vega penned a number of plays about aloof women characters. The reader may recall two of these plays, *El perro del hortelano* and *La vengadora de las mujeres*, which concern highborn women whose desire to remain single vanishes when they become enamored of and marry their social inferiors (real and apparent, respectively). In another play, *Los melindres de Belisa*, the haughty, spoiled (*melindres*) Belisa and her widowed mother *both* fall in love with a man who they believe is a slave. Really a prince in disguise, he rejects the two rivals for his affection and weds his beloved. Poor Belisa ends up married to a man whom she does not love, a just form of retribution, she sadly acknowledges, for having snubbed countless other suitors.

Calderón de la Barca also wrote a play, *Guárdate del agua mansa*, in which the haughtily nonconformist Eugenia winds up having to marry a man whom she despises. Eugenia is as rebellious a daughter as her sister Clara is obedient. She does not give a fig for what people think or say. Clara, on the other hand, recognizes the value of appearances, which are worth more in her and society's estimation than virtue unnoticed. It is better to be bad and appear good, she says, than to be good and appear bad: ". . . Y no es tan malo / No ser bueno y parecerlo, / Como serlo y no mostrarlo."[4] Their father, a greedy *indiano* (a man of dubious origins who has amassed a fortune in the New World), urges Eugenia to marry the boorish, illiterate, but "*limpio*" Don Toribio. Eugenia refuses. In the meantime, Clara believes that Don Félix, the man whom she hopes to wed, loves Eugenia. Beware (*guárdate*) of calm water (*agua mansa*), warns the title of this play, for a storm will make it churn and engulf its victims. Jealousy transforms the seemingly placid, gentle Clara into a troublemaker who almost ruins her sister's reputation as well as her own. Forging Eugenia's signature, she writes Félix to meet her in her sister's bedroom. He gladly does her bidding but is discovered leaving the room. When he finally unravels the sisters' identities, he chooses to marry Clara and thus salvages her good name. As for Eugenia, only now that her reputation is compromised does she learn its true importance. Fearful that it will suffer permanent injury, she humbles herself and begs Toribio to wed her. Now it is his turn to refuse her, since she rejected him and insulted him to his face. Fortunately for her reputation, however, another suitor graciously asks for her hand. Under the circumstances, she has no alternative but to accept his proposal.

Agustín Moreto penned one of the best-known and most entertaining comedies of this type, *El desdén con el desdén*. The young lady, a countess, snubs the Count's overtures of love. But the Count is wise to the ways of women. If he counters her true disdain with pretended disdain, he surmises, he will wound her pride and will arouse her interest. He sets his plan in motion, and it works like magic, but not before the two engage in a hilarious battle of wits. At one point, he declares his love for her and then retracts his declaration. Infuriated, she announces her intention to marry another man, and she asks the Count to assist her in selecting a suitable suitor. In retaliation, the Count informs her that he too has decided to wed another woman. Eventually, and with great reluctance, she admits that she has grown to love him, and all ends happily. Love has cured her of her former elusiveness, and she meekly relinquishes her freedom and espouses the wifely role she once loathed.

As we have noted, however, not all disdainful young ladies are destined to marry the men who have captured their hearts. Tisbea, for example, arrogantly proclaimed her immunity from Cupid's arrows, only to succumb to Don Juan's poisonous entreaties. Her Sevillian seducer's death left her humbled, and she would not readily find an antidote to the dishonor and heartsickness he bequeathed her. The peasant *bandolera* Gila also rejected love and marriage, for she did not want any man to subject her or to imagine himself her master. She sought freedom, she declared, not imprisonment: "No quiero ver que nadie me sujete, / No quiero que ninguno se imagine / Dueño de mí; la libertad pretendo."[5] In contrast to Tisbea, she never loved her seducer, the infamous Captain whose cruelty precipitated her descent into criminality and her subsequent death.

In the course of all these plays, dramatists, echoing societal attitudes, break the young women's haughty, individualistic spirit. The ladies finally see the "error" of their ways and accept the punishment their nonconformity has earned them.

One of the very few fictional young women who are permitted to live single and independent is Marcela, the shepherdess in Cervantes' *Don Quijote*. The reader may recall that the goatherds hurled harsh accusations at her and blamed her for Grisóstomo's death. But she paid no heed to the idea that she must love a man just because he loved her. True love, she asserted, stems from the heart, not from duty, gratitude, or fear. She defended her right to lead an unencumbered, solitary way of life. Cervantes and Don Quijote sided with this strong-minded individual despite the outrage of the goatherds, who could not comprehend why she should be allowed to disdain the social conventions they held so dear.

THE PLIGHT OF THE UNHAPPILY MARRIED WOMAN

Aside from the occasional nun, *bandolera*, and independent-minded nonconformist, most young female characters are

264

either destined to wed or are already married. Of the latter, nevertheless, many are unhappy. Parental pressure or other circumstances have deprived them of the freedom to wed their beloveds and have coerced them into loveless states of matrimony, from which they cannot escape. Since authors seldom present separation and annulment as solutions to disastrous marriages (the Church having traditionally prohibited divorce and remarriage),[6] these ladies must remain wed until death parts them from their spouses.

The motif of the unhappily married woman (*malmaridada* or *malcasada*) figures prominently in Spanish literature of the Middle and Golden Ages. Unlike the heroines in comedies of intrigue, who succeeded in circumventing the social demands placed on them, these young ladies cannot bring themselves to disobey their fathers or other male guardians, even if disobedience means sacrificing love.

Frequently, the bride's former sweetheart confronts her and insists on knowing why she has married against her wishes. One such young woman is the shepherdess Diana in Jorge de Montemayor's famed sixteenth-century pastoral novel *Los siete libros de la Diana*. Her parents compelled her to wed the wealthy Delio. When her beloved Sireno accuses her of faithlessness, she responds that he is wrong to blame her; instead, he should blame her parents: "¡Bueno es que me pongas tú culpa por haberme casado, teniendo padres!"[7] When Sireno argues that she should not have married for any reason other than love, the dutiful Diana replies that the obedience she owed her parents required her to forsake all else, including love: "¿Y qué parte era el amor, adonde estaba la obediencia que a los padres se debía?"[8] Luckily for the seemingly ill-fated lovers, however, Gaspar Gil Polo wrote a continuation of their tale, *Diana enamorada*, in which Delio conveniently dies. Now a wealthy widow, Diana is free to wed Sireno, the man whom she, not her parents, has chosen.

The *malmaridada* or *malcasada* is the primary motif of many traditional, anonymous Spanish poems. Like her counterpart, the unhappy young novice, she herself laments her plight, a literary device that serves to intensify her feelings of anguish and impotence. One *malcasada* expresses the hope that her husband will one day find himself a captive, just as he has made a captive of her:

> De ser malcasada
> No lo niego yo,
> Cautivo sea
> Quien me cautivó.[9]

So miserable is she that she even wishes for death to claim her:

> Yo, triste cuitada,
> La muerte deseo
> Y nunca la veo,
> Que soy desdichada.[10]

Several of these poems touch on a particularly grave consequence of unhappy wedlock—adultery. One lady, for example, explains that God has given her a churlish husband who is killing her and whom she despises. In order not to be always under his power, she offers herself to another man whom she adores; presumably, he will treat her better than her husband has:

> Y pues yo muero por vos,
> Querámonos bien los dos
> Pues me dio un marido Dios
> Que me mata, el grosero.
> A vos quiero yo querer,
> Que me sabréis conocer,
> Por no estar siempre en poder
> De un hombre que tan mal quiero.[11]

Traditional poetry also refers to other motives for a *malmaridada*'s infidelity: her husband's coldness and his extramarital affairs. The hapless wife may have already been wronged by an oppressive father. To compound her woes, her husband ignores her and leaves her unfulfilled.

266

María de Zayas y Sotomayor, writing in the seventeenth century from the woman's perspective, dares to place the blame for a wife's infidelity squarely on the husband's shoulders. During the first year of marriage, Zayas forthrightly complains, husbands deplete their reserves of caresses and affection, after which time they make their wives die of frustration. Perhaps, if not for certain, Zayas continues, this is why abandoned wives become involved in base, adulterous relationships. As a result, the husbands lose their honor, and the wives, their lives:

> [Las caricias] las gastan todas al primer año, y después, como se hallan fallidos del caudal del agasajo, hacen morir a puras necesidades de él a sus esposas, y quizá, y sin quizá, es lo cierto ser esto la causa por donde ellas, aborrecidas, se empeñan en bajezas, con que ellos pierden el honor y ellas la vida.[12]

Men, Zayas warns, deceive themselves if they think that vigilance, locks, and keys will keep their spouses from mischief. Rather than guard them and conceal them, husbands should love them, caress them, and give them what they are lacking, because a satisfied wife will guard and conceal herself, if not out of virtue, then at least out of obligation:

> Piensan que por velarlas y celarlas se libran y las apartan de travesuras, y se engañan. Quiéranlas, acarícienlas y denlas lo que les falta, y no las guarden ni celen, que ellas se guardarán y celarán, cuando no sea de virtud, de obligación.[13]

WIFE MURDER

Forced marriage and/or an inattentive husband are the causes underlying most wife characters' infidelity, a motif that constitutes the framework of the so-called "dramas of honor". The antagonist in these Golden Age plays is the wife's impassioned admirer. In the majority of these dramas, she and he had been in love and had contemplated marriage. For a variety of reasons, however, she was forced to marry another man. Although she still loves her former sweetheart, and he professes to love her, his feelings are baser than hers. Believing that she wronged him when she wed, he vows to avenge himself on her and her husband by seducing her. This adulterous act will heal his wounded pride and will satisfy his sexual desire for her as well as his thirst for revenge. Little does he know that he is the tragic victim of the obsessive passions he cannot control, passions that will ultimately lead him and the wife to their deaths.

When the antagonist makes his first amorous overtures, the wife usually rejects them, for she has promised to remain faithful to her husband. Furthermore, she sees reality more clearly than does her would-be lover, and she realizes that he seeks to dishonor her. Knowing that her husband would kill them both, should they besmirch his honor in any way, she understandably fears for her reputation and for their lives. Gradually, however, the antagonist's pleas make her vacillate between duty to her husband and love for his rival, between the role of faithful wife, which God and society expect her to play, and personal fulfillment, which she can only find in the arms of her beloved. Eventually, passionate love overpowers her and so blinds her to reason and duty that she fatally agrees to yield to his entreaties.

In some honor plays, the husband discovers his wife's adulterous intent before she actually carries it out; in others, he catches the lovers in the act of adultery. Her infidelity, whether in word or deed, emasculates him and ruins his self-esteem. Should his wife's affair become public knowledge, the esteem in which society holds him would also plummet, and people would insultingly refer to him as a cuckold. Bereft of dignity, his reputation in jeopardy, he must exert his manliness by murdering the lovers, for only in this way can he redeem his honor.

The husband feels no remorse whatsoever when he slays the wife's lover, who is at once the catalyst of and the witness to the husband's dishonor. According to the honor code, however, he must murder his wife as well. Even if she is innocent of real adultery, even if the husband acknowledges in his heart

268

the tragic chain of events that has led her to wed against her will and to surrender to another man against her better judgment, and even if the husband truly loves her and might wish to spare her life, why, the reader might wonder, must he still wreak vengeance on her?

The answer to this question lies in the husband's and society's interpretation of the conjugal bond, an interpretation the honor code reflects: once a woman becomes one in flesh with her husband, she becomes an integral part of him (and not vice versa, which explains the double standard regarding extramarital sexual behavior). Her illicit love affair dishonors her and her husband alike and destroys the integrity of their marriage. It is like a cancerous cell, which threatens to contaminate the entire organism. The only way to prevent the impurity from causing more harm is to destroy it. The husband realizes that the wife loves his rival and that she would have preferred to marry him. He knows that her feelings for her lover go deeper than transitory sexual attraction, for she has given—or thought of giving—herself to him, body and soul. Therefore, the husband cannot eliminate the passionate love that has defiled their marriage without eliminating her in the process.

The husband who loves his wife perceives the vengeance he exacts to be a sacrifice he must make for honor's sake. His soliloquies (which rank among the finest in Golden Age theater) express the apparent conflict raging within him: he wavers between rationalizing his wife's conduct and even forgiving her, on the one hand, and carrying out his duty to himself and to society, on the other. In reality, however, he has no choice to make. In the struggle between what he might want to do as an individual and what he must do as a social being, duty prevails. His wife's affair has grievously injured his honor, on which are based his two most precious possessions (which are even more precious than his wife): his self-respect and his membership in society. Since there is no way to heal his honor other than to kill his wife, then kill her he must. Should he refrain from sacrificing her, people would judge him cowardly and unmanly. Moreover, they might ostracize him, thereby relegating him to a state worse than death itself.

The honor-driven husband character undoubtedly feels anger, resentment, betrayal, and jealousy. In the final analysis, nonetheless, his reason, not his emotions, compels him to slay the woman whom he may still love. So impotent is he in the face of societal pressures, which have influenced his reason, that he never even ponders the transcendental consequences of his deed. Never does it occur to him that vengeance clashes with the fundamental precepts of Christianity and that it imperils his chance of eternal salvation.

Of all Golden Age honor plays, Calderón de la Barca's trilogy figures among the best known. Readers and spectators never forget the husbands' horrifying acts of vengeance. These acts, however, are not unique to Calderón's dramas. What accounts for their enduring popularity is the chain of events that inexorably culminates in tragedy.

Two of Calderón's three plays, *A secreto agravio, secreta venganza* and *El pintor de su deshonra,* involve a wife who contemplates adultery and one who is abducted by her lover, respectively. These women are victims of error. Distraught at the erroneous news that their beloved fiancés had perished abroad, they submitted to parental pressure and reluctantly wed men whom they did not love. When their trueloves return home, they upbraid the ladies for their faithlessness and for the haste in which they married. Anger, thirst for vengeance, and passion transform the men into negatively individualistic antagonists, and they recklessly determine to possess the women whom circumstances beyond their control took from them.

When Don Luis, the antagonist of *A secreto agravio,* confronts Doña Leonor, she expresses concern for her reputation, but her resolve soon begins to weaken. Finally, she tells him that a suitable occasion for their affair will shortly materialize. Don Lope, her husband, finds Luis in the house and immediately suspects that his honor is imperiled. Fearing that the King is also suspicious, he at first plans to avenge himself publicly, thereby winning back the high esteem in which the King has always held him. But after he gives the matter further consideration, he concludes that public vengeance would prompt people to refer to him as a dishonored man, not as an avenger; in other words, people would remember his offense, not his vengeance. Since so few people know of Leonor's adulterous intent, he now decides to keep it a secret. As the title of the play indicates, an offense (*agravio*) committed in secret calls for secret vengeance (*venganza*); therefore, he will slay the lovers in such a way that they will seem to the world to have perished of natural causes. The few people who suspect the lovers may also surmise the real reason for their deaths; as no one will be able to prove that he murdered them, however, his reputation will remain virtually intact.

Meanwhile, Leonor retires to her country home, an opportune site for the tryst she has in mind. She writes Luis to join her, and Luis, not realizing that Lope recognizes him, foolishly accepts Lope's offer to row him there in a boat. Lope then slays him and makes it appear that he accidentally drowned. When he tells Leonor of Luis's death, she faints, and her reaction quells any doubt he may have had of her guilt. He then sets the house ablaze, and Leonor perishes. Water and fire have purified Lope's honor; consequently, he is able to face his King once again.

The King, nevertheless, learns the truth about the lovers' demises, but he will not divulge Lope's secret; in effect, he rules that Lope's acts of vengeance were fully justified. The symbol and font of honor, the King must uphold the harsh, informal honor code, according to which adultery in word is tantamount to adultery in deed. But he conveniently disregards the formal code he ought to uphold, whereby a husband could only kill his wife and her lover if he caught them in flagrante delicto.

El pintor de su deshonra concerns a painter, Don Juan, whose wife Doña Serafina resolutely refuses to yield to Don Álvaro's advances. Her determination incites Álvaro to abduct her against her will to Italy. All that Juan ever desired was an heir and peaceful surroundings in which to practice his craft. To his utter consternation, he now finds himself dishonored and his life in disarray, and the worst part of his quandary is the helplessness he feels. In a moving soliloquy, he denounces (as do many husband characters who share his plight) the honor code for besetting him with such woes. Accursed be the man who invented such a rigorous law, he laments. That tyrannical legislator placed a man's reputation in someone else's hands. How unjust that another person should subject and enslave a man's honor and that a man should be condemned by another person's will for a crime he did not commit. How does the barbarous world, he wonders, consent to such an infamous rite?

> ¡Mal haya el primero, amén,
> Que hizo ley tan rigurosa!
> ¡Poco del honor sabía
> El legislador tirano,
> Que puso en ajena mano
> Mi opinión, y no en la mía!
> ¡Que a otro mi honor se sujete,
> Y sea (¡oh injusta ley traidora!)
> La afrenta de quien la llora,
> Y no de quien la comete!
> . . .
> ¿El honor que nace mío,
> Esclavo de otro? Eso no.
> ¡Y que me condene yo
> Por el ajeno albedrío!
> ¿Cómo bárbaro consiente
> El mundo este infame rito?[14]

Notwithstanding his protestations, however, Juan must abide by the terms of the code he calls treacherous if he is to recapture his honor.

Disguised, Juan follows the lovers to Italy and meets a prince who is also enamored of Serafina. Unaware that Juan is her husband, the Prince commissions him to paint her portrait. Juan seizes the opportunity and packs his bag with paint and pistols to do what he must. He goes to the home where she and Álvaro are staying, and he watches her in secret. Sensing his presence, Serafina has a premonition of her imminent death. Álvaro embraces his frightened lover, whereupon Juan, who has hitherto vacillated, now has no alternative but to kill them. Since their adultery was not a secret, Juan's vengeance is public, and he paints his dishonor in blood for all the world to see. Although people may refer to him as a dishonored painter, he reasons, they will at least recognize that he was man enough to exact retribution.

As in Don Lope's case, the Prince's endorsement of Juan's act signifies that the lovers deserved to perish for having disobeyed the laws of society; it also means that Juan merits full reinstatement to society for having dutifully obeyed its code of honor.

While Calderón's dramas of honor are generally better known than Lope de Vega's, it was Lope who established the precedent of the Golden Age honor play. With one possible exception, nonetheless, the dramas he wrote concerning adulterous wives who perish have failed to spark the same degree of lasting interest as Calderón's, a failure that can be partially attributed to Lope's unsympathetic portrayal of the wife characters.

The wives in two of Lope's honor plays, *El sufrimiento del honor* and *Los comendadores de Córdoba*, are blatantly adulterous. War has beckoned their dutiful husbands, whose extended absences from home leave the wives lonely and bored. Hardly latter-day Penelopes, these women waste no time in finding other men to ease the dreariness of their lives. Lope characterizes the wives as such superficial malcontents that the reader feels no sympathy whatsoever for the fate awaiting them once their husbands arrive home. The husband's vengeance in *Los comendadores de Córdoba* is especially gruesome: he puts to death every living creature—man, woman, and animal—that has witnessed his dishonor. The King, what is more, praises the husband's horrific but (in the King's opinion) justifiable deed.

One of Lope's more popular dramas of honor is *El castigo sin venganza*, a play based on a tale by the Italian novelist Matteo Bandello. Casandra, the wife, arouses more sympathy than

Lope's other wife characters. Betrothed against her wishes to the dissolute Duke of Ferrara, she and his illegitimate son Federico fall in love. Under more fortuitous circumstances, they might have married, but duty compels her to wed the Duke, a man who she knows does not love her. Shortly thereafter, the Duke goes off to war. Anger, wounded pride, loneliness, and the love she feels for her stepson combine to push her to the threshold of adultery. Both Casandra and Federico are torn between loyalty to the Duke and love for each other, but passion finally overcomes them.

In the meantime, the Duke returns home in triumph and, ironically, resolves to transform his lecherous ways. When he discovers that his son and his wife are lovers, however, his noble intentions immediately turn to thoughts of vengeance. He determines to restore his honor in secret; in this way, he will not disclose his dishonor to his subjects. In which capacity, he asks himself, should he act? As husband, father, or ruler? If he were to play the role of avenging husband, he would have to slay both his wife and his son; besides, he might run the risk of publicizing their affair. Therefore, he decides to act as father and ruler: instead of avenging himself on the lovers, he will punish his son. Accordingly, he devises a grimly ingenious plan. Since he must also rid himself of the woman who has betrayed him, he orders Federico to murder a traitor, whose face is concealed beneath a hood. Federico obeys his father and unwittingly slays his beloved Casandra. Then the Duke sentences Federico to death for murdering his stepmother. In effect, the Duke has secretly avenged his dishonor. Although his subjects may believe that he meted out punishment (*castigo*) and not vengeance, he has deceived neither himself nor us.[15]

That a woman must pay with her life for committing or even contemplating adultery may fill the modern reader with horror. What is even more horrifying, however, than the plays in which a real or would-be adulteress perishes are the tales about a husband who murders his *totally* innocent wife. The wife characters in these short stories and dramas are victims of tragic circumstance. Their monomaniac husbands are so exclusively concerned with their reputations that they hastily slay their wives without considering the circumstantial nature of the evidence with which they have been presented.

Four of María de Zayas' ten *Desengaños amorosos* involve star-crossed, guiltless wives who perish. Zayas acknowledges having written this collection of short stories in order to warn women of men's cruelty; as a result, these tales, while they are most entertaining, may strike even the most credulous reader as farfetched. Nevertheless, Zayas' intentional exaggeration does emphasize a fundamental reality about medieval and Golden Age women—their vulnerability. As a man's honor depended so heavily on his wife's appearance of virtue, she had to be on guard at all times. Should she inadvertently convey the impression, mistaken or not, that her heart belonged to another man, or should she indicate that another man had expressed an interest in her, she would endanger her reputation and her husband's honor, and she might very well court death.

The most horrifying of Zayas' tales depict husbands who quickly tire of their wives, a marital risk to which Zayas frequently alludes. Her husband characters grab at any opportunity to rid themselves of their hapless spouses; some even make a concerted effort to believe the falsely incriminating evidence their mistresses have planted in an attempt to frame their rivals.

A relatively small number of Golden Age plays also treats the innocent wife put to death by her husband. Some of these noble-born wives had fallen in love with princes who, for a variety of reasons, coerced them into wedding other men. The princes, nonetheless, continue to pursue them. While the wives still love their former sweethearts, they remain faithful to their husbands in word and deed (though not necessarily in thought). They pay dearly for a crime they never committed, but royal blood immunizes the antagonists from vengeance.

The most famous of these dramas is undoubtedly Calderón's *El médico de su honra*, the third in his trilogy of honor plays.

Doña Mencía, the wife, resists Prince Enrique's efforts to seduce her, just as she had done before she married Don Gutierre. In desperation, the Prince bribes a slave and gains entry into Mencía's boudoir. At that very moment, Gutierre comes home, and the Prince flees. Panic-stricken, Mencía imprudently cries out that a man has hidden in her bedroom, whereupon Gutierre rushes in and finds the dagger the Prince had left behind.

Gutierre's suspicions, which are already aroused, mount when Mencía speaks in her sleep. Addressing him as "Enrique", she asks him to leave. Even though Gutierre believes that she is technically innocent, his honor cannot suffer the thought that she once cared for another man and that she may have been making love to him in her dreams; therefore, he determines to murder her. As the doctor (*médico*) of his honor, he will prescribe a cure for the dread disease that afflicts him—dishonor. The cure he has in mind will restore his honor to health, but during the course of the treatment, the cause of his disease—Mencía—will be eradicated. After granting his wife two hours in which to prepare her soul, he forces a barber to bleed her to death. In this awful perversion of the essence of Christianity, Mencía's blood is sacrificed so that Gutierre can attain temporal life. But Mencía fares better in the long run than her husband, for the crucifix hanging in her room provided her with solace during those long two hours and symbolizes the redemption to which the shedding of her innocent blood has entitled her.

Gutierre, meanwhile, lies to the King about his wife's death, but the King eventually discovers the truth. Even if he were tempted to punish Gutierre, however, he cannot, for he must now order him to marry a woman whom he had seduced and then abandoned in order to wed Mencía. Gutierre willingly accedes to the King's demand and offers her his hand, which is stained with Mencía's blood. Poor woman! She knows full well what fate may await her, should she ever give the appearance of infidelity. For her, nevertheless, as for Gutierre, honor takes precedence over life itself.[16]

Francisco de Rojas Zorrilla, who wrote several plays about

guiltless wives and their narrow escapes from death, penned one tragedy in which the innocent wife perishes. This play, *Casarse por vengarse*, differs from Calderón's *El médico de su honra* in certain important points: for one thing, the Prince would have married his beloved, but she was under the mistaken impression that he would not have, and she subsequently married another man in vengeance; for another, the Prince still truly loves her despite her rash marriage, and he tries to protect her from her vengeful husband, who belatedly discovers that her heart does not belong to him; finally, when the King learns that her death was not accidental, he swears to himself that he will one day avenge her murder without disclosing the details. Many of Rojas Zorrilla's dramas contain veiled criticisms of the excesses of the honor code, and this play is no exception. The King's refusal to condone an atrocious act of murder committed for honor's sake reflects Rojas' abhorrence of the extremes to which the code might impel its honor-bound adherents.

Readers of Golden Age literature often wonder how true to life these honor plays really were. If we are to believe the testimony of writers who witnessed the corruption and decadence of seventeenth-century cities—in particular, of Madrid—adultery was not all that uncommon. Yet documentary evidence suggests that vengeance in the form of murder was not a normal occurrence either in Madrid or in the smaller towns and countryside, where adultery was certainly committed less frequently than in the larger metropolises.[17] What is difficult to ascertain, however, is the number of wife murders that went unreported. In all probability, an indeterminable number of husbands did take advantage of the legal code in effect during the sixteenth and seventeenth centuries, whereby a man could kill his wife and her lover if he caught them in the adulterous act. Other husbands, particularly those who merely suspected their wives, would have refrained from murdering them; instead, they might have sent them back in disgrace to their families, or they might have even forgiven them. As for these wives' real or alleged lovers, the ones who did not flee the husbands' wrath might have been challenged to fight them in a duel.

If honor plays do not necessarily portray the everyday reality of the sixteenth and seventeenth centuries, the reader may wonder, what motivated dramatists to write them? And why were they so popular?

Lope de Vega provides a partial answer to both questions in his *Arte nuevo de hacer comedias,* a poetic treatise he penned in order to explain the art of writing the *Comedia nueva* (the new form of plays for which he was largely responsible). Dramas involving honor, he states, forcefully move one and all: "Los casos de la honra son mejores, / Porque mueven con fuerza a toda gente."[18] Although his explanation does not distinguish between true honor plays (those in which the wife perishes) and plays in which the wife's life is spared, the former surely would have moved theatergoers and readers to an even greater extent than the latter. Sixteenth- and seventeenth-century men and women alike certainly responded to the timeless and universal emotions of unhappiness, love, fear, betrayal, and insecurity, and to the tragedy that ensues when passion, having consumed the antagonist of a drama and perhaps the wife, inevitably collides with the husband's sense of honor.

While spectators may have been stunned and even repelled at the severity of the punishment meted out to the wife character, men in the audience would have understood what prompted the husband to take such drastic action: the fear of society's ridicule and outright rejection. Even though men viewing the play might have been incapable of wreaking similar vengeance, honor plays offered them the chance to identify, for one brief moment, with the husband's loss of dignity and with his dread of losing face. Women, in turn, could have related to the tragic wife. A woman who had married for reasons other than love, for example, would have empathized with the wife's conflict between love and duty, between the individualistic role she would like to play and the social one she ought to play. A woman who was wed to a jealous husband quite possibly lived in fear that he would accuse her of infidelity, just as the husband character accuses his wife.

The fact that most vengeful husband characters are exonerated of any wrongdoing leads us to conclude, moreover, that these dramas were also written to exalt the ideals and values of duty, dignity, fidelity, manliness, and reputation. Does it follow, then, that dramatists personally approved of the acts of vengeance they depict, especially of wife murder? This question cannot be answered in general terms, since playwrights who wrote the same type of plays did not necessarily share the same opinion of the deeds they portray.

With regard to Calderón, his views on vengeance are difficult to glean for the simple reason that he neither states nor implies them in his honor plays. Some literary critics doubt whether Calderón, a devout Catholic, could have espoused vengeance, particularly the murder of an innocent wife; indeed, they conclude, he uses the symbols of water, fire, and blood in order to stress the perversity of the honor code. Other critics think that the monarch characters' sanctioning of the three wife murders signifies Calderón's tolerance of the code as an effective means for society to quell an individual's real or potential defiance of social order. Calderón, in their estimation, would have written these plays not only to move and entertain his public but also to admonish wives and would-be seducers against indiscretion. According to this interpretation, Calderón did not reject the ideal of forgiveness (an ideal he reiterates in his religious *autos sacramentales*); he did, however, recognize that an individual might have to disregard forgiveness if his honor and the harmony of his family life were at stake.

Lope de Vega, in contrast to Calderón, does make known his position regarding vengeance in a short story he wrote, "La más prudente venganza". This tale contains all the ingredients of an honor play and is about a husband who secretly murders his wife and her would-be lover. In his concluding remarks, Lope states that no one should imitate this example of vengeance. Rather, it should serve as a warning to women whose inordinate sexual appetite drives them to risk life and honor for such a brief moment of pleasure; in doing so, they offend God, their parents, their husbands, and their reputations: "No es ejemplo que nadie debe imitar, aunque aquí se escriba para que lo sea a las mujeres que con desordenado apetito aventuran la vida y la honra a tan breve deleite, en grave ofensa de Dios, de sus padres, de sus esposos y de su fama."[19]

Lope goes on to say that he opposes vengeance, since the offender's blood does not wash away the stain of dishonor. Because what was cannot stop being, it is foolish, Lope maintains, for an offended man to believe that he can remove the offense by killing the offender:

> Y he sido de parecer siempre que no se lava bien la mancha de la honra del agraviado con la sangre del que le ofendió, porque lo que fue no puede dejar de ser, y es desatino creer que se quita, porque se mata al ofensor, la ofensa del ofendido.[20]

In other words, vengeance does not restore the dishonored man's honor, for he must always live with the knowledge that it was violated and that nothing will ever bring it back to its original, pristine state.

Even if we did not know of this passage, other factors point to Lope's aversion to vengeance: his own extramarital affairs, which would have made him regard certain instances of infidelity with leniency, and the many plays he wrote in which he spares the lives of wives accused of loving other men.

WIFE MURDER AVERTED

In numerous plays written by Lope de Vega and other playwrights, the husband either lends credence to slander or misinterprets circumstantial evidence; consequently, he wrongly concludes that his wife is guilty of adultery. She endures unimaginable agony, for his accusation has thrust her from the security of marriage into the solitude and despair of impending doom. She might very well have perished, had the truth not surfaced. Although her husband ultimately spares her, he does exact retribution from the antagonist who has maligned or pursued her—except, of course, if the person's blood is royal.

In several such Golden Age dramas, a sovereign's wife is the victim of malicious slander. This motif, which Lope popularized but did not originate, sets the framework for a well-known play written by the sixteenth-century dramatist Francisco Agustín Tárrega, *La duquesa constante*. The Duchess displays a constancy to her husband, the Duke, that would have weakened the resolve of many a less resolute wife. Just before he goes off to war, the Duke entrusts the Duchess to his friend Torcato's care, and he leaves Torcato a sealed envelope, which Torcato is to open only in the event of the Duke's death. The Duke's prolonged absence from home spurs the evil Torcato to woo the Duchess. In a fit of jealousy, Torcato's wife writes the Duke that the Duchess has betrayed him. Time passes, and Torcato mistakenly believes that the Duke has died. Eventually he opens the envelope, reads the Duke's note, and discovers that the Duke has commanded him to poison the Duchess in order to ensure her fidelity. Torcato tells the Duchess about the contents of the note and promises her that he will not carry out the Duke's order if she will agree to wed him (once, of course, he slays his wife). The faithful Duchess, however, chooses to die, since life without her Duke would be no life at all. But fortunately for her, the Duke returns home just in the nick of time, learns of his wife's constancy, and kills Torcato. As for Torcato's jealous wife, the Duke heeds the Duchess' magnanimous plea for mercy on her behalf and refrains from slaying her.

Lope de Vega's plays involving this motif are chivalrous in tone, for the wronged royal-born wife, unlike her noble or peasant counterpart, is permitted to seek a champion to defend her cause in public. Her fate hangs on his ability to vanquish the wicked antagonist. One such play is *El testimonio vengado,* which Lope based on an historical episode in the lives of the medieval King Sancho III Garcés "el Mayor" of Navarre and his Queen. The King's spiteful sons become so irate when their mother forbids them to ride horseback that they wrongly accuse her of adultery. She vows to clear her name and chooses for her champion her stepson, the gallant Ramiro, whose feelings for her contrast markedly with her own sons'. Ramiro routs his half brothers and avenges the false testimony they bore against their mother. The King spares their lives but disinherits them in punishment for their baseness.[21]

This motif also appears in one of María de Zayas' short stories, "La perseguida triunfante". Zayas' tale, however, differs from Tárrega's and Lope's in two ways: the intervention of the Virgin Mary, who repeatedly saves the Queen from misfortune, and the royal couple's amicable separation after the truth is revealed. The outcome of Zayas' story is more realistic than that of the plays, for Zayas, an astute observer of feminine nature, realizes that the Queen has suffered so greatly because of her husband's vengeful streak that she cannot possibly resume married life; accordingly, the King and the Queen decide to end their days in a monastery and a convent, respectively.

Several of Lope's plays treat a monarch depicted not as a believer and co-victim of slander but as an antagonist whose lustful pursuit of an innocent noblewoman threatens her life. These plays are similar to those we have seen in which a monarch attempted to seduce an unmarried girl. His royal blood prevents the husband from killing him; were it not for his repentance, the wife might also have met an untimely end. In *La corona merecida*, for example, the King comes to his senses— but only after he sees the hideous burns that the wife has inflicted on herself in a desperate effort to cool his ardor. The King's remorse proves him worthy (*merecida*) of the crown (*corona*) he wears.

Many Golden Age plays concern noble-born wives who are pursued or maligned by men of their rank. As they cannot call on a gallant man to champion their cause, they must either defend themselves as best they can or pray that the truth will come to light before they perish. One such play, Lope's *En los indicios la culpa*, examines the dangerous effects of misconstruing circumstantial evidence. All indications (*indicios*) point to the wife's guilt (*culpa*), and the husband makes plans to murder her. But the truth, which he learns just before he is about to carry out his plan, bears no resemblance to his erroneous conclusion. As it turns out, an admirer whom the wife had spurned planted a note falsely incriminating her of infidelity with her husband's best friend. The husband's fortuitous discovery reconciles him to his wife and his friend; the evildoer, however, manages to flee for his life.

While many of Lope's husband characters are so exclusively preoccupied with their honor that they determine to redress their wives' alleged adultery without fully examining the facts, not all husbands in Golden Age theater would pull the proverbial trigger at the first hint of their wives' infidelity.

Tirso de Molina wrote one drama, *El celoso prudente,* in which he commends the jealous (*celoso*) husband for exercising prudence. The husband's sense of reason eventually leads him to find out that the Prince's love letter and portrait, which he spotted in his wife's boudoir, were not intended for her but for her sister. Had he not sought to learn the truth, his wife would have paid for a crime she never even gave a thought to committing.

Rojas Zorrilla's husband characters also tend to react prudently to the mistaken news of their wives' adulterous relationships. In the words of one such husband, it is foolish to punish the offense without ascertaining the transgression: ". . . y es necio / Quien castiga las ofensas / Sin averiguar los yerros."[22] The husbands' circumspection is especially praiseworthy since they know full well that their wives never loved them and that they wed them against their wishes. These circumstances, warns Rojas Zorrilla (like his predecessor Guillén de Castro), make infidelity a distinct possibility. Nevertheless, the wives reject adultery, for they have and will always put duty and honor before any other considerations.

Rojas Zorrilla's *Santa Isabel, reina de Portugal,* despite its title, is a secular play about this motif of alleged infidelity and the husband's initial reluctance to murder his wife. The heroine is the Aragonese Princess Isabel (1271–1336), who married the Portuguese King Diniz ("Dionís" in Spanish) by proxy. Although her exceeding piety and reputed miracles convinced the Church to canonize her in 1625, Rojas treats the nonreligious side of her life—in particular, her unhappy marriage to the King.

Isabel had wanted to become a nun but was compelled to wed Dionís for reasons of state. Alone in a strange land, virtually abandoned by her dissolute husband, her only friend is her secretary Don Ramiro. He and Don Carlos, the antagonist of the story and Dionís' confidant, are both in love with Doña Blanca, but she favors Ramiro. In a vindictive plot to rid himself of his rival, Carlos insinuates to the King that the Queen and Ramiro are betraying him. Although the King is already jealous of the innocent friendship between the two, he refrains from vengeance, even when he is confronted with evidence that would seem to lend credence to Carlos' slander. Carlos, however, goads the King so incessantly that the King finally resolves to take his honor into his own hands. But when he enters Isabel's bedroom to murder her, he sees her garbed as a nun and kneeling in front of a crucifix. Her religious devotion, which he always belittled, deters him from taking the fatal step. As for the villainous Carlos, his treachery comes to light, and he winds up dead. Ramiro marries Blanca, and the King, now thoroughly *desengañado,* repents his lascivious ways and returns to his long-suffering, saintly Queen.

Peasant wives falsely accused of adultery also appear in Golden Age theater, but less frequently than do royal or noble-born wives. The best-known play about the plight of such a peasant woman happens to be one of Lope's most famous dramas, his *Peribáñez y el comendador de Ocaña.* The antagonist, the Commander of the Order of Ocaña, becomes smitten with Peribáñez' wife Casilda on their wedding day. As in many of the plays involving lustful noblemen who pursue unmarried peasant girls, the Commander fails to comprehend why Casilda does not surrender to his entreaties. This Commander, how-

284

ever, is not as cruel as the overlords in Lope's *Fuenteovejuna* and *El mejor alcalde, el rey;* to the contrary, his feelings for Casilda border on the courtly, and he acknowledges that his one flaw, which will prove tragic, is the passionate love from which he cannot escape.

Since his pleas of love have gotten him nowhere, he reckons that generosity just might win Casilda's heart—and Peribáñez' acquiescence. Accordingly, he showers the couple with gifts and masks the dishonorable intentions of his ostensibly honorable gestures.

One day, Peribáñez passes by a painter's studio and notices a portrait of his wife. He recognizes that his honor is at stake and belatedly realizes how foolish he was to have accepted the Commander's gifts. To his great relief, however, the painter assures him of Casilda's innocence. Then he hears the reapers sing a ballad about the Commander's love for Casilda. Like Pedro Crespo in Calderón's *El alcalde de Zalamea*, Peribáñez is a wealthy, Old Christian peasant, and he fears that the ballad will cause his hitherto enviable reputation to plummet.[23] In touching soliloquies, Peribáñez bemoans having married a beautiful woman (a familiar lament in literature) and the fragility of honor, which shatters at the slightest blow as if it were made of the finest crystal: "¡Ay honra, al cuidado ingrata! / Si eres vidrio, al mejor vidrio / Cualquiera golpe le basta."[24]

To ensure Peribáñez' absence from home, the Commander appoints him captain of a band of soldiers, but Peribáñez, now fully aware of his rival's intentions, requests the Commander to knight him, thereby elevating him to the rank of a nobleman. Knighthood will technically make Peribáñez and the Commander equal and will subsequently enable Peribáñez to avenge any wrong that the Commander may do him. Perplexed at Peribáñez' request, the Commander agrees, and Peribáñez then entrusts Casilda and her honor to the Commander's safekeeping.

The Commander has sworn to protect Casilda from harm, and yet he means to dishonor her. The gentleman in him senses the dilemma he faces, but desire overpowers honor. Promising

Casilda's cousin to wed her to his lackey, he elicits her help, and she lets him into Casilda's house.

The suspicious Peribáñez, meanwhile, leaves his soldiers and heads for home. On the way, he ponders his predicament. He believes in his heart that Casilda is not guilty, but people may suspect otherwise. On the one hand, he loves her and wishes to spare her; on the other, honor bids him to kill her. What he, as an individual, would like to do conflicts with what he feels he must do in order to restore the reputation he fears is already sullied. He will not resolve this conflict, however, until he sees for himself the extent of his dishonor.

When Peribáñez arrives home, he finds Casilda valiantly resisting the Commander's amorous advances, and he is convinced of her innocence. He then begs the Commander's pardon for what he is about to do, whereupon he mortally wounds him. The Commander, unlike his infamous, insensitive counterparts in *Fuenteovejuna* and *El mejor alcalde, el Rey*, begs Peribáñez' forgiveness in return and confesses that he deserves to die for having offended him.

After Peribáñez slays the treacherous cousin and the lackey in revenge, he and Casilda set forth to inform the King of the events surrounding the Commander's death. The King not only sanctions Peribáñez' deed but confirms his captaincy, and the Queen bestows on Casilda lovely garments befitting a captain's wife. Their just and generous acts spell an end to the turmoil that the impassioned Commander's presence has signified in Peribáñez' and his wife's lives; furthermore, they guarantee that Peribáñez' peers will hold him in even greater esteem than before the Commander entered the picture.[25]

In a handful of Golden Age plays, the wife manages to escape death, not because the truth has proved her innocent of wrongdoing but because she herself kills the man who wronged her and, by extension, her husband. In spite of the fact that she defies social custom in usurping the husbandly role of avenger, her courage and sense of honor so impress her husband that he "forgives" her for having been dishonored and for wreaking vengeance. Occasionally, the King gives his stamp of approval to the wife's act of justice, as occurs in a play attributed to Lope de Vega, *Audiencias del rey don Pedro*. Let even the wisest of men take a lesson from this heroic woman, exclaims King Pedro (in this play, "the Just"): "Escarmienten los más sabios / En esta heroica mujer."[26]

The antagonists of these stories are often the husbands' best friends. In pursuing their wives, they have not only dishonored them and the husbands but have betrayed their friends' trust as well.

This wicked friend type appears in one of Rojas Zorrilla's most startling and powerful dramas, *Cada cual lo que le toca*. Typical of Rojas' wife characters, Doña Isabel married her husband Don Luis against her will. She had warned him that wedlock would bring neither of them joy. When she shunned him on their wedding night and thereafter, he realized—to his credit—that he, as well as her domineering father, was to blame for their miserable marriage. Time passes, and Luis discovers the reason behind his wife's reluctance to wed and her frigidity: she was not a virgin when she married (a most unusual state of affairs for Golden Age theater to portray). The extraordinarily sensible Luis, however, determines not to murder her since she had warned him not to wed her in the first place. Nevertheless, he still wants her to reveal her ex-lover's identity.

One day, he spots his "friend" Don Fernando sneaking into the house and cannot believe his eyes. As it turns out, the donjuanesque Fernando had taken Isabel to bed under the promise of marriage and had then abandoned her. Unable to resist the challenge of re-seducing the woman who is now his best friend's wife, he has furtively entered their home. Isabel begs her husband to give her the opportunity to avenge her dishonor. To each his—and her—own, states the title of the play: *cada cual lo que le toca*. It is Luis's place to wish Fernando dead, but it is her place, she tells her husband, to kill him. Acknowledging the wisdom of her words, Luis allows her one day in which to wreak vengeance. She duly slays Fernando, whereupon she puts her tainted past behind her and eagerly yields to her husband's embraces.[27]

After avenging their dishonor, most wife characters become reconciled with their husbands. However, in one of María de Zayas' stories, "Al fin se paga todo", circumstances are such that the wife finds it impossible to resume marital life. The couple's happiness came to an abrupt halt when the husband's brother, whose sexual overtures she had long spurned, impersonated her husband one night when the husband was away from home. When she realized who had enjoyed her, she slew him. Notwithstanding her innocence and her husband's willingness to welcome her back with open arms, she feels that her presence would serve as a constant reminder of the dishonor that has, in her opinion, put a wall between them. The hapless husband dies of a broken heart, but she fares rather well indeed: she inherits his wealth and weds another man.

The majority of wife characters whose husbands refrain from murdering them are totally innocent. In a very few cases, however, women guilty of intended or real adultery also avoid death. What is even more unusual is that their lovers do not perish either. These rare plays are truly exceptional because they depict individuals who succeed in defying society and what it most reveres: the honor code, marriage, and the principle of wifely fidelity.

Most full-length plays in which the wives' and lovers' lives are spared were written by Lope de Vega (although this solution to dishonor frequently appears in the farcical, one-act *entremeses* penned by a variety of dramatists).

Why did Lope challenge the honor code, which was such an essential component of Golden Age theater as well as a hallowed societal institution?

Lope occasionally places the blame for the wife character's infidelity on her wayward husband. If he had remained faithful to his wife instead of visiting his paramour, the wife would never have contemplated adultery. Lope knew firsthand that a wife's unhappiness and feeling of rejection could prompt her to search for love outside wedlock, for he was involved during the course of his tempestuous life in a number of extramarital affairs, both as the unmarried lover of married women and as the married lover of single women. His amorous adventures might very well have led him to an understanding of the extenuating circumstances surrounding certain instances of adultery. If we accept as sincere the comments he wrote in his aforementioned "La más prudente venganza", we must conclude that he was basically opposed to wife murder. These plays, then, would seem to reflect his personal approach to the problem of dishonor, an approach that experience had perhaps tempered.

The wife and husband characters of these plays often reconcile if she has not consummated her illicit love. For example, in Lope's humorous *El castigo del discreto* (another play he modeled after a tale by Bandello), the husband intercepts a love letter his wife wrote to her admirer Felisardo. But the husband is more sensible (*discreto*) than most husbands in Golden Age plays. He recognizes that he himself whetted his wife's interest in the man when he extolled his virtues to her. Therefore, as he is partially to blame for what she intends to do, he devises an ingenious plan whereby he will kill not *her* but only her adulterous intent. Should the plan work, she never will give infidelity another thought. Forging Felisardo's signature, he sends her a letter inviting her to a tryst. Delighted, she hurries to the appointed place. Meanwhile, her husband impersonates his rival, and when she embraces him in the dark, he gives her a sound thrashing and then leaves! Needless to say, she is utterly astonished and indignant. When the real Felisardo enters the room, she angrily berates him for having beaten her! Thoroughly confused, he too leaves. The chastened wife then returns to her husband, never to err again.

In several other plays, Lope daringly kills off the husband so that the wife can wed her lover. One such husband, who appears in Lope's *Las ferias de Madrid*, is an exceedingly unsympathetic, arrogant philanderer. One day, the wife goes to the fair (*ferias*), meets a charming man, and the two fall in love.

The husband gains possession of a love letter the man has sent her and vows to wreak vengeance the moment he catches the pair in the act. Luckily for the lovers, however, unforeseen events continually frustrate their efforts to meet one another in bed. The husband then confronts his wife's father, Don Belardo (not coincidentally, Lope's pseudonym), and demands that he murder his daughter in imitation of an "exemplary" Roman father. Belardo not only refuses but slays the husband instead. Without killing his daughter, Belardo has defended his honor from the threats of impending infidelity and ensuing death. Immediately afterward, he gives his blessing to the lovers' marriage.[28]

One of the most potentially tragic dramas concerning two adulterous lovers whom Fortune ultimately blesses is Juan Ruiz de Alarcón's *La crueldad por el honor*. The play centers around the husband, Don Nuño, whom Ruiz portrays as a positive-turned-negative individual. Nuño becomes so driven by the desire to wreak vengeance that he radically changes the course of his life and almost succeeds in reshaping the history of Aragon. On his wedding night, Nuño discovered that his wife Doña Teodora was not a virgin. Shortly thereafter, he spotted her and her lover Don Bermudo together. As Bermudo out-ranked him, he could not deter his powerful rival from protecting Teodora and sending her to a convent for safekeeping. Nuño then accompanied his king, the twelfth-century Alfonso I of Aragon, on a crusade to the Holy Land. Unbeknownst to the Aragonese, King Alfonso died, but his loyal subjects never gave up the hope that he would one day return home alive.[29] Alfonso's death offers Nuño the perfect chance to quench his thirst for vengeance, which has consumed him every minute of the twenty-eight years he has spent abroad. Accordingly, he impersonates the King and returns home in triumph. Now, he reasons, nothing will prevent him from slaying the lovers.

Nuño only reveals his identity to Sancho, the young man who he believes is his son. Sancho vacillates between "filial" duty to the imposter king and fealty to the rightful Queen whose crown Nuño has usurped. Loyalty to the Queen, however, prevails, and he denounces his "father". Just as Nuño is about to murder Bermudo, he is seized. Sancho implores him to commit suicide in order to spare him, Sancho, further humiliation. Realizing that he cannot escape the tangled web of vengeance and deceit that he has spun, Nuño agrees to die, but only if Sancho will kill him. The two then embrace, and Sancho reluctantly carries out the terms of their agreement. Nuño goes to his grave without realizing what Sancho eventually learns—that Sancho is not his son but Bermudo's. Following Nuño's death, the Queen accedes to the throne, and Teodora marries Bermudo. All ends happily for the vindictive Nuño's victims as well as for Aragon.

Aside from these rare full-length plays in which extramarital love is not punished, most Golden Age dramas involving adultery end tragically for the lovers, who must pay the fatal price that society has prescribed for such defiant individuals. The death penalty, in the case of lovers caught in flagrante, reflects the formal legal code in effect during the sixteenth and seventeenth centuries. In the case of intended adultery, it reflects the informal honor code. That lovers—in particular, wife characters who are technically innocent—must die does not, however, reflect the Christian principles of love and forgiveness, principles that were supposed to govern the lives of all Spaniards.

The one author whose husband characters consistently forgive their adulterous wives is Miguel de Cervantes. In several of his works, Cervantes explores the reasons underlying infidelity and holds society ultimately responsible for creating many of the conditions that may motivate a woman to carry on an illicit affair. The circumstances that, in Cervantes' opinion, mitigate her guilt are the same as those to which Guillén de Castro and Rojas Zorrilla alluded: a materialistic father who coerces his daughter to wed a man often many years her senior, a jealous husband who also robs her of her free will, and/or a husband who expects the impossible from his wife.

One of Cervantes' short "exemplary" novels, "El celoso extremeño", treats the not uncommon motif of the wife who was forced to marry an older man. The father and the husband are greatly to blame for the disastrous consequences of the match, for they have frustrated the girl's natural desire for sexual gratification. Moreover, her jealous husband deprives her of her freedom by keeping her under lock and key. In Cervantes' view, she is the victim of selfishness and oppression. Although she might have resisted the impulse to look elsewhere for love, society should not sentence her to death since its values influenced her father and her husband to mistreat her.

In contrast to Lope's spared adulteress characters, nonetheless, this wife does not wed her beloved once her husband dies—despite the fact that the mortally ill husband recognizes his responsibility for their affair and begs her to marry her lover. Instead, the contrite wife ends her days in a convent, and her disappointed lover goes off to the Indies.[30]

Another well-known tale of adultery is "El curioso impertinente", a short story that Cervantes included in *Don Quijote*. This tale is about a husband, Anselmo, whose impertinent curiosity compels him to test his wife Camila's fidelity. To this end, he asks his friend Lotario to try to seduce her, and Lotario reluctantly agrees. Anselmo then absents himself in order to facilitate the seduction, and Camila eventually surrenders to Lotario. When Anselmo discovers the affair, he forgives her. He was to blame, he admits, for having tested her beyond the limits of her endurance. *Desengañado* and heartbroken, he dies. Lotario, in the meantime, takes Camila to a convent and goes off to war; soon after, he dies in battle.

Cervantes' position regarding vengeance is one of understanding and compassion. Like Lope's, his outlook may very well have been shaped in part by personal experience, since several women in his immediate family were involved in scandalous love affairs. Perhaps these sad events led Cervantes to reject vengeance for the same reasons that Lope gave in his "La más prudente venganza": acts of vengeance, Cervantes writes, punish, but they do not remove guilt; and they always remain alive in people's memories, at least for as long as the wronged man lives: "Las venganzas castigan, pero no quitan las culpas; . . . siempre están vivas en las memorias de las gentes, a lo menos, en tanto que vive el agraviado."[31] Instead of restoring a man's reputation, vengeance only harms it further. Because vengeance is, in effect, counterproductive, what is an offended man to do? Cervantes advises him to act charitably toward his wayward wife, forgive her, take her back, suffer her, and admonish her to mend her ways: "Sería mejor caridad perdonarla, recogerla, sufrirla, y aconsejarla."[32]

Cervantes shares with most playwrights a recognition of the wronged husband's sense of impotence in the face of dishonor and shame. Like Lope, moreover, he implies that the rationale underlying the honor code is false. Men who abide by it avenge themselves in the belief that they are ensuring their continuing membership in society. In reality, however, they only deceive themselves, for vengeance usually publicizes the very offense they would have preferred not to disclose. The moment people learn of a man's dishonor, his reputation begins to suffer. Rather than aggravate his plight, he should endure it with dignity and resignation. While sensible, virtuous conduct may not ever redeem the wronged individual in the eyes of society, it will prove him worthy of redemption in the eyes of God.

Cervantes' stories figure among the very few secular works of fiction that openly express the Christian viewpoint concerning wife murder. (*Pícaros* also "pardon" their adulterous wives, but their tolerance does not reflect their forgiving nature as much as their self-interest.) With few exceptions, nonreligious plays, novels, and short stories seldom explicitly censure society for imbuing the honor code with religious symbolism or for equating vengeance with justice; nor do they warn husbands of the peril that may befall their souls if they obey honor's commandment of vengeance. Instead of addressing the individual's relationship with God, secular literature explores the individual's relationship with society and depicts those actions that provoke, prevent, and eliminate conflict between them.

ENDNOTES

[1] In *Antología de la poesía española: Lírica de tipo tradicional*, ed. D. Alonso and J.M. Blecua, 2nd ed. (Madrid: Gredos, 1964), p. 48.

[2] Ibid., p. 26.

[3] For detailed studies on women characters who shun love and marriage, see M. McKendrick's "Women Against Wedlock: The Reluctant Brides of Golden Age Drama" and her *Woman and Society in the Spanish Drama of the Golden Age: A Study of the Mujer Varonil*, espec. Ch. 5: "The *mujer esquiva*."

[4] Pedro Calderón de la Barca, *Guárdate del agua mansa*, Act I, in *Obras completas*, ed. A. Valbuena Briones, 2nd ed. (Madrid: Aguilar, 1973), II, 1300.

[5] Luis Vélez de Guevara, *La serrana de la Vera*, Act II, ed. E. Rodríguez Cepeda (Madrid: Alcalá, 1967), p. 99.

[6] The setting of Cervantes' farcical *entremés*, *El juez de los divorcios*, is a divorce court, although the judge refuses to grant divorces.

[7] Jorge de Montemayor, *Los siete libros de la Diana*, Bk. VI, ed. F. López Estrada, 5th ed. (Madrid: Espasa-Calpe; CC, 1970), p. 273.

[8] Ibid.

[9] In *El cancionero español de tipo tradicional*, ed. J.M. Alín (Madrid: Taurus, 1968), p. 375.

[10] Ibid.

[11] Ibid., p. 370 ("Queredme bien, caballero").

[12] María de Zayas y Sotomayor, "La inocencia castigada," in *Novelas completas*, ed. M. Martínez del Portal (Barcelona: Bruguera, 1973), p. 408.

[13] Ibid.

[14] Pedro Calderón de la Barca, *El pintor de su deshonra*, Act III, in *Obras completas*, ed. A. Valbuena Briones, 5th ed. (Madrid: Aguilar, 1969), I, 897.

[15] Agustín Moreto based his *Antíoco y Seleuco* on Lope de Vega's *El castigo sin venganza;* Moreto's play, however, ends more happily than Lope's because Seleuco, the king-father, is only engaged—not married—to the woman whom his son loves; therefore, he magnanimously permits the pair to wed.

[16] Calderón based his *El médico de su honra* on a play of the same name by Lope de Vega; Lope's play in turn served as the basis for Antonio Enríquez Gómez' tragic drama of honor *A lo que obliga el honor*. Lope's *La desdichada Estefanía* also concerns an innocent wife suspected of adultery and killed by her husband.

[17] See C.A. Jones, "*Honor* in Spanish Golden-Age Drama: Its Relation to Real Life and to Morals."

[18] Lope de Vega, *Arte nuevo de hacer comedias*, in *Obras escogidas*, ed. F.C. Sainz de Robles, 4th ed. (Madrid: Aguilar, 1964), II, 880.

[19] Ibid., "La más prudente venganza," p. 1373.

[20] Ibid.

[21] Another play by Lope de Vega in which the maligned wife seeks a cham-

pion is his *El gallardo catalán* (a.k.a. *El valeroso catalán*). And in Lope's *La discordia en los casados*, the wife, who is a duchess in her own right, leads an army against her husband the King in order to defend her good name against his accusations. Fortunately for the couple, discord and strife turn into bliss at the end of the play. Tirso de Molina also wrote variants on the motif of the maligned queen, but in his plays the queens are unmarried. One such play, his *La prudencia en la mujer*, is similar in plot to Lope's *El testimonio vengado* and concerns the successful attempts of King Sancho IV's widow to clear her name.

[22] Francisco de Rojas Zorrilla, *La traición busca el castigo*, Act II, in BAE, LIV, 247. Another of Rojas Zorrilla's plays in which the prudent husband examines the facts rather than kill his innocent wife in haste is *Peligrar en los remedios*.

[23] The motif of the honor-threatening song also occurs in Lope de Vega's *Porfiar hasta morir*, a play based on the life of the fifteenth-century Galician troubadour Macías and his fatal love for a married woman.

[24] Lope de Vega, *Peribáñez y el comendador de Ocaña*, Act II, in *Obras escogidas*, ed. F.C. Sainz de Robles, 5th ed. (Madrid: Aguilar, 1966), I, 776.

[25] Lope's *La llave de la honra* is similar to *Peribáñez* except for the fact that the husband is not a peasant but an *hidalgo*. Vélez de Guevara borrowed from *Peribáñez* and *Fuenteovejuna* to create his *La luna de la sierra*. Unlike in Lope's plays, however, the antagonist does not die, since the Queen's rebuke more than suffices to deter him from continuing his reckless pursuit of the faithful wife.

[26] Lope de Vega (attributed to), *Audiencias del rey don Pedro*, Act III, in *Obras escogidas*, ed. F.C. Sainz de Robles, 3rd ed. (Madrid: Aguilar, 1974), III, 1009.

[27] Rojas Zorrilla also treats the motif of the woman avenger in his *Progne y Filomena*, a play based on the mythological story about a king who rapes his wife's sister, and the vengeance both women wreak.

[28] In another of Lope's plays, *El galán escarmentado*, the father kills the *Converso* husband of his potentially unfaithful daughter, and she eventually marries her lover; J. Silverman discusses the *Converso* aspect of this play in his "Del otro Teatro Nacional de Lope de Vega: El caso insólito de *El galán escarmentado*." Lope's most shocking play of this type is *Los embustes de Fabia*, which he set in ancient Rome. So desperate is the wife character to wed her lover that she plots to murder her husband. When he learns of her plan, he refrains from vengeance but later commits suicide. The wife then repents her cruelty and proceeds to marry her lover.

[29] King Alfonso's death and the hope that he would one day return predate a similar episode in Portuguese history concerning King Sebastião. Notwithstanding the news that Sebastião had died in Morocco in 1578, many Portuguese refused to give up hoping that he would claim his throne once again. This messianistic belief inspired several imposters to impersonate him, although they met with no lasting success.

295

[30] This motif of the adulterous young wife who was forced to wed an old man also appears in Cervantes' *entremés*, *El viejo celoso*, as well as in Castillo Solórzano's pseudopicaresque tale *La garduña de Sevilla y anzuelo de bolsas*.

[31] Cervantes, *Los trabajos de Persiles y Sigismunda*, Bk. III, Ch. vii, in *Obras completas*, ed. A. Valbuena Prat, 12th ed. (Madrid: Aguilar, 1962), p. 1649.

[32] Ibid.

Conclusion

While it is misleading to interpret Spanish medieval and Golden Age literary works as undistorted mirror images of social life, the patterns of conflict they recreate, as well as the means whereby conflict is resolved, do undeniably reflect which ideals, values, and norms of conduct established society expected the individual to uphold and which ones it allowed him or her to oppose.

For example, however horrifying and perverse are the husband character's acts of vengeance, this solution to the problem of conflict does dramatize the significance that Spanish society traditionally attached to the sanctity of marriage and honor. The husband who avenges potential or real infidelity believes that he is affirming his allegiance to these ideals, and his belief far outweighs any personal impulse to overlook or forgive a threat to his dignity and, subsequently, to his sense of belonging.

To the contrary, the seducer's unrestrained individualism impels him to challenge the ideals of marriage and honor. Having ruptured the bonds that join him and the object of his desire to society, he must die for his defiant acts.

Similarly, the wife who betrays her husband in thought, word, or deed must normally pay with her life. With few exceptions, however, authors portray her in a slightly more favorable light than the male antagonist; depicted as the victim of circumstances beyond her control, she attests to the social evils of materialism and forced marriage, which have nullified her free will in the choice of a husband and have deprived her of love within the framework of marriage. Yet the chain of causality that marks her existence does not wield sufficient strength to mitigate her guilt in the eyes of her world, for her adulterous feelings have conflicted with the most crucial imperative underlying her wifely role—fidelity.

Like her married counterpart, many an unmarried female protagonist falls victim to venality and parental tyranny. Some of these characters are further wronged by rapists or by seducers who promise to wed them in return for their sexual favors. Having lost their virginity, the young ladies realize that they court death at the hands of their honor-driven male guardians. Desperate to redeem their right to live in the state of matrimony, they pursue the antagonists, thereby circumventing the social convention that relegates the duty of restoring honor to their menfolk. Most of these young women manage to snare the men into marriage, which wipes clean the stain of dishonor and puts an end to the conflict in which the couples have lived with society.

Another female type who usurps the male prerogative of vengeance is the *bandolera*. She has suffered from oppression and deceit, but rage at the particular men who have wronged her transforms her justifiable desire for justice into an insatiable thirst for revenge against men in general. The *bandolera's* eventual repentance usually serves to placate society, although in some tales the enormity of her crimes warrants that she be sentenced to death.

All of these women characters have collided with society's mores and must consequently either pay for their misdeeds or struggle to redeem their honor. Other young ladies depicted in literature, on the other hand, strive not to recapture what they have lost but to attain what they fear may never be theirs—personal fulfillment. Whether or not their endeavors meet with success depends on the nature of their aspirations.

Most of these young women fervently desire marriage but insist, nonetheless, on the right to wed on their own terms. Refusing to bow to the will of their mercenary and domineering kinsmen, these plucky characters plot to marry the men whom they love. In doing so, they defy convention and imperil their reputations. Since matrimony is their goal, however, society forgives their transgressions and allows them to wed their sweethearts. Without causing lasting injury to their family honor, the young ladies have triumphed over materialism and the custom of arranged marriage, social ills that condemn less determined women to a life of misery.

Other female characters are so extremely unconventional that they eschew love and marriage altogether. In most stories, however, they fall in love despite their convictions, and they forsake the "unnatural" and disreputable ways of life that they had charted for themselves. They meekly assume the conjugal role society expects them to play, and their conformity to convention eliminates the conflict that has ensued as a result of their individualistic notions.

Numerous male protagonists share with these women the desire to alter their foreordained roles. They are blessed with the proper pedigree but still suffer because Fortune has not showered them with wealth. Hardly content to lead the dreary, humiliating existence of impoverished noblemen, they aspire to membership in the world of the rich and the powerful. Their dilemma underscores the harsh realities of their world, which debases the ideal of true honor and holds wealth and the appearance thereof in greater esteem than integrity. The most prevalent solution to such a nobleman's predicament lies in wedding his affluent ladylove. Before he can win her hand, however, he must feign wealth in order to meet with her and her father's approval. Only by resorting to deception can he eliminate the conflict waging between his ambitions and established society's expectations of him. Once conflict is removed, he is welcomed to the world that would not have accepted him as he was.

Other men and women, nevertheless, refuse to compromise their integrity in order to satisfy societal demands; instead, these individuals—characters like the shepherd, the shepherdess, and Don Quijote, as well as many poets—repudiate the corruption and falsity that permeate courtly and urban circles. They determine to live in accordance with their principles, and

299

they seek the freedom to modify their roles in keeping with their authentic identities. They may live as they choose for as long as they wish, provided that they do not clash with the structure and norms of estate society, and that their pursuits of individuality and freedom are firmly rooted in reality and are not harmful to themselves or to society. Shepherds and shepherdesses generally meet these stipulations. Don Quijote, however, fails to meet the latter two and is restrained from continuing his quest; *desengañado*, he realizes on his deathbed the extent to which fantasy and folly had deluded him.

While certain literary voices crave the positive solitude they encounter only in dissociating themselves from courtly and urban mainstream society, the majority of the marginal men and women who appear in literature seek just the opposite: they hope to become permanently associated with that very milieu. These individuals—*conversos* and *pícaros*—yearn to escape the negative solitude that established society, in excluding them from birth, has forced on them. Their attempts to forge new identities and roles reveal the gap separating the theory from the reality of estate society; like impoverished but ambitious noblemen, they too learn that money is the ultimate key to respectability, for it buys the fraudulent documents and the trappings that might enable them to win acceptance. As these men and women struggle to free themselves of the atavistic forces that narrowly prescribe the boundaries of their existences, they inevitably collide with the dominant society responsible for their marginal status. As counterproductive as it usually proves to be, the sole means by which they can secure a foothold in that world is to sacrifice a part of their integrity. Their efforts, however, often fail when mainstream society unmasks their ruses and their former identities and then casts them out. Once again, they find themselves in a state of estrangement from the world they had tried to penetrate. And even when they do succeed, they must live in constant fear of exposure. Their plight bears witness, indeed, to the impotence of an individual when faced with circumstances beyond his control.

300

Similarly, many prisoners and destitute commoners portrayed in literature are victims of societal forces they are powerless to sway. They have no alternative but to resign themselves to the inequities that characterize their earthly existences. In the case of peasants, the only form of oppression against which writers allow them to rebel is the sexual victimization of their womenfolk; their actions, however, do not signify a revolt against the nobility in general or against the social order but against particular noblemen who abuse the authority vested in them by society.

Dramas involving peasants exalt the hierarchical arrangement of estate society and the theoretically harmonious network of obligations and privileges that should link monarchs, nobles, and commoners. In the ideal world that playwrights created, most villeins are content to play the same roles their ancestors played. An occasional peasant does, nonetheless, fall in love with a noble, and their desire to wed one another places them in potential conflict with their world, which frowns on socially mixed marriages. Luckily for the lovers, a fortuitous turn of events resolves their quandary and enables them to marry: either the monarch elevates the commoner to the nobility, or it is discovered that the "commoner" is really a noble after all. Thus, he or she is allowed to find happiness without disregarding social convention.

An analysis of the patterns of conflict recreated in Spanish medieval and Golden Age literature, therefore, leads us to conclude that the vast majority of characters who exert their individuality *fail* in the end if their aspirations violate the following interrelated canons, which established society considered the bedrock of an orderly and harmonious world:

1. *Acceptance of inherited roles and the duties underlying them*: Male and female characters must abide by the obligations and limitations governing the roles to which they were born to play, and their responsibility to their roles should supercede any personal inclination that might hinder them from discharging their duties effectively. Men should manifest courage and loyalty,

301

defend their honor, and respect the honor of other individuals. Women ought to safeguard their chastity; single women, in particular, are discouraged from acting in an "unfeminine" fashion or otherwise jeopardizing their reputations and their marriageability.

2. *Honor*: Marriage repairs honor shattered by premarital sexual activity. When circumstances rule out marriage, however, death and/or the isolation of a convent provide the only other reputable solutions to the problem of dishonor.

3. *Social stratification*: Although literary works condone social ascent within the second and the third estates, relatively few commoners rise—or even harbor a desire to rise—to the ranks of the nobility. The marginal men and women who make their appearance in literature rarely are able to carve a permanent niche for themselves in mainstream society.

Characters who exert their individuality and who ultimately *succeed* in reaching their goals seldom challenge the structure and the mores of established society; rather, they limit their defiance to injustice and to certain societal conventions and attitudes they (and their creators) view as harmful:

1. *Injustice*: Characters who have been prevented by unjust individuals from playing their foreordained roles frequently redeem their birthright.

2. *Forced marriage*: Numerous heroines reject the prospect of a loveless marriage and connive to wed the men whom they, not their menfolk, have chosen.

3. *Materialism and falsity*: Authors present these motifs in various ways. In some comedies, for instance, they explain why a father wishes to marry off his daughter against her will; in other works, they are related to corruption and inordinate ambition, evils that many writers and characters denounce. While these men and women achieve contentment by opposing venality and hypocrisy, others, ironically, discover that the key to their fulfillment lies not in renouncing materialism and falsity but in acquiescing to them.

4. *Male prerogative of restoring honor*: Female characters occasionally take the matter of righting their dishonor into their

own hands. In some tales, the young ladies force the men who have wronged them into wedlock; in others, they resort to vengeance.

5. *Droit du seigneur*: Peasant protagonists often avail themselves of the honor code in order to avenge the intended or real abduction of their womenfolk by sexually aggressive noblemen.

In the final analysis, then, the destinies of these individuals generally depend on the nature of their conflictive relationships with society. Conflict is resolved to the disadvantage of individuals who have challenged the fundamental tenets regulating their roles and who consequently threaten social order and harmony. Conflict, to the contrary, is resolved to the advantage of individuals who oppose injustice and those customs and values they deem detrimental to their pursuits of honor and happiness and to the well-being of society.

Selected Reading List

Selected Reading List of Secondary Sources Applicable to All Parts and Chapters of this Book

Alborg, Juan Luis. *Historia de la literatura española*. 2nd ed. Madrid: Gredos, 1970. Vols. I and II.

Arco y Garay, Ricardo del. *La sociedad española en las obras dramáticas de Lope de Vega*. Madrid: n.p., 1941.

Beneyto, Juan. *Historia social de España y de Hispanoamérica*. Madrid: Aguilar, 1961, pp. 1–266.

Blanco Aguinaga, Carlos; Julio Rodríguez Puértolas; and Iris M. Zavala. *Historia social de la literatura española (en lengua castellana)*. Madrid: Castalia, 1979. Vol. I.

Cros, Edmond. "Fundamentos de una sociocrítica: Presupuestos metodológicos y aplicaciones." *I&L*, 1 (1977), 60–68.

Davies, R. Trevor. *The Golden Century of Spain: 1501–1621*. London: Macmillan; New York: St. Martin's, 1964.

—. *Spain in Decline: 1621–1700*. London: Macmillan; New York: St. Martin's, 1961.

Defourneaux, Marcelin. *Daily Life in Spain in the Golden Age*. Trans. N. Branch. New York: Praeger, 1971.

Domínguez Ortiz, Antonio. *La sociedad española en el siglo XVII*. Vols. I and II. Madrid: C.S.I.C., 1963 and 1970.

Fernández Álvarez, Manuel. *La sociedad española del Renacimiento*. Salamanca: Anaya, 1970.

Glick, Thomas F. *Islamic and Christian Spain in the Early Middle Ages*. Princeton: Princeton U.P., 1979.

Kamen, Henry. *Spain in the Later Seventeenth Century, 1665–1700*. London and New York: Longman, 1980.

O'Callaghan, Joseph F. *A History of Medieval Spain*. Ithaca: Cornell U.P., 1975.

Piétri, François. *La España del Siglo de Oro*. Trans. F. Ximénez de Sandoval. Madrid: Guadarrama, 1959.

Ruiz Ramón, Francisco. *Historia del teatro español (Desde sus orígenes hasta 1900)*. Madrid: Alianza, 1967, pp. 1–380.

Valbuena Prat, Ángel. *Historia de la literatura española*. 7th ed. Barcelona: Gustavo Gili, 1964. Vols. I and II.

Wilson, Margaret. *Spanish Drama of the Golden Age*. Oxford, Eng., and Elmsford, NY: Pergamon, 1969.

Introduction

Casa, Frank P. "Aspects of Characterization in Golden Age Drama." In *Critical Perspectives on Calderón de la Barca*. Ed. F.A. De Armas, D.M. Gitlitz, and J.A. Madrigal. Lincoln, NE: Society of Spanish and Spanish-American Studies, 1981, pp. 37–47.

Green, Otis H. "The Medieval Tradition: *Sic et Non*." Ch. 1 of his *Spain and the Western Tradition: The Castilian Mind in Literature from El Cid to Calderón*. Madison: U. of Wisconsin P., 1968. Vol. I. (Also Ch. 1 of his *The Literary Mind of Medieval & Renaissance Spain*. Lexington: U.P. of Kentucky, 1970.)

—. "Truancy and Recantation." Ch. 7 of his *Spain and the Western Tradition*. Vol. I.

Chapter 1: "Estate Society"

Boase, Roger. "The Aristocratic Theory of Society." Pt. I of his *The Troubadour Revival: A Study of Social Change and Traditionalism in Late Medieval Spain*. London and Boston: Routledge & Kegan Paul, 1978.

Hamilton, Bernice. "The Position of the Ruler." Ch. 3 of her *Political Thought in Sixteenth-Century Spain: A Study of the Political Ideas of Vitoria, De Soto, Suárez, and Molina*. London: Oxford U.P., 1963.

Maravall, José Antonio. "La sociedad estamental castellana y la obra de don Juan Manuel." In his *Estudios de historia del pensamiento español*: Serie primera: *Edad Media*. Madrid: C.H., 1967, pp. 451–472. (A review of L. de Stefano's book; see below.)

Rodríguez Puértolas, Julio. "Juan Manuel y la crisis castellana del siglo XIV." In his *Literatura, historia, alienación*. Barcelona: Labor, 1976, pp. 45–69.

Schafler, Norman. "Don Juan Manuel and the Changing Structure of Society: A Conflict." *KRQ*, 26 (1979), 181–187.

Stefano, Luciana de. *La sociedad estamental de la baja Edad Media española a la luz de la literatura de la época*. Caracas: Univ. Central de Venezuela; Facultad de Humanidades y Educación; Instituto de Filología "Andrés Bello", 1966.

Ullman, Walter. *The Individual and Society in the Middle Ages*. Baltimore: Johns Hopkins U.P., 1966.

Chapter 2: "Literary Treatments of Social Ascent"

Ciavarelli, Maria Elisa. *El tema de la fuerza de la sangre*. Madrid: Porrúa Turanzas, 1980. (On Cervantes' "La gitanilla".)

Díez Borque, José María. *Sociología de la comedia española del siglo XVII*. Madrid: Cátedra, 1976. (See espec. Pts. I and III.)

Maravall, José Antonio. "Relaciones de dependencia e integración social: Criados, graciosos y pícaros." *I&L*, 1 (1977), 3–32.

—. *Teatro y literatura en la sociedad barroca*. Madrid: Seminarios y Ediciones, 1972. (See espec. Ch. 2.)

Márquez Villanueva, Francisco. "Amantes en la Sierra Morena." In his *Personajes y temas del Quijote*. Madrid: Taurus, 1975, pp. 15–75. (On Cervantes' character Dorotea.)

Stern, Charlotte. "Lope de Vega, Propagandist?" *BCom*, 34 (1982), 1–36.

Szanto, George H. *Theater and Propaganda*. Austin: U. of Texas P., 1978.

Wiltrout, Ann E. "Role Playing and Rites of Passage: *La ilustre fregona* and *La gitanilla*." *Hispania*, 64 (1981), 388–399.

Chapter 3: "Negative Solitude and the Marginal Individual"

Caro Baroja, Julio. *Inquisición, brujería y criptojudaísmo*. Barcelona: Ariel, 1970.

—. "El Señor Inquisidor." Ch. 1 of his *El Señor Inquisidor y otras vidas por oficio*. 2nd ed. Madrid: Alianza, 1970.

Casa, Frank P. "Pleberio's Lament for Melibea." *ZRP*, 84 (1968), 20–29.

Castro, Américo. "*La Celestina* coma contienda literaria." Pt. II of his *La Celestina como contienda literaria* (*Castas y casticismos*). Madrid: *RO*, 1965.

—. "Cervantes y el 'Quijote' a nueva luz." Pt. I of his *Cervantes y los casticismos españoles*. Madrid: Alfaguara, 1966.

—. "Los hispano-hebreos y el sentimiento de la honra." Ch. 3 of his *De la edad conflictiva*. Madrid: Taurus, 1961.

—. *La realidad histórica de España*. 3rd ed. Mexico City: Porrúa, 1966.

—. *Sobre el nombre y el quién de los españoles*. Madrid: Taurus, 1973.

Domínguez Ortiz, Antonio. *La clase social de los conversos en Castilla en la Edad Moderna*. Madrid: C.S.I.C., 1955.

Dunn, Peter N. "Pleberio's World." *PMLA*, 91 (1976), 406–419.

Durán, Manuel. *Luis de León*. New York: Twayne, 1971. (See espec. Ch. 2: "Luis de León, the Man and the Humanist.")

Gilman, Stephen. *The Spain of Fernando de Rojas: The Intellectual and Social Landscape of La Celestina*. Princeton: Princeton U.P., 1972.

Kamen, Henry. *The Spanish Inquisition*. London: Weidenfeld and Nicolson, 1965.

Márquez, Antonio. "Dos procesos singulares: Fray Luis de León y Antonio Enríquez Gómez." Ch. 5 of his *Literatura e Inquisición en España* (*1478–1834*). Madrid: Taurus, 1980.

Márquez Villanueva, Francisco. "La criptohistoria morisca (Los otros conversos)." *CHA*, 390 (1982), 517–534.

—. "El morisco Ricote o la hispana razón de estado." In his *Personajes y temas del Quijote*. Madrid: Taurus, 1975, pp. 229–335.

—. "El problema historiográfico de los moriscos." *BH*, 86 (1984), 61–135.

—. "El problema religioso de los conversos." In Hernando de Talavera. *Católica impugnación*. Ed. F. Martiń Hernández. Barcelona: Juan Flors, 1961, pp. 43–53.

Oelman, T. "The Religious Views of Antonio Enríquez Gómez: Profile of a Marrano." *BHS*, 60 (1983), 201–209.

Redondo, Augustin. "Le jeu de l'énigme dans l'Espagne du XVIe siècle et du début du XVIIe siècle: Aspect ludique et subversion." In *Les Jeux à la Renaissance*. Ed. P. Ariès and J.-C. Margolin. Actes du XXIIIe Colloque International d'ètudes humanistes; Tours, 1980. Paris: Vrin, 1982, pp. 445–458.

Rodríguez Puértolas, Julio. "El Romancero, historia de una frustración." In his *Literatura, historia, alienación*. Barcelona: Labor, 1976, pp. 105–146. (On the "Romance del prisionero".)

Rogers, Francis M. "Fernão Mendes Pinto, His *Peregrinaçam*, and the Spanish Play." In Antonio Enríquez Gómez. *Fernán Méndez Pinto*. Ed. L.G. Cohen, F.M. Rogers, and C.H. Rose. Cambridge, MA: Harvard Univ.; Dept. of Romance Languages and Literatures, 1974, pp. 9–27.

Rose, Constance H. *Alonso Núñez de Reinoso: The Lament of a Sixteenth-Century Exile*. Rutherford, NJ: Fairleigh Dickinson U.P., 1971.

—. "Enríquez Gómez and the Literature of Exile." In Antonio Enríquez Gómez. *Fernán Méndez Pinto*. Ed. L.G. Cohen, F.M. Rogers, and C.H. Rose, Cambridge, MA: Harvard Univ.; Dept. of Romance Languages and Literatures, 1974, pp. 47–63.

Scholberg, Kenneth R. "Los conversos en la sátira e invectiva del siglo XV." Ch. 6 of his *Sátira e invectiva en la España medieval*. Madrid: Gredos, 1971. (On Cota and Montoro.)

Wardropper, Bruce W. "Pleberio's Lament for Melibea and the Medieval Elegiac Tradition." *MLN*, 79 (1964), 140–152.

Yerushalmi, Josef Hayim. *From Spanish Court to Italian Ghetto: Isaac Cardoso: A Study in Seventeenth-Century Marranism and Jewish Apologetics*. New York: Columbia U.P., 1971. (See espec. Ch. 1: "Marranos in the Seventeenth Century.")

Chapter 4: *"Pícaros* and *Pícaras"*

The Picaresque

Bjornson, Richard. *The Picaresque Hero in European Fiction*. Madison: U. of Wisconsin P., 1977. (See espec. Chs. 1–6.)

Blackburn, Alexander. *The Myth of the Picaro: Continuity and Transformation of the Picaresque Novel (1554–1954)*. Chapel Hill: U. of North Carolina P., 1979. (See espec. Chs. 1 and 2.)

Carrillo, Francisco. "Raíz sociológica e imaginación creadora en la picaresca española." In *La Picaresca: Orígenes, textos y estructuras*. Ed. M. Criado de Val. Actas del I Congreso Internacional sobre la Picaresca (organizado por el Patronato "Arcipreste de Hita"). Madrid: F.U.E., 1979, pp. 65–77.

Castro, Américo. "Perspectiva de la novela picaresca." In Pt. I of his *Hacia Cervantes*. 3rd ed. Madrid: Taurus, 1967, pp. 118–142.

Cros, Edmond. "Aproximación a la picaresca." In *La Picaresca: Orígenes, textos y estructuras*. Ed. M. Criado de Val. Actas del I Congreso Internacional sobre la Picaresca (organizado por el Patronato "Arcipreste de Hita"). Madrid: F.U.E., 1979, pp. 31–38.

Dunn, Peter N. *The Spanish Picaresque Novel*. Boston: G. K. Hall; Twayne, 1979.

Francis, Alán. *Picaresca, decadencia, historia: Aproximación a una realidad histórico-literaria*. Madrid: Gredos, 1978.

Frutos Gómez de las Cortinas, J. "El antihéroe y su actitud vital (Sentido de la novela picaresca)." *Cuadernos de Literatura*, 7 (1950), 97–145.

Guillén, Claudio. "Toward a Definition of the Picaresque." In his *Literature as System: Essays toward the Theory of Literary History*. Princeton: Princeton U.P., 1971, pp. 71–106.

Herrero García, Miguel. "Nueva interpretación de la novela picaresca." *RFE*, 24 (1937), 343–362.

Maravall, José Antonio. "La aspiración social de 'medro' en la novela picaresca." *CHA*, 312 (1976), 590–625.

—. "Pobres y pobreza del medievo a la primera modernidad (Para un estudio histórico-social de la picaresca)." *CHA*, 367–368 (1981), 189–242.

—. "Relaciones de dependencia e integración social: Criados, graciosos y pícaros." *I&L*, 1 (1977), 3–32.

Miller, Stuart. *The Picaresque Novel*. Cleveland: Case Western Reserve U.P., 1967.

Molho, Maurice. *Introducción al pensamiento picaresco*. Trans. A. Gálvez-Cañero y Pidal. Salamanca: Anaya, 1972.

Monte, Alberto del. *Itinerario de la novela picaresca española*. Barcelona: Lumen, 1971.

Parker, Alexander A. *Los pícaros en la literatura: La novela picaresca en España y Europa (1599–1753)*. Trans R. A. Mackry. Madrid: Gredos, 1971. (See espec. Chs. 1–3.)

Rico, Francisco. *La novela picaresca y el punto de vista*. Barcelona: Seix Barral, 1970.

Ripoll, Carlos. "Notas sobre la novela picaresca." In his *"La Celestina" a través del Decálogo y otras notas sobre la literatura de la Edad le Oro*. New York: Las Americas, 1969, pp. 89–124.

Sieber, Harry. *The Picaresque*. London: Methuen, 1977.

Zalazar, Daniel Eduardo. "Libertad y determinismo en la novela picaresca española." *CHA*, 301 (1975), 47–68.

Lazarillo de Tormes

Alter, Robert. "Lazarillo and the Picaresque Code." Ch. 1 of his *Rogue's Progress: Studies in the Picaresque Novel*. Cambridge, MA: Harvard U.P., 1964.

Brancaforte, Benito. "La abyección en el *Lazarillo de Tormes*." *CHA*, 387 (1982), 551–566.

Carey, Douglas M. "*Lazarillo de Tormes* and the Quest for Authority." *PMLA*, 94 (1979), 36–46.

Fiore, Robert L. *Lazarillo de Tormes*. Boston: G.K. Hall; Twayne, 1984.

Gilman, Stephen. "The Death of Lazarillo de Tormes." *PMLA*, 81 (1966), 149–166.

Herrero, Javier. "Renaissance Poverty and Lazarillo's Family: The Birth of the Picaresque Genre." *PMLA*, 94 (1979), 876–886.

Mancing, Howard. "The Deceptiveness of *Lazarillo de Tormes*." *PMLA*, 90 (1975), 426–432.

—. "El pesimismo radical del *Lazarillo de Tormes*." In *La Picaresca: Orígenes, textos y estructuras*. Ed. M. Criado de Val. Actas del I Congreso Internacional sobre la Picaresca (organizado por el Patronato "Arcipreste de Hita"). Madrid: F.U.E., 1979, pp. 459–467.

Márquez Villanueva, Francisco. "La actitud espiritual del *Lazarillo de Tormes*." In his *Espiritualidad y literatura en el siglo XVI*. Madrid: Alfaguara, 1968, pp. 67–137.

McGrady, Donald. "Social Irony in *Lazarillo de Tormes* and its Implications for Authorship." *RPh*, 23 (1970), 557–567.

Rodríguez Puértolas, Julio. "'Lazarillo de Tormes' o la desmitificación del Imperio." In his *Literatura, historia, alienación*. Barcelona: Labor, 1976, pp. 173–199.

Sánchez Blanco, Francisco. "El 'Lazarillo' y el punto de vista de la alta nobleza." *CHA*, 369 (1981), 511–520.

Windler, Victoria C. "Alienación en el 'Lazarillo de Tormes': La fragmentación del 'yo' narrativo." *EFil*, No. 8 (1972), pp. 225–253.

Guzmán de Alfarache

Eoff, Sherman. "The Picaresque Psychology of Guzmán de Alfarache." *HR*, 21 (1953), 107–119.

Jones, J.A. "The Duality and Complexity of Guzmán de Alfarache: Some Thoughts on the Structure and Interpretation of Alemán's Novel." In *Knaves and Swindlers: Essays on the Picaresque Novel in Europe*. Ed. C.J. Whitbourn. London and New York: Oxford U.P., 1974, pp. 25–47.

McGrady, Donald. *Mateo Alemán*. New York: Twayne, 1968.

Nagy, Edward. "La honra familiar en el *Guzmán* de Mateo Alemán." *Hispano*, 8 (1960), 39–45.

Ramírez, Genevieve M. "Guzmán de Alfarache and the Concept of Honor." *REH*, 14 (1980), 61–77.

El Buscón

Bleznick, Donald W. *Quevedo*. New York: Twayne, 1972. (See espec. Ch. 4.)

Cros, Edmond. "'Le Buscón' de Quevedo: Interprétation." *LdD*, 10 (1980), 57–68.

Dunn, Peter N. "El individuo y la sociedad en *La vida del Buscón*." *BH*, 52 (1950), 375–396.

Geisler, Eberhard. "La identidad imposible: En torno al Buscón." *Nuevo Hispanismo*, 1 (1982), 39–54.

Johnson, Carroll B. "*El Buscón*: Don Pablos, don Diego y don Francisco." *Hispano*, 51 (1974), 1–26.

—. "Quevedo in Context: Personality, Society, Ideology." *Mester*, Vol. 9, No. 2 (1980), pp. 3–16.

May, T.E. "Good and Evil in the 'Buscón': A Survey." *MLR*, 45 (1950), 319–335.

Parker, Alexander A. "The Psychology of the 'Pícaro' in 'El Buscón'." *MLR*, 42 (1947), 58–69.

Redondo, Augustin. "Del personaje de don Diego Coronel a una nueva interpretación de 'El Buscón'." In *Actas del Quinto Congreso Internacional de Hispanistas*. Ed. M. Chevalier et al. Bordeaux: Univ. de Bordeaux; Instituto de Estudios Ibéricos e Iberoamericanos, 1977. Vol. II, pp. 699–711.

Rose, Constance H. "Pablos' *Damnosa Heritas*." *RF*, 82 (1970), 94–101.

Bataillon, Marcel. *Pícaros y picaresca: La pícara Justina.* Madrid: Taurus, 1969. (See espec. Pts. I–III.)

Brownstein, Leonard. *Salas Barbadillo and the New Novel of Rogues and Courtiers.* Madrid: Playor, 1974. (See espec. Ch. 4.)

Damiani, Bruno M. *Francisco Delicado.* New York: Twayne, 1974.

—. *Francisco López de Úbeda.* Boston: G.K. Hall; Twayne, 1977.

Dunn, Peter N. *Castillo Solórzano and the Decline of the Spanish Novel.* Oxford, Eng.: Blackwell, 1952. (See espec. Ch. 7.)

Hanrahan, Thomas. *La mujer en la novela picaresca española.* 2 vols. Madrid: Porrúa Turanzas, 1967.

Márquez Villanueva, Francisco. "El mundo converso de 'La Lozana andaluza'." *ArH*, Nos. 171–173 (1973), pp. 87–97.

Peyton, Myron A. *Alonso Jerónimo de Salas Barbadillo.* New York: Twayne, 1973. (See espec. Ch. 3.)

Soons, Alan. *Alonso de Castillo Solórzano.* Boston: G.K. Hall; Twayne, 1978. (See espec. Ch. 4.)

Chapter 5: "Wealth, Appearances, and the Impoverished Nobleman"

Beysterveldt, Antonie A. van. *Repercussions du souci de la pureté de sang sur la conception de l'honneur dans la "Comedia nueva" espagnole.* Leiden: E. J. Brill, 1966.

Díez Borque, José María. *Sociología de la comedia española del siglo XVII.* Madrid: Cátedra, 1976. (See espec. Ch. 1 of Pt. II and Chs. 2 and 3 of Pt. III.)

Maravall, José Antonio. *Teatro y literatura en la sociedad barroca.* Madrid: Seminarios y Ediciones, 1972. (See espec. Chs. 11 and 12.)

Parr, James A. "Honor-Virtue in *La verdad sospechosa* and *Las paredes oyen.*" *REH*, 8 (1974), 173–188.

Poesse, Walter. *Juan Ruiz de Alarcón.* New York: Twayne, 1972. (See espec. Chs. 1 and 5.)

Chapter 6: "The Plight of the Destitute, Oppressed Commoner"

Alonso, Dámaso. "Pobres y ricos en los libros de 'Buen Amor' y de 'Miseria de Omne'." In his *De los siglos oscuros al de Oro (Notas y artículos a través de 700 años de letras españolas).* Madrid: Gredos, 1971, pp. 105–113.

Deyermond, Alan D. "El ambiente social e intelectual de la *Danza de la Muerte.*" In *Actas del Tercer Congreso Internacional de Hispanistas.* Ed. C.H. Magis. Mexico City: Colegio de México, 1970, pp. 267–276.

Maravall, José Antonio. *El mundo social de "La Celestina"*. 2nd ed. Madrid: Gredos, 1968.

Ortiz Griffin, Julia. "Class Struggle in *La Celestina*." In *Homenaje a Humberto Piñera: Estudios de literatura, arte e historia*. Madrid: Playor, 1979, pp. 187–195.

Parker, Alexander A. "'El gran teatro del mundo'." Ch. 3 of his *The Allegorical Drama of Calderón: An Introduction to the Autos Sacramentales*. Oxford, Eng.: Dolphin, 1968.

Rodríguez Puértolas, Julio. "La Celestina o la negación de la negación." In his *Literatura, historia, alienación*. Barcelona: Labor, 1976, pp. 147–171.

—. "Nueva aproximación a *La Celestina*." In his *De la Edad Media a la Edad Conflictiva: Estudios de literatura española*. Madrid: Gredos, 1972, pp. 217–242.

—. *Poesía de protesta en la Edad Media castellana: Historia y antología*. Madrid: Gredos, 1968. (See espec. pp. 11–57.)

Scholberg, Kenneth R. *Sátira e invectiva en la España medieval*. Madrid: Gredos, 1971. (See espec. Chs. 3 and 5.)

Whyte, Florence. *The Dance of Death in Spain and Catalonia*. Baltimore: Waverly, 1931.

Chapter 7: "Positive Solitude and Freedom"

Durán, Manuel. *Luis de León*. New York: Twayne, 1971. (See espec. Chs. 4 and 5.)

Johnson, Carroll B. *Madness and Lust: A Psychoanalytical Approach to Don Quixote*. Berkeley: U. of California P., 1983. (See espec. Ch. 4.)

Jones, Joseph R. *Antonio de Guevara*. Boston: G.K. Hall; Twayne, 1975. (See espec. Ch. 6.)

Marañón, Gregorio. "Gloria y miseria del conde de Villamediana." In his *Don Juan: Ensayos sobre el origen de su leyenda*. 10th ed. Madrid: Espasa-Calpe; Austral, 1964, pp. 67–116.

Salinas, Pedro. "The Idealization of Reality: Garcilaso de la Vega." Ch. 3 of his *Reality and the Poet in Spanish Poetry*. Trans. E. Fishtine Helman. Baltimore: Johns Hopkins U.P., 1966.

—. "The Escape from Reality: Fray Luis de León and San Juan de la Cruz." Ch. 4 of his *Reality and the Poet*. . . . (See above.)

Sieber, Harry, "Society and the Pastoral Vision in the Marcela-Grisóstomo Episode of *Don Quijote*." In *Estudios literarios de hispanistas norteamericanos dedicados a Helmut Hatzfeld con motivo de su 80 aniversario*. Barcelona: Hispam, 1974, pp. 185–194.

Unamuno, Miguel de. "De mística y humanismo." Ch. 4 of his *En torno al casticismo*. 6th ed. Madrid: Espasa-Calpe; Austral, 1964.

Vossler, Karl. *La poesía de la soledad en España*. Buenos Aires: Losada, 1946.

Chapter 8: "The Quest for Self-Realization and Freedom in Cervantes' Characters"

Arco y Garay, Ricardo del. "La crítica social en Cervantes." In his *Estudios de historia social de España*. Madrid: 1952. Vol. II, pp. 291–326.

—. *La sociedad española en las obras de Cervantes*. Madrid: Patronato del IV Centenario del Nacimiento de Cervantes, 1951.

Basave Fernández del Valle, Agustín. *Filosofía del Quijote*. Mexico City: Espasa-Calpe; Austral, 1959. (See espec. Chs. 7 and 12.)

Castro, Américo. "Cervantes." Pt. II of his *Hacia Cervantes*. 3rd ed. Madrid: Taurus, 1967.

—. "Cervantes y el 'Quijote' a nueva luz." Pt. I of his *Cervantes y los casticismos españoles*. Madrid: Alfaguara, 1966.

—. *El pensamiento de Cervantes*. New ed. Barcelona: Noguer, 1972. (See espec. Chs. 2 and 4.)

Durán, Manuel. *Cervantes*. New York: Twayne, 1974. (See espec. Chs. 2, 5, and 7.)

Forcione, Alban K. *Cervantes' Christian Romance: A Study of Persiles y Sigismunda*. Princeton: Princeton U.P., 1972. (See espec. pp. 118–121 for parallels between Transila, a character in *Persiles*, and Preciosa.)

Gilman, Stephen. *Cervantes y Avellaneda: Estudio du una imitación*. Mexico City: F.C.E., 1951.

Green, Otis H. "*El Licenciado Vidriera*: Its Relation to the *Viaje del Parnaso* and the *Examen de Ingenios* of Huarte." Ch. 10 of his *The Literary Mind of Medieval & Renaissance Spain*. Lexington: U.P. of Kentucky, 1970.

Johnson, Carroll B. *Madness and Lust: A Psychoanalytical Approach to Don Quixote*. Berkeley: U. of California P., 1983. (See espec. Ch. 3.)

Lerner, Isaías. "Marginalidad en las Novelas Ejemplares: I: *La gitanilla*." *Lexis*, 4 (1980), 47–59.

Maravall, José Antonio. *El humanismo de las armas en Don Quijote*. Madrid: Instituto de Estudios Políticos, 1948.

Márquez Villanueva, Francisco. "¿Historia de amor?" In his *Personajes y temas del Quijote*. Madrid: Taurus, 1975, pp. 115–146. (On Zoraida.)

Morel-Fatio, A. "Social and Historical Background." In *Cervantes across the Centuries: A Quadricentennial Volume*. Ed. A. Flores and M.J. Benardete. New York: Gordian, 1969, pp. 101–127. (On *Don Quijote*.)

Ortega y Gasset, José. "Ensimismamiento y alteración." Ch. 1 of his *El hombre y la gente*. 7th ed. Madrid: *RO*, 1972. Vol. I.

Parker, Alexander A. "El concepto de la verdad en el 'Quijote'." *RFE*, 32 (1948), 287–305.

Predmore, Richard L. *The World of Don Quixote*. Cambridge, MA: Harvard U.P., 1967.

Río, Ángel del. "El equívoco del *Quijote*." *HR*, 27 (1959), 200–221.

Rosales, Luis. *Cervantes y la libertad*. 2 vols. Madrid: Sociedad de Estudios y Publicaciones, 1960.

Salinas, Pedro. "Lo que debemos a Don Quijote." In his *Ensayos de literatura hispánica: Del "Cantar de Mío Cid" a García Lorca*. 2nd ed. Madrid: Aguilar, 1961, pp. 85–105.

Weiger, John G. *The Individuated Self: Cervantes and the Emergence of the Individual*. Athens: Ohio U.P., 1979.

Chapter 9: "The Undeceived Individual"

Colonello, Pio. "*Honra* e *honor* nelle *Coplas por la muerte de su padre* di J. Manrique: Loro ambito semantico." Naples: Istituto Universitario Orientale: Sezione Romanza: *Annali*, 19 (1977), 417–434.

Foster, Virginia Ramos. *Baltasar Gracián*. Boston: G.K. Hall; Twayne, 1975.

Green, Otis H. "*Desengaño*." Ch. 3 of his *Spain and the Western Tradition: The Castilian Mind in Literature from El Cid to Calderón*. Madison: U. of Wisconsin P., 1968. Vol. IV. (Also Ch. 8 of his *The Literary Mind of Medieval & Renaissance Spain*. Lexington: U.P. of Kentucky, 1970.)

Hafter, Monroe Z. *Gracián and Perfection: Spanish Moralists of the Seventeenth Century*. Cambridge, MA: Harvard U.P., 1966. (See espec. Chs. 4–6.)

Hesse, Everett W. *Calderón de la Barca*. New York: Twayne, 1967. (See espec. Ch. 11 on *La vida es sueño*.)

—. "Calderón de la Barca." Ch. 4 of his *Análisis e interpretación de la comedia*. 3rd ed. Madrid: Castalia, 1970. (On *Eco y Narciso* and *La vida es sueño*.)

Lida de Malkiel, María Rosa. *La idea de la fama en la Edad Media castellana*. Mexico City: F.C.E., 1952.

Maravall, José Antonio. "Antropología y política en el pensamiento de Gracián." Ch. 7 of his *Estudios de historia del pensamiento español: Serie tercera: Siglo XVII*. Madrid: C.H., 1975.

Montesinos, José F. "Gracián o la picaresca pura." In his *Ensayos y estudios de literatura española*. Madrid: RO, 1970, pp. 141–158.

Mujica, Barbara. "Freedom, Power, and Self-Assertion: *La Vida es Sueño*." Ch. 4 of her *Calderón's Characters: An Existential Point of View*. Barcelona: Puvill, 1980.

Parker, Alexander A. "'El gran teatro del mundo'." Ch. 3 of his *The Allegorical Drama of Calderón: An Introduction to the Autos Sacramentales*. Oxford, Eng.: Dolphin, 1968.

Rosales, Luis. *El sentimiento del desengaño en la poesía barroca*. Pt. I. Madrid: C.H., 1966.

Serrano de Haro, Antonio. *Personalidad y destino de Jorge Manrique*. Madrid: Gredos, 1966. (See espec. Pt. I.)

Vossler, Karl. *La poesía de la soledad en España*. Buenos Aires: Losada, 1946.

Part V: "The Individual and the Societal Code of Honor" (The following works relate to Chapters 10–13.)

Artiles, Jenaro. "La idea de la venganza en el drama español del siglo XVII." *Segismundo*, 3 (1967), 9–38.

Beysterveldt, Antonie A. van. *Repercussions du souci de la pureté de sang sur la concéption de l'honneur dans la "Comedia nueva" espagnole*. Leiden: E.J. Brill, 1966.

Casa, Frank P. "Aspects of Characterization in Golden Age Drama." In *Critical Perspectives on Calderón de la Barca*. Ed. F.A. De Armas, D.M. Gitlitz, and J.A. Madrigal. Lincoln, NE: Society of Spanish and Spanish-American Studies, 1981, pp. 37–47.

—. "Conflicto y jerarquía de valores en el teatro del Siglo de Oro." In *Estudios sobre el Siglo de Oro en homenaje a Raymond R. MacCurdy*. Ed. Á. González, T. Holzapfel, and A. Rodríguez. Albuquerque: Univ. of New Mexico; Dept. of Modern and Classical Languages, 1983. Madrid: Cátedra, 1983, pp. 15–24.

—. *The Dramatic Craftsmanship of Moreto*. Cambridge, MA: Harvard U.P., 1966.

Castro, Américo. "Algunas observaciones acerca del concepto del honor en los siglos XVI y XVII." *RFE*, 3 (1916), 1–50, 357–386.

—. "El drama de la honra en la literatura dramática." Ch. 1 of his *De la edad conflictiva*. Madrid: Taurus, 1961.

Correa, Gustavo. "El doble aspecto de la honra en el teatro del siglo XVII." *HR*, 26 (1958), 99–107.

Díez Borque, José María. *Sociología de la comedia española del siglo XVII*. Madrid: Cátedra, 1976.

Gutiérrez Nieto, Juan Ignacio. "Honra y utilidad social (En torno a los conceptos de honor y honra)." In *Calderón: Actas del Congreso Internacional sobre Calderón y el teatro español del Siglo de Oro*. Ed. L. García Lorenzo. Madrid: C.S.I.C., 1983 (Anejos de *Segismundo*, No. 6). Vol. II, pp. 881–895.

Hesse, Everett W. *Calderón de la Barca*. New York: Twayne, 1967.

Honig, Edwin. *Calderón and the Seizures of Honor*. Cambridge, MA: Harvard U.P., 1972. (See espec. Chs. 1–3.)

MacCurdy, Raymond R. *Francisco de Rojas Zorrilla*. New York: Twayne, 1968.

—. "Women and Sexual Love in the Plays of Rojas Zorrilla: Tradition and Innovation." *Hispania*, 62 (1979), 255–265.

Maravall, José Antonio. "La función del honor en la sociedad tradicional." *I&L*, 2 (1978), 9–27.

—. *Teatro y literatura en la sociedad barroca*. Madrid: Seminarios y Ediciones, 1972.

McKendrick, Melveena. *Woman and Society in the Spanish Drama of the Golden Age: A Study of the Mujer Varonil*. Cambridge, Eng.: Cambridge U.P., 1974. (See espec. Chs. 4, 5, and 9.)

Menéndez Pidal, Ramón. "Del honor en el teatro español." In his *De Cervantes y Lope de Vega*. 5th ed. Madrid: Espasa-Calpe; Austral, 1958, pp. 145–173.

Mujica, Barbara. "Honor from the Comic Perspective: Calderón's *Comedias de capa y espada*." *BCom*, 38 (1986), 7–24.

Northup, G.T. "Cervantes' Attitude Toward Honor." *MP*, 21 (1924), 397–421.

Parker, Alexander A. "The Approach to the Spanish Drama of the Golden Age." *TDR* (Autumn, 1959), pp. 42–59.

—. "Towards a Definition of Calderonian Tragedy." *BHS*, 39 (1962), 222–237.

Piluso, Robert V. *Amor, matrimonio y honra en Cervantes*. New York: Las Américas, 1967.

—. "Honor in Valdivielso and Cervantes." *KRQ*, 17 (1970), 67–81.

Reichenberger, Arnold G. "The Uniqueness of the *Comedia*." *HR*, 27 (1959), 303–316.

Salomon, Noël. *Recherches sur le thème paysan dans la "comedia" au temps de Lope de Vega*. Bordeaux: Univ. de Bordeaux; Institut d' Etudes Ibériques et Ibéro-Américaines, 1965.

Spitzer, Leo. "*Soy quien soy*." *NRFH*, 1 (1947), 113–127.

Sponsler, Lucy A. *Women in the Medieval Spanish Epic and Lyric Traditions*. Studies in Romance Languages, No. 13. Lexington: U.P. of Kentucky, 1975.

Wilson, Margaret. *Tirso de Molina*. Boston: G.K. Hall; Twayne, 1977.

Chapter 10: "Honor and Dishonor"

Arias Arias, Ricardo. "El *Caballero Cifar*." In his *El concepto del destino en la literatura medieval española.* Madrid: Ínsula, 1970, pp. 222–248.

Caro Baroja, Julio. "Honor y vergüenza: Examen histórico de varios conflictos populares." Pt. III of his *Ciudad y campo*. Madrid and Barcelona: Alfaguara, 1966. (Also in *El concepto del honor en la sociedad mediterránea*. Ed. J.G. Peristiany. Barcelona: Labor, 1968, pp. 77–126.)

Carreño, Antonio. "La vergüenza como valor sociológico y narrativo en Don Juan Manuel: El exemplo L de 'El conde Lucanor'." *CHA*, 314–315 (1976), 495–510.

Correa, Gustavo. "El tema de la honra en el *Poema del Cid*." *HR*, 20 (1952), 185–199.

Dutton, Brian. "The Semantics of Honor." *RCEH*, 4 (1979), 1–17.

Lida de Malkiel, María Rosa. *La idea de la fama en la Edad Media castellana*. Mexico City: F.C.E., 1952.

Márquez Villanueva, Francisco. "La génesis literaria de Sancho Panza." In his *Fuentes literarias cervantinas*. Madrid: Gredos, 1973, pp. 63–83. (On the *villano* in literature.)

Martin, Georges. "La marginalidad cidiana: Textos, mitos." *Imprévue*, 1 (1980), 53–61.

Pitt-Rivers, Julian. "Honor y categoría social." In *El concepto del honor en la sociedad mediterránea*. Ed. J.G. Peristiany. Barcelona: Labor, 1968, pp. 21–75.

Poesse, Walter. "Utilización de las palabras 'honor' y 'honra' en la comedia española." In *Homenaje a don Agapito Rey: Trabajos publicados en su honor*. Ed. J. Roca-Pons. Bloomington: Indiana Univ.; Dept. of Spanish and Portuguese, 1980, pp. 289–303.

Resina, Juan Ramón. "El honor y las relaciones feudales en el Poema de mío Cid." *REH*, 18 (1984), 417–428.

Salinas, Pedro. "El 'Cantar de Mío Cid' (Poema de la honra)." In his *Ensayos de literatura hispánica: Del "Cantar de Mío Cid" a García Lorca*. 2nd ed. Madrid: Aguilar, 1961, pp. 27–43.

Sánchez Albornoz, Claudio. "Honor, orgullo y dignidad." Ch. 10 of his *España, un enigma histórico*. Buenos Aires: Editorial Sudamericana, 1962. Vol. I.

Chapter 11: "Honor in Conflict with Love"

Holmberg, Arthur. "Variaciones sobre el tema del honor en *La dama duende* de Calderón." In *Calderón: Actas del Congreso Internacional sobre Calderón y el teatro español del Siglo de Oro*. Ed. L. García Lorenzo. Madrid: C.S.I.C., 1983 (Anejos de *Segismundo*, No. 6). Vol. II, pp. 913–923.

Honig, Edwin. *Calderón and the Seizures of Honor*. Cambridge, MA: Harvard U.P., 1972. (See Ch. 7 on *La dama duende*.)

Mujica, Barbara. "Freedom and Reason: *La Dama Duende*." Ch. 2 of her *Calderón's Characters: An Existential Point of View*. Barcelona: Puvill, 1980.

Oostendorp, Henricus Th. "El conflicto entre el honor y el amor en la literatura española del siglo XV." Ch. 3 of his *El conflicto entre el honor y el amor en la literatura española hasta el siglo XVII*. Utrecht: Univ.; Instituto de Estudios Hispánicos, Portugueses e Iberoamericanos, 1962. (On "sentimental" novels.)

Petrov, D.K. "El amor, sus principios y dialéctica en el teatro de Lope de Vega." *Escorial*, 16 (1944), 9–41.

Ruiz de Conde, Justina. *El amor y el matrimonio secreto en los libros de caballerías*. Madrid: Aguilar, 1948.

Wardropper, Bruce W. "Lope's *La dama boba* and Baroque Comedy." *BCom*, 13 (1961), 1–13.

Whinnom, Keith. *Diego de San Pedro*. New York: Twayne, 1974. (See espec. Ch. 7 on *Cárcel de amor*.)

Chapter 12: "Honor, Illicit Passion, and the Unmarried Woman"

Bleznick, Donald W. *Quevedo*. New York: Twayne, 1972. (See Ch. 7 concerning Quevedo's views about tyrannicide.)

Cao, Antonio F. "La mujer y el mito de Don Juan en Calderón: *La niña de Gómez Arias.*" In *Calderón: Actas del Congreso Internacional sobre Calderón y el teatro español del Siglo de Oro*. Ed. L. García Lorenzo. Madrid: C.S.I.C., 1983 (Anejos de *Segismundo*, No. 6). Vol. II, pp. 839–854.

Casanova, Wilfredo O. "Honor, patrimonio del alma y opinión social, patrimonio de casta en *El alcalde de Zalamea* de Calderón." *Hispano*, 33 (1968), 17–33.

Correa, Gustavo. "Naturaleza, religión y honra en *La Celestina.*" *PMLA*, 77 (1962), 8–17.

Delgado Morales, M. "Guillén de Castro y las teorías políticas sobre el tiranicidio y el derecho de resistencia." *BH*, 85 (1983), 65–82.

Dunn, Peter N. *Fernando de Rojas*. Boston: G.K. Hall; Twayne, 1975. (See espec. Ch. 8.)

—. "Honour and the Christian Background in Calderón." *BHS*, 37 (1960), 75–105. (Also in *Critical Essays on the Theatre of Calderón*. Ed. B.W. Wardropper. New York: New York U.P., 1965, pp. 24–60.)

—. "'Patrimonio del alma'." *BHS*, 41 (1964), 78–85. (On Calderón's *El alcalde de Zalamea*.)

Edwards, Gwynne. "The Closed World of *El alcalde de Zalamea.*" In *Critical Perspectives on Calderón de la Barca*. Ed F.A. De Armas, D.M. Gitlitz, and J.A. Madrigal. Lincoln, NE: Society of Spanish and Spanish-American Studies, 1981, pp. 53–67.

Gijón, Esmeralda. "Concepto del honor y de la mujer en Tirso de Molina." Madrid: *Estudios*, 5 (1949), 479–655.

Gilman, Stephen. *The Art of La Celestina*. Madison: U. of Wisconsin P., 1956. (See espec. Ch. 5.)

Honig, Edwin. *Calderón and the Seizures of Honor*. Cambridge, MA: Harvard U.P., 1972. (See Ch. 5 on *La devoción de la Cruz*, Ch. 6 on *El alcalde de Zalamea*, and Ch. 8 on *La vida es sueño*.)

Jones, Cyril A. "Honor in *El alcalde de Zalamea.*" *MLR*, 50 (1955), 444–449. (Also in *Critical Essays on the Theatre of Calderón*. Ed. B.W. Wardropper. New York: New York U.P., 1965, pp. 193–202.)

La Du, Robert R. "Honor and the King in the *Comedias* of Guillén de Castro." *Hispania*, 45 (1962), 211–216.

Larson, Donald R. *The Honor Plays of Lope de Vega*. Cambridge, MA: Harvard U.P., 1977. (See espec. pp. 82–112 on *Fuenteovejuna*.)

Lida de Malkiel, María Rosa. *La originalidad artística de La Celestina*. Buenos Aires: Eudeba, 1962. (See espec. pp. 283–658.)

Lundelius, Ruth. "Tirso's View of Women in *El Burlador de Sevilla.*" *BCom*, 27 (1975), 5–14.

Márquez Villanueva, Francisco. "Amantes en la Sierra Morena." In his *Personajes y temas del Quijote*. Madrid: Taurus, 1975, pp. 15–75. (On the seduction of Dorotea.)

Matas, Julio. "El honor en *Fuenteovejuna* y la tragedia del Comendador." In *Lope de Vega* y los orígenes del teatro español: Actas del I Congreso Internacional sobre Lope de Vega. Ed. M. Criado de Val. Madrid: EDI-6, 1981, pp. 385–391.

Mujica, Barbara. "The Rapist and his Victim: Calderón's 'No hay cosa como callar'." Hispania, 62 (1979), 30–46.

Oostendorp, Henricus Th. "El conflicto entre el honor y el amor en La Celestina." Ch. 4 of his El conflicto entre el honor y el amor en la literatura española hasta el siglo XVII. Utrecht: Univ.; Instituto de Estudios Hispánicos, Portugueses e Iberoamericanos, 1962.

Parker, Alexander A. "The Father-Son Conflict in the Drama of Calderón." Forum for Modern Language Studies, 2 (1966), 99–113.

—. "Santos y bandoleros en el teatro español del Siglo de Oro." Arbor, 13 (1949), 395–416. (The English version of this article, "Bandits and Saints in the Spanish Drama of the Golden Age," appears in Critical Studies of Calderón's Comedies. Ed. J.E. Varey. London: Gregg International and Tamesis, 1973, pp. 151–168.)

Podol, Peter. "Non-Conventional Treatment of the Honor Theme in the Theater of the Golden Age." REH, 7 (1973), 449–463. (On El alcalde de Zalamea.)

Pring-Mill, R.D.F. Introduction to Lope de Vega. Five Plays. Trans. J Booty. New York: Hill and Wang, 1961, pp. xxii–xxvi. (On Fuenteovejuna.)

Roca Franquesa, J.M. "Un dramaturgo de la Edad de Oro: Guillén de Castro: Notas a un sector de su teatro." RFE, 28 (1944), 378–427. (On regicide and El amor constante.)

Rodríguez, Alfred. "Tirso's Don Juan as Social Rebel." BCom, 30 (1978), 46–55.

Rodríguez Cepeda, Enrique. Introduction to Luis Vélez de Guevara. La serrana de la Vera. Madrid: Alcalá, 1967, pp. 7–45.

Rougemont, Denis de. "Don Juan." In his Love Declared: Essays on the Myths of Love. Boston: Beacon, 1963, pp. 99–107.

Scott, Nina M. "Honor and Family in La fuerza de la sangre." In Studies in Honor of Ruth Lee Kennedy. Ed. V.G. Williamsen and A.F.M. Atlee. Estudios de Hispanófila, No. 46. Chapel Hill, NC: 1977.

Sloman, Albert E. The Dramatic Craftsmanship of Calderón: His Use of Earlier Plays. Oxford, Eng.: Dolphin, 1958. (See Ch. 8 on El alcalde de Zalamea.)

Sylvania, Lena E.V. "Doña María de Zayas y Sotomayor: A Contribution to the Study of her Works." RR, 13 (1922), 197–213, and 14 (1922), 197–232.

Whitby, William M. "Rosaura's Role in the Structure of La vida es sueño." HR, 28 (1960), 16–27. (Also in Critical Essays on the Theatre of Calderón. Ed. B.W. Wardropper. New York: New York U.P., 1965, pp. 101–113.)

Wiltrout, Ann E. "Murder Victim, Redeemer, Ethereal Sprite: Women in Four Plays by Calderón de la Barca." In Perspectivas de la comedia, Vol. II: Ensayos sobre la comedia del Siglo de Oro español, de distintos autores. Ed. A.V. Ebersole. Valencia: Albatros Hispanófila, 1979, pp. 103–120. (About La vida es sueño and other plays.)

Chapter 13: "Women, Wedlock, and the Threat of Adultery"

Ayala, Francisco. "Sobre el punto de honor castellano." RO, 2 (2ª Época) (1963), 151–174.

Bataillon, Marcel. "Cervantes y el 'matrimonio cristiano'." In his Varia lección de clásicos españoles. Madrid: Gredos, 1964, pp. 238–255.

Bryans, John. "Coquín's Conversion: Honour, Virtue, and Humour in 'El médico de su honra'." *MLR*, 77 (1982), 597–605.

Casa, Frank P. "Honor and the Wife-Killers of Calderón." *BCom*, 29 (1977), 6–23.

—. "Honor as a Mediating Myth." In *La Chispa '81: Selected Proceedings*. Ed. G. Paolini. Second Louisiana Conference on Hispanic Languages and Literatures. New Orleans: Tulane Univ., 1981.

Castro, Américo. "'El celoso extremeño', de Cervantes." In his *Hacia Cervantes*. 3rd ed. Madrid: Taurus, 1967, pp. 420–450.

—. "El honor." In his *El pensamiento de Cervantes*. New ed. Barcelona: Noguer, 1972, pp. 355–386.

Chauchadis, Claude. "Risa y honra conyugal en los entremeses." In *Risa y sociedad en el teatro español del Siglo de Oro*. Actes du 3ᵉ Colloque du Groupe d'Etudes Sur le Théâtre Espagnol; Toulouse, 1980. Paris: Centre National de la Recherche Scientifique, 1980, pp. 165–173.

Correa, Gustavo. "El doble aspecto de la honra en *Peribáñez y el Comendador de Ocaña*." *HR*, 26 (1958), 188–199.

Cruickshank, D.W. "The Metaphorical *Criptojudaísmo* of Calderón's Gutierre." *BHS*, 59 (1982), 33–41. (On *El médico de su honra*.)

Dille, Glen F. "Antonio Enríquez Gómez's Honor Tragedy *A lo que obliga el honor*." *BCom*, 30 (1978), 97–111.

Dunn, Peter N. "Honour and the Christian Background in Calderón." *BHS*, 37 (1960), 75–105. (Also in *Critical Essays on the Theatre of Calderón*. Ed. B.W. Wardropper. New York: New York U.P., 1965, pp. 24–60.)

Ebersole, Alva V. "El tema del adulterio en 'Los comendadores de Córdoba'." In *Estudios sobre el Siglo de Oro en homenaje a Raymond R. MacCurdy*. Ed. Á. González, T. Holzapfel, and A. Rodríguez. Albuquerque: Univ. of New Mexico; Dept. of Modern and Classical Languages, 1983. Madrid: Cátedra, 1983, pp. 59–65.

Fichter, William L. "A Study of Conjugal Honor in [Lope's] Theatre." Introduction to his *Lope de Vega's El castigo del discreto together with a Study of Conjugal Honor in his Theatre*. New York: Instituto de las Españas, 1925, pp. 28–72.

Hesse, Everett W. "Honor and Behavioral Patterns in *El médico de su honra*." *RF*, 88 (1976), 1–15.

Honig, Edwin. *Calderón and the Seizures of Honor*. Cambridge, MA: Harvard U.P., 1972. (See Ch. 4 on *A secreto agravio*. . . .)

Jones, Cyril A. "*Honor* in Spanish Golden-Age Drama: Its Relation to Real Life and to Morals." *BHS*, 35 (1958), 199–210.

—. "Spanish Honour as Historical Phenomenon, Convention and Artistic Motive." *HR*, 33 (1965), 32–39.

Larson, Donald R. *The Honor Plays of Lope de Vega*. Cambridge, MA: Harvard U.P., 1977.

McGrady, Donald. "The Comic Treatment of Conjugal Honor in Lope's *Las ferias de Madrid*." *HR*, 41 (1973), 33–42.

McKendrick, Melveena. "Celebration or Subversion?: *Los comendadores de Córdoba* Reconsidered." *BHS*, 61 (1984), 352–360.

—. "Honour/Vengeance in the Spanish 'Comedia': A Case of Mimetic Transference?" *MLR*, 79 (1984), 313–335.

—. "Women Against Wedlock: The Reluctant Brides of Golden Age Drama." In *Women in Hispanic Literature: Icons and Fallen Idols*. Ed. B. Miller. Berkeley: U. of California P., 1983, pp. 115–146.

318

Mujica, Barbara. "Absudity and Alienation: 'A secreto agravio, secreta venganza'." Ch. 3 of her *Calderón's Characters: An Existential Point of View*. Barcelona: Puvill, 1980.

Podol, Peter. "Non-Conventional Treatment of the Honor Theme in the Theater of the Golden Age." *REH*, 7 (1973), 449–463.

Pring-Mill, R.D.F. Introduction to Lope de Vega. *Five Plays*. Trans. J. Booty. New York: Hill and Wang, 1961, pp. xx–xxii (on *Peribáñez*) and xxxi–xxxvi (on *El castigo sin venganza*).

Rodríguez Puértolas, Julio. "Alienación y realidad en Rojas Zorrilla." In his *De la Edad Media a la Edad Conflictiva: Estudios de literatura española*. Madrid: Gredos, 1972, pp. 339–363.

Rogers, Daniel. "'Tienen los celos pasos de ladrones': Silence in Calderón's *El médico de su honra*." *HR*, 33 (1965), 273–289. (Also in *Critical Studies of Calderón's Comedies*. Ed. J.E. Varey. London: Gregg International and Tamesis, 1973, pp. 1–16.)

Rosales, Luis. "El naturalismo cervantino." In his *Cervantes y la libertad*. Madrid: Sociedad de Estudios y Publicaciones, 1960. Vol. II, pp. 383–435.

Sánchez, Galo. "Datos jurídicos acerca de la venganza del honor." *RFE*, 4 (1917), 292–295.

Silverman, Joseph H. "Del otro Teatro Nacional de Lope de Vega: El caso insólito de *El galán escarmentado*." *Hispania*, 67 (1984), 23–27.

Sloman, Albert E. *The Dramatic Craftsmanship of Calderón: His Use of Earlier Plays*. Oxford, Eng.: Dolphin, 1958. (See Ch. 2 on *El médico de su honra*.)

Sylvania, Lena E.V. "Doña María de Zayas y Sotomayor: A Contribution to the Study of her Works." *RR*, 13 (1922), 197–213, and 14 (1922), 197–232.

Toro, Alfonso de. "Sistema semiótico: Estructura del drama de honor de Lope de Vega y Calderón de la Barca." In *Lope de Vega y los orígenes del teatro español: Actas del I Congreso Internacional sobre Lope de Vega*. Ed. M. Criado de Val. Madrid: EDI-6, 1981, pp. 283–301.

—. "Sistema semiótico-estructural del drama de honor en Lope de Vega y Calderón de la Barca." *RCEH*, 9 (1985), 181–202.

Valbuena Briones, Ángel. Prologue to Calderón de la Barca. *Dramas de honor*. 2nd ed. Madrid: Espasa-Calpe; CC, 1967. Vol. I, pp. xi–civ.

Wade, Gerald E. "Spain's Golden Age Culture and the 'Comedia'." *Hispania*, 61 (1978), 832–850. (On *El castigo sin venganza*.)

Wardropper, Bruce W. "*Honor* in the Sacramental Plays of Valdivielso and Lope de Vega." *MLN*, 66 (1951), 81–88.

—. "Poetry and Drama in Calderón's *El médico de su honra*." *HR*, 49 (1958), 3–11.

—. "The Unconscious Mind in Calderón's 'El pintor de su deshonra'." *HR*, 18 (1950), 285–301.

—. "The Wife-Murder Plays in Retrospect." *RCEH*, 5 (1981), 385–395. (On Calderón's plays.)

Watson, A. Irvine. "*El pintor de su deshonra* and the Neo-Aristotelian Theory of Tragedy." *BHS*, 40 (1963), 17–34. (Also in *Critical Essays on the Theatre of Calderón*. Ed. B.W. Wardropper. New York: New York U.P., 1965, pp. 203–223.)

Wilson, Edward M. "La discreción de don Lope de Almeida." *Clavileño*, 2 (1951), 1–10. (The English version of this article, "The Discretion of Don Lope de Almeida," appears in *Critical Studies of Calderón's Comedies*. Ed. J.E. Varey. London: Gregg International and Tamesis, 1973, pp. 17–36.) (On *A secreto agravio. . . .*)

Wiltrout, Ann E. "Murder Victim, Redeemer, Ethereal Sprite: Women in Four Plays by Calderón de la Barca." In *Perspectivas de la comedia*, Vol. II: *Ensayos sobre la comedia del Siglo de Oro español, de distintos autores*. Ed. A.V. Ebersole. Valencia: Albatros Hispanófila, 1979, pp. 103–120. (On *A secreto agravio* . . . , *El médico de su honra*, and other plays.)

Zuckerman-Ingber, Alix. *El bien más alto: A Reconsideration of Lope de Vega's Honor Plays*. Gainesville: U.P. of Florida, 1984.

—. "Honor Reconsidered: *Los comendadores de Córdoba*." JHP, 4 (1979), 59–75.

Index

Vladimir Honsa

OLD SPANISH GRAMMAR
OF «LA GRAN CONQUISTA DE ULTRAMAR»
With Critical Edition of Book IV, Chapters 126–193, The Conquest of
Jerusalem by Sultan Saladin

American University Studies: Series 2 (Romance Languages and Literature).
Vol. 43
ISBN 0-8204-0315-6   249 pages   hardback sFr. 88.00

Recommended prices – alterations reserved

This work is a complete grammar of an Old Spanish text of the 13th century. It includes
a critical edition of an important part of a medieval chronicle on which the study is
based. The grammar consists of three parts:
(1) phonology, reconstructed from graphemic references, (2) description and classification of morphosyntactic structures, and (3) analysis of stylistic devices. In addition,
it contains a chronological identification of the language and its interrelation with
languages of the Mediterranean area and other Hispano-Romance dialects. A glossary
shows the origin, medieval usage and Modern Spanish equivalent of the words of the
text with references to their use in other Old Spanish literary works and to their counterparts in the Old French version of the chronicle. An exhaustive bibliography concludes the book.
Contents: Grammar of Old Spanish based on a critical edition of a 13th-century chronicle: phonology, morphosyntax, and stylistics. Descriptive approach with historical,
comparative and dialectological considerations.

PETER LANG PUBLISHING, INC.
62 West 45th Street
USA – New York, NY 10036

Vladimir Honsa

AN OLD SPANISH READER

Episodes from «La gran conquista de Ultramar»
With Introduction, English Summary of the Chronicle, and Etymological
Vocabulary

American University Studies: Series 2 (Romance Languages and Literature).
Vol. 32
ISBN 0-8204-0265-6   77pages   hardback US $ 15.00 / sFr. 34.50

Recommended prices – alterations reserved

This Old Spanish Reader is suitable for classes or individual study in medieval Spanish
literature and historical linguistics. It presents a selection of episodes from the Crusades
and the conquest of the Kingdom of Jerusalem by Sultan Saladin. These episodes are
excerpted from a 13th-century chronicle which is representative of the medieval Spanish
language and style.
Content: The Reader consists of: (a) an introduction dealing with the history and sources of the text, (b) an English summary of the chronicle, (c) the Old Spanish text based
on manuscripts, (d) a vocabulary with etymologies and translations into Modern Spanish
and English, and (e) a selected bibliography.

 PETER LANG PUBLISHING, INC.
62 West 45th Street
USA – New York, NY 10036